T0304087

Integrated Cost-Schedule Risk Analysis

To my wife Judie, who always thought that integrating cost and schedule risk analysis was important

Integrated Cost-Schedule Risk Analysis

DAVID HULETT

Routledge
Taylor & Francis Group

LONDON AND NEW YORK

First published 2011 by Gower Publishing

Published 2016 by Routledge
2 Park Square, Milton Park, Abingdon, Oxon OX14 4RN
711 Third Avenue, New York, NY 10017, USA

Routledge is an imprint of the Taylor & Francis Group, an informa business

British Library Cataloguing in Publication Data
Hulett, David T.
  Integrated cost-schedule risk analysis.
  1. Project management--Finance. 2. Cost control.
  3. Financial risk management. 4. Risk assessment. 5. Risk
  assessment--Mathematical models.
  I. Title
  658.1'552-dc22

  ISBN: 978-0-566-09166-7 (hbk)

Library of Congress Cataloging-in-Publication Data
Hulett, David T.
  Integrated cost-schedule risk analysis / David Hulett.
    p. cm.
  Includes index.
  ISBN 978-0-566-09166-7 (hbk) -- ISBN 978-1-4094-2812-1 (ebook) 1. Project management--
  Cost control. 2. Costs, Industrial. 3. Risk assessment. I. Title.
  HD69.P75H85 2011
  658.15'52--dc22

                                                            2010049003

Contents

List of Figures

List of Tables

Foreword

PHILIP RAWLINGS
Director, Euro Log Ltd, Teddington, UK/

It is a truth universally acknowledged (or at least fairly-commonly accepted) that the cost of any project is to some extent influenced by the time taken to complete the project; if we are delayed by bad weather we still have to pay the project manager; if construction takes longer, there will be some extra costs, notwithstanding that we may have negotiated a fixed-price contract (we have additional management costs and will expect to see some claims – inevitably, not all of those can be rejected). In an uncertain environment, i.e. on real projects where risk and uncertainty is the expectation, the link between time, cost and risk is all too clear.

A familiar approach to quantitative risk analysis is to conduct analyses of the risks and uncertainties as separately applied to the schedule and to the cost; just maybe, there will be some line item in the cost analysis to account for project overruns – this will necessarily be a crude and clumsy approximation to the true impact.

A far more realistic approach is to integrate all aspects of the analysis into a single model such that the inter-relationships between cost, time, risk and uncertainty can be modelled in a way that is representative of the real-world situation, and which is itself readily presented for validation. In this way, time-dependent costs (cost items whose magnitude varies as the time taken to perform those tasks) may be individually modelled and related to their particular schedule drivers.

David Hulett is well-known for his practical approach to risk management; his previous book *"Practical Schedule Risk Analysis"* introduced a practical approach to developing risk models to account for risks and uncertainties that are inevitably encountered in "real-world" projects: that is the ones that you and I actually get involved with. Hulett's approach is a very hands-on exposition of dealing with the Quantitative analysis portion of the Analyse step of the Risk Management Process – how to translate the risks and uncertainties that you have identified into possible schedule outcomes of the project.

Many is the book or learned paper describing the risk management process and many are the standards leading you on the way to setting up an environment that will encourage you and your organisation to identify, analyse and manage the risks that conspire to de-rail your venture, or to give you the opportunity to seize the advantage over competitors.

Not so common is the medium that will show or tell you how to perform those steps. There seems to be an assumption that integrated cost and schedule in a single model is in some way too difficult – perhaps it is now time to lay that idea to rest and to emphasise the benefits of a more realistic predictive analysis of the venture. Only in this way can informed decisions be made as to the optimum scenario in which to pursue the project's objectives.

Hulett's latest book takes the approach further and describes how one can (and really should) develop risk models that consider both cost and schedule and, more importantly, the interaction between the two.

Although the approach considered in this book uses Primavera Risk Analysis software from Oracle (which used to be called Pertmaster not that long ago) to demonstrate the ideas within, models could be built in other software. Hulett's exposition here, though, makes considerable use of Risk Drivers, a facility to apply common risks or uncertainties across many project components – this takes us some way from the seemingly high overhead of attempting to assign uncertainty distributions to each and every cost and duration in the model.

The Risk Drivers approach (particularly as now implemented in Primavera Risk Analysis) encourages the analyst to concentrate on those uncertainties or risks (i.e. uncertainties that may or may not happen and with an associated finite probability of occurrence) that are key to successful project completion. A Risk Driver may be applied to several components of the model – e.g. productivity uncertainty applies to all relevant construction activity durations. Further, this method applies an implicit correlation between parameters using the same Risk Driver, thus avoiding the problematic estimating of correlation factors to be applied between various risk distributions. It is to be hoped that Primavera Risk Analysis will be further developed to extend Risk Driver capability to *all* risk parameters and to allow drivers to be added/multiplied as well as applied in parallel and series to further extend this very effective and transparent method.

Using Risk Drivers as a sensitivity tools (i.e. by suppressing Risk Drivers one-by-one) highlights those risks that are worth serious mitigation attention, thus focussing effort (which usually translates into money) onto those risks that will best improve project prospects if they can be reduced.

It is to be hoped that Hulett's approach will be adopted, no doubt adapted to suit each individual practitioner, to produce more realistic (let us not say 'accurate') projections of project outcomes – to set more achievable targets and to point towards more effective risk mitigation actions.

Foreword

CHARLES BOSLER
Chairman of the Risk Management SIG (www.risksig.com) and
President of RiskTrak International

Over the years, I have worked together with David Hulett on a number of projects but one in particular comes to mind as I read this book. The Architect of the Capitol (AOC) hired me to do risk assessment on the U.S. Capitol Visitor Center Project while David was analyzing the cost and schedule risk for the US Government Accountability Office (GAO). This project was the largest construction project in the government, at that time. The requirements for this project were real and immediate. The scale was large however pre-9/11 the funding was questionable.

The Capitol Visitor Center (CVC) is located underground below the East Capitol Grounds, to enhance rather than detract from the appearance of the Capitol and its' historic Frederick Law Olmsted landscape. The completed CVC contains over 580,000 square feet on three levels, requiring a 196,000-square-foot excavation, or "footprint" for purposes of comparison, the Capitol itself encompasses 775,000 square feet.

The CVC was designed to preserve and maximize public access to the Capitol while greatly enhancing the experience for the millions who come each year to walk its historic corridors and experience the democratic process in action.

Despite the clear need for this project Congress was pilloried in the press for the changes to the schedule and the projected cost over-runs. In 2005 Congress demanded an assessment and analysis of the project. David was hired by the GAO to provide quantitative risk analysis of cost and schedule and I was contracted by the AOC to provide an Independent Verification and Validation (IV&V) of the project that was to be presented to the CPC and Congress before the project could proceed.

When I finished reading David's book I began to consider the impact of the Risk Driver method on those of us who perform cost and schedule risk analysis. We work everyday to help people understand uncertainty and improve our estimates of the "unknowable" —the *future impacts* of the risks we face on every project.

We can consider all of the; "known-knowns" these are the risks and events that we know, then all of the "known-unknowns" which are those things that we know we don't know, we can even find ways to consider the "unknown-knowns" those things that we aren't aware that we actually already know, and there will always be the remaining "unknown-unknowns" those risks or events that we don't know. However, the real "unknowable" is the impact of these risks or opportunities on our project. Yet that is our task—to estimate the *future impact* of risk and events based on the best available information at our disposal. This was the very reason that the AOC contracted me to work on this project for Congress.

Along the way, as the CVC project progressed from an idea to an operating part of the government it was a very large construction project which included; an antiquities preservation project, a large IT project, a couple of food services projects, a security project, a human resources project, commissioning of the safety, fire and smoke systems,

xvi Integrated Cost-Schedule Risk Analysis

etc., and each of these project efforts, at some point, faced the same constraints as any other project. They all had to conform to the "iron-triangle" of project management ... scope, cost and schedule. All of which was unknown in the beginning and became a virtual certainty as time progressed and the date for the "Grand Opening" approached.

Obviously since each of these projects relate to the same government facility the risks and costs are all inter-related and the costs and impacts can be correlated using the Risk Driver approach, which allows us to consider the cross-project risks and dependencies of each of the sub-projects.

Additionally, when we perform a sensitivity analysis using the Risk Driver approach we can tell the Program Executive of the CVC, the CPC and Congress which risks drive the greatest overall risk to the project. Using the Risk Driver approach to risk analysis is a significant improvement over the more traditional 3-point estimate because it uses the high priority risks identified in the Risk Register that have been rank ordered through qualitative risk factors.

Congress conducts the business of our Nation. David reminds us what every businessman knows ... "Time is Money" and as such they can not, or better yet, should not be considered separately and exclusively, since they are the very same thing. To consider one without the other surely misses half the equation, which will lead to errors in both cost and schedule estimates. David gives us an effective means to integrate cost & schedule risk, which allows us to realize and analyze cost risks that cause schedule uncertainty and vice versa. Regardless of the cause, as schedule slips to the right cost will increase accordingly so we *must* look at the integrated cost and schedule risk (and/or opportunities) in a new way if we are ever to succeed.

Congress knows that they are ultimately accountable to the people of the United States and that their every action will face scrutiny in the press. That's why they take a deliberative and careful approach to planning. The reasons are many but the fact is—the Congress values analysis. Analysis that prioritizes and allocates 100's of Billions of dollars every year. So we know that analysis works. Why then do so many of us ignore this monumental testament to the success of statistics, modeling and simulation? I ask this because in this book David gives us an effective approach and all the tools we need to improve our cost and schedule estimates, which will increase the chance for success in our projects. Once armed with the tools and techniques necessary we can all improve. We can never know the "unknowable" ... the future will always be uncertain, but we can surely decrease the cone of uncertainty to a manageable level.

Preface

This book, *Integrated Cost and Schedule Risk Analysis*, is a logical successor to *Practical Schedule Risk Analysis* (Gower, 2009), though it can be read separately. Logically the integration of cost and schedule risk analysis is performed on a resource-loaded project schedule, so the issues surrounding project scheduling and the notions of schedule risk analysis were introduced in the first book.

In the early chapters of this book there is a fair amount of commonality with the earlier book for two reasons:

- First, many of the concepts of project risk and methods of its analysis are the same whether one is analyzing schedule risk or cost risk. Since the first six chapters of this book deal with cost risk analysis by itself without reference to project schedule there is some repetition. The methods of analysis have similarities, though the schedule risk analysis in the first book uses the schedule as a platform and the early chapters of this book use a cost spreadsheet as the platform.
- Second, I cannot be sure that the reader of this book has also read the earlier book on schedule risk analysis, so some of the material, for example on risk concepts, risk data, basic Monte Carlo simulation and corporate risk culture, which are common to both cost and schedule risk analysis are covered in both books. Also, in introducing the project schedule as a platform to the integrated cost and schedule risk, beginning in Chapter 7, some material specifically what makes up a good schedule is essentially summarized from the earlier book.

If the main issue with the project is timely completion of the schedule, schedule risk analysis can be performed without considering cost risk. However, in my view, cost risk cannot be fully analyzed without considering the implication of schedule risk. Many activities require resources that are paid more if they work longer (time-dependent resources such as labor, rented equipment and the like), so any activity that takes longer or shorter than scheduled will have a cost that is different from its baseline estimate. We often find that the most important risks to cost are actually important because they affect the schedule. Put another way, a significant amount of the cost contingency reserve should be held against uncertainties in schedule that, if they happen, will cause individual work activities as well as level of effort (LOE) activities to cost more.. It is not possible confidently to estimate the effect of schedule risk on cost risk without combining the resources into the schedule and evaluating the schedule uncertainty simultaneously with any cost-type risks in a Monte Carlo simulation. Resources may be specified at a summary level (we have used as few as eight resources for multi-billion dollar projects), if they can put the entire budget (free of embedded contingency and not including below-the-line contingency reserve) onto the right activities of the schedule.

In addition to uncertainty in the activity duration there are other factors that affect project cost risk. Even if the project worked to the original schedule, the cost might be uncertain because of the uncertain number of resources and their compensation, leading to an uncertain cost or "burn rate" per day. Also, some inputs such as procured equipment and raw materials have costs that are uncertain for reasons other than uncertainty in burn rate or activity duration, such as those stemming from uncertainty in the markets for raw materials or equipment because of industry-specific activity or the general economic uncertainty. These other cost risk factors are also analyzed, along with the analysis of the schedule uncertainty's implication for cost.

In addition to explaining a powerful approach to integrating cost and schedule using resource-loaded schedules, I have introduced, as I did in *Practical Schedule Risk Analysis*, the use of the project risks to drive the analysis. The Risk Driver Method of analysis starts with the risks in the risk register and characterizes them by their probability of occurring, the range of impacts they will have on the activity durations, burn rates and uncertainty of cost of equipment and raw materials, assigning them to affect specific activities that are included in the schedule if they occur. The benefits of the Risk Driver Method include that a risk can be applied to one or many activities and we can estimate the whole impact of a risk on all the activities that it affects through the analysis. Also, the risk is characterized by its probability as well as impact, which is natural given the definition of project risk. Finally, correlations between activity durations are caused during the Monte Carlo simulation if there is a risk that is applied to more than one activity, as many of the risks are. The Risk Driver Method can be applied to simple cost risk analysis on a spreadsheet (see Chapter 6) or to both schedule and cost when simulating the resource-loaded schedule (see Chapter 8 and following).

The Risk Driver Method contrasts with the traditional approach that starts with uncertainty in the activity durations or project component costs using 3-point estimates of activity durations that combine the impact of potentially several risks on an activity, do not maintain any linkage with other activities that those risk may affect, and generally does not take account of the probability that the risk will or will not occur. Fundamentally, the 3-point estimate approach deals with an intermediate product, the impact of risks or multiple risks on an activity duration or project element cost, not the risks themselves.

The Risk Driver Method takes one step back to fundamentals to the actual risks that are causing those impacts, and models how the activity durations or element costs might vary as they are influenced by risks that may or may not occur and have a range of possible impacts if they do occur. In short, the Risk Driver Method models how the uncertain durations of activities or costs of the project elements arise based on the fundamental risks.

Since a 3-point estimate combines in an often-murky way the influences of multiple risks on specific activities, and does not model the impact of any risk on multiple activities or costs, the traditional approach cannot determine which risks are important, only which activities are important. Specifically, if a risk affects multiple activities its importance may far exceed its impact on any one activity. Hence, the Risk Driver Method results flow naturally into risk mitigation by allowing us to prioritize the risks, which management can manage, so the analysis becomes a tool for project performance improvement.

Of course other methods of cost and schedule risk analysis can be combined with the Risk Driver Method. Some risks, analyzed as risk register risks by some Monte Carlo software systems, can be added when a risk under given circumstances causes an activity or several activities to appear in the schedule. These are sometimes called probabilistic branches or existence activities. In addition, uncertainties such as schedule or cost estimating error, due to the immaturity of the data available at any point, can be added as 3-point estimates because the uncertainty has a 100 percent chance of existing in all iterations (there is always cost estimating error until financial completion of the project). The Risk Driver Method applies to duration and cost uncertainty of activities and resources that are already in the schedule.

These methods are in use today and have provided clarity of analysis leading to acceptance by project managers and owners. The field of project risk analysis is dynamic and these methods of integrating cost and schedule risk and of using the Risk Drivers Method are becoming accepted.

Many thanks go to Charles Bosler and Philip Rawlings for reading the book in manuscript form and providing the forewords.

David T. Hulett, Ph.D.
Los Angeles, CA
January 23, 2011

1 *Introduction: Why Conduct Cost Risk Analysis?*

Introduction

Key areas covered in this chapter include:

- some relevant experience of cost overruns from experience
- the nature of cost estimates including the components that make up most estimates
- why typical contingency estimates do not provide for risk on the subject project
- how corporate culture biases the estimates of cost and contingency reserve
- project risks are defined and discussed in general
- why project risk tends to cause overruns (as opposed to underruns or on-budget performance).

Project cost estimates are statements made by knowledgeable people such as engineers or estimators expressing their views about how much a completed project will cost. However, because events in the future are never completely known, it is wise to investigate the conditions and events that may make these projects cost more or less than the official estimate.

This is not a criticism of estimating, which is a prerequisite of cost risk analysis. Rather it is an explicit recognition of a conceptual difference between trying to estimate a single value for project cost (estimating) and performing a risk analysis of that single value. The risk analysis explicitly assesses the risks to that estimate and provides a range of possible costs with their probability as well as the risks that cause the difference between them and the estimate.

Using quantitative methods of project cost risk analysis (and its integral companion schedule risk analysis) provides the means to examine the impact of individual risks on the overall project cost. Cost risk analysis is the way to determine the likelihood of finishing the project on budget as well as to estimate the requisite contingency reserve needed to provide the desired amount of certainty about achieving the cost plus reserve. Cost risk can also identify the most important risks to project cost so risk mitigation can be effective.

Experience shows us that cost estimating on projects is rarely successful because cost overruns routinely occur. One study of public transportation infrastructure projects found that 9 out of 10 projects had overrun their initial estimates and that overruns of 50 to 100 percent were common. "We make the following observations regarding the distribution of inaccuracies of construction cost estimates. Costs are underestimated in almost 9 out of 10 projects. For a randomly selected project, the likelihood of actual costs being larger than estimated costs is 86 percent. The likelihood of actual costs being lower than or equal to estimated costs is 14 percent" (Flyvbjerg et al. 2002).

For IT projects, an industry study by the Standish Group found that average cost overrun was 43 percent and that 71 percent of projects were over budget, over time and under scope. Spectacular examples of cost overrun include the Sydney Opera House with 1,400 percent, and the Concorde supersonic airplane development with 1,100 percent. The cost overrun of Boston's Big Dig or Central Artery/Tunnel Project was 275 percent. The cost overrun for the Channel Tunnel between the UK and France was 80 percent for Construction costs alone. Each of these projects also experienced increases in financing costs (Wikipedia 2009).

Edward Yourdon's book *Death March* cites the generally accepted assessment of IT projects' performance that the average IT project is likely to be 6 to 12 months late and 50 percent to 100 percent over budget (Yourdon 1997).

With this experience fresh in all project managers' minds, and the minds of the public, is there a way to find out what these projects will really cost? Is there some way to identify risks to the project plan and its cost so we can mitigate them to achieve a better result? How can cost risk analysis help the project management community to avoid the worst of the cost overruns? In describing cost risk and its extension, integrated cost – schedule risk analysis, this book provides answers to these questions.

Project Cost Risk Analysis Purpose and Summary

Project cost risk analysis examines the risks to the project and specifies how they may affect the project schedule and costs. (Schedule risk analysis performs the same functions for the project schedule. See Hulett 2009). The analysis of cost risk can be conducted in the project's conceptual development phase as soon as there is a notional budget, and should be continued periodically throughout project execution as the estimate is refined and more risks are identified and quantified.

In summary, the process of performing cost risk analysis using quantitative methods, particularly Monte Carlo simulation, can be described as follows:

- Quantitative cost risk analysis methods require gathering risk data, usually from in-depth interviews about project risks. Interviewees are carefully selected and interviews may be intense.
- A Monte Carlo simulation approach is used to develop the possible costs of the particular project plan under consideration. Monte Carlo simulation is internationally recognized as best practice.
- We strip the contingency reserve that has been included "below the line" or embedded in line item estimates from the estimate and start from line item estimates that are without contingency reserve or padding.

- Using simulations we then estimate a contingency reserve that is explicitly based on the risks of the specific projects. This contingency is appropriate for the plan that is in place and is based on the risks identified and quantified. Hence the accuracy of the result depends on the accuracy of information developed during the risk analysis as well as the underlying estimate.
- The estimation of possible project costs enables management or other stakeholders to adopt a budget that will provide their desired level of certainty (given the plan and the risks that have been identified, quantified and analyzed). Management or other stakeholders determine their desired level of certainty.
- The risks that contribute to the contingency so estimated can be identified and prioritized using various quantitative measures. The list of high-risk line items or high priority risks to the project cost forms the basis of risk mitigation efforts. In this way the quantitative risk analysis leads to a better project plan because it drives toward early mitigation of the important risks.

Project Cost Estimates

Project managers, sponsors or owners expect to be told how much a project will cost when it is completed. To gather project cost information they turn to their estimators or to an engineering company that is engaged to assist in the early stages of developing the project plan, including developing its schedule and cost parameters, to agree on a cost number. Those experts, in their turn, will have developed the work breakdown structure (WBS) for the project and populated the cost line items with estimates based on material take-offs for the specified equipment, the estimated cost of equipment, raw materials and labor, as well as many other project cost elements.

Estimators often have available to them cost results from prior projects to use in developing the estimates of cost for a current project. Estimators may have experience to bring to bear, often taking data from prior projects and adjusting them for project size and complexity or new technology, to be applicable to the project they are estimating.

In some cases, particularly on aerospace or defense projects, estimators have done statistical or *parametric* analysis of the relationships of cost to cost-driving project elements such as weight, power, capacity, function points or other quantity measures deemed to be relevant to indicating project cost. Technology readiness is sometimes a cost factor as well. Parametric estimating, using a database of past projects costs and cost-driving elements, involves computing regression parameters that can be used to extrapolate the cost of the current project based on its design parameters for those same cost-driving elements.

Cost estimators also use information from the market to determine costs. Equipment suppliers are asked to indicate (1) whether they are interested in supplying the equipment for the project and (2) at what price the services or equipment would be supplied. Information from the suppliers, which is not yet a formal fixed-price bid, will be used in developing cost estimates for the equipment. For other project elements such as labor and bulk material the estimators may conduct a market survey, although most large companies will have that information continually under review by a separate department or a standing subscription to a service that monitors labor or material markets.

Ultimately, when procurements are made at a fixed price and when contracts are signed for project management, fabrication, construction, installation and commissioning, the estimator has some pretty hard numbers to use in the estimate. Of course, *fixed price* or *lump-sum turnkey* may not mean that there is no longer any cost risk, because of external compensable factors and changes to the original plan, but those contracts are good bases for the cost estimate.

Ultimately the estimates of individual line items are combined to generate a bottom line number that represents what the project *will cost* based on myriad assumptions and calculations, sources of information and adjustments. In many projects there is an element of new work that cannot be estimated based on historical precedent, however, which means that detailed cost estimates will be built up from engineering information that should describe the new work accurately.

If the project is large and expensive, estimates and worksheets may be scrutinized and checked by third parties against technical specifications and data from market information.

Still, consumers of these estimates need to understand that the estimates calculated this way are based on specific assumptions that may turn out to be wrong, and hence are subject to uncertainty that usually delays the project schedule and often increases the cost of the project above the estimates, even with contingency added. Some of those assumptions are that specific risks will not occur, yet experience shows that risk occur on every project.

Contingency Reserves

Project cost estimators recognize the uncertainty in their estimates and almost always add a contingency reserve to the estimate *below the line* to make provision for the risks that might occur. In fact project stakeholders require the estimate and addition of a contingency reserve of cost before they take the cost estimate seriously.[1] If this contingency reserve were correctly calibrated to cover the cost uncertainty in the estimate, then the sum of the estimates and the contingency reserve for risk should be enough to provide an estimated target that is a safe for planning and budgeting purposes.

Often the estimators have approved institutional contingency-sizing rules, usually percentages applied to specific components of the estimate. Sometimes percentage contingencies are even applied to numbers that already contain contingencies. Contingency amounts following these rules are historically based and can help to determine a believable total cost for the finished project. However:

- The process of developing a contingency reserve is complex and based on data that may not be correct for this project.
- There may be risks affecting this project that have not been encountered before and therefore are not incorporated in the reserve calculation.

---

1   It is interesting that these same consumers of project planning and control information usually refuse to consider a contingency reserve of time for schedules while they insist on contingency on cost estimates. The estimation of realistic costs and of durations is similarly affected by project risk and should be treated similarly, with contingency reserve for project risk required by both.

The typical contingency reserve appears to provide for the average or expected (in the statistical sense, the mean value) level of uncertainty whereas the stakeholders typically want to be protected against more than the average level of risk. Often estimates have contingency costs or padding built into or allocated (spread) to the specific line items in addition to the contingency below the line. If this occurs, the estimator may be able to reconstruct contingency-free estimates that were generated and can be used for quantitative risk analysis. Contingency-free estimates are needed for a cost risk analysis.

Do Contingency Reserves Provide for Project Risk?

Contingency estimates that rely on percentages determined by engineering practice or history may not be appropriate for managing risk in the project.

Overall project risk is determined by the individual risks that affect the project, how likely those risks are to occur on the project, and what impact those risks may have on the project if they occur. Deciphering these currents and cross-currents without a formal risk analysis is a daunting task. It is often not performed in estimating the contingency reserve that accompanies the estimate, in favor of applying historical percentages and factors.

In addition to not knowing the extent of risk on the project, the estimator generally does not know the degree of risk aversion of the customer on this project. The degree of protection of the cost objective (degree of certainty) required by management or the customer is influenced by many factors including how the project fits within or advances the organization's strategic objectives; the financial situation of the performing and customer organizations; the inherent degree of risk aversion of the organizations; the risk-taking behavior of the industry, and other factors.

It would be difficult for the estimator to gauge all of these factors simultaneously in sizing the contingency reserve of cost. How is the estimator to know the risks without examining them? Even if armed with a risk register that has risks prioritized using qualitative risk analysis methods (APM 2004; Hopkinson et al. 2008; PMI 2008) the estimator will not know how they fit together to affect overall project cost risk. The estimator generally falls back on institutionally fixed percentages to calculate cost contingency reserves. The estimates of contingency reserve generally provide for an average project contingency even if the stakeholders would prefer to have more protection from overrun risk.

The contingency reserve percentages used by the estimator and the estimating engineering organization may, but rarely do, provide for risk on a specific project. Since the project owners understand that the contingency is somewhat arbitrary (at least as it pertains to the specific project) the contingency is susceptible to adjustment by the owner. On some projects, the project owners have been known to persuade the estimator or engineering company to reduce the contingency reserve to serve a political purpose – reducing the apparent cost of the project – for the consumption of management, owners or other stakeholders.

In one instance the estimate of cost (before contingency) increased from the first to the second estimate, and the owner forced the engineering company to reduce the contingency reserve by a like amount so that the total estimate including contingency stayed the same in the two estimates. Although this example is extreme, owners' disregard for the integrity of the contingency reserve is not uncommon and may be based on their lack of respect for the process by which the contingency is estimated. Wanting to please the owner and gain future estimating business, and realizing that the institutional contingency reserve percentages are subject to interpretation, the estimators at the engineering company may bow to owner pressure and *revise* the contingency reserve estimate. (*Revise*, in this context, means, in most cases, *reduce it to whatever the customer will accept.*)

There has to be a better approach to determining the cost contingency that provide both for the specific risks that may affect cost and the customer's degree of risk aversion. This approach is quantitative cost risk analysis. In fact, since uncertainty in time influences uncertainty in cost, we need to apply both quantitative integrated cost and schedule risk analysis.

Why Do So Many Projects Overrun their Cost Estimates?

In many cases, project managers know that other projects have overrun their budgets, but they may feel that (1) this project will be secure from overruns because they are good project managers, (2) if the project overruns its budget the causes of those overruns will be evident to all and will not be judged to be their fault, or (3) since all projects overrun there will be no personal consequence to them. There is a fair amount of self-deception in the project management world about both cost estimates and schedules.

The main reasons for costs to overrun the estimates, assuming that the cost estimators are competent, relate to the corporate culture and to the risk in the project.

* Corporate management, including those responsible for selling the project to the customer, contributes to cost overruns by influencing project cost estimates to be underestimated. This is the corporate culture that tends to prefer estimates and schedules that are optimistic, perhaps calling them *challenges* or *stretch goals*.
* Risk in the project, including estimating uncertainty, is often more likely to push the costs higher than lower. This *cost growth* or upward pressure is often the result of making estimates based on optimistic rather than realistic assumptions.

Each of these factors can lead to estimates and schedules that are not, and have never been, achievable. Both the influence of corporate culture and the presence of serious project risks are often ignored, underestimated, denied or otherwise not analyzed and corrected.[2]

How Corporate Culture Influences the Adequacy of Project Cost Estimates

To emphasize the point, project managers may adopt cost estimates (and schedules) that are significantly optimistic or *aggressive* to the point that the project team does not believe

---

2   These observations are based on 20 years of project risk analysis experience. Since project risk analysis may be practiced on projects that are already in trouble, the sample may be biased. However, it does us no good to assume a perfect world of unbiased cost estimates and fair dealing when it comes to bidding a cost figure, when there is evidence that this is not always practiced.

them. A common refrain amongst project teams in this situation is that; "everything has to go according to plan" for the cost or schedule to be achieved. This statement is shorthand for "I do not believe the plan as it is reflected in the cost estimate and the project schedule." A corollary to this statement is "Why should I work nights and weekends to achieve an imposed budget and schedule that cannot be achieved no matter how hard I work?"

When someone wants to discuss project cost or schedule risk, the corporate culture may suppress the discussion, deflect or postpone it. When someone has objective evidence that the project is underestimated or that the schedule is not going to be achieved, the corporate culture is such that influential managers may rise up and (1) argue with the results, the method or the data, (2) suppress the results, or (3) take the *know-nothing* approach of saying "I am not going to give up on my dates or budget" without explanation, invoking the power they have over others.

A culture that ignores or downplays project risks has an inherently negative effect on the project cost estimate, and hence will lead to overruns of the estimate. When these factors are at work with the requirement to make a lump-sum-turnkey (LSTK) bid, the contractor may seriously underbid the contract, hoping that the overruns will be revealed somewhat later. When the customer is deciding which projects (if any) to execute, these two forces of risk and corporate culture may seriously skew the information available to the decision-makers. If a government agency is presenting its acquisition budget to the administration or to the legislative body those bodies will have difficulty gaining truthful and realistic information on which to make decisions. Congressional investigations and hearings are likely to follow.

We need to be clear about the institutional pressures and the competitive environment within which the cost estimates are produced. We have to realize that the cost estimates are not necessarily unbiased estimates produced by professional estimators and engineers. There are many forces that influence the cost estimates to be biased toward the low side – in fact there are immediate rewards to underestimation – that trump the countervailing force in favor of adding padding (overestimation) in order to make it possible to finish on budget.

It would be a mistake to assume that cost estimates and schedules are unbiased estimates of a realistic project plan. We always have to check the risks to the plan's cost estimate and schedule to see if they represent a feasible result.

Underbidding a project to win the work may be a successful strategy in the end. In many cases, external events and change orders from the customer may provide the opportunity to bill more and make a profit in the end. While it is human nature for individual task managers to add padding in the initial estimate to ensure budget success, the institutional factors described here seem to squeeze any excess out of the project's budget (and schedule) to result in an estimate for which it is at least improbable and may be impossible to finish on budget or on schedule from the outset.

DeMarco and Lister indicate several reasons why estimated costs are not sufficient to get the job done. In part companies "try to emphasize positive thinking by ignoring the possible unfortunate consequences of the risk they are taking. This is an extreme variant of the can-do attitude … If there are things that could go wrong, that would make your project a total fiasco, for example, they would just have you not think about those things at all" (DeMarco and Lister 2003).

DeMarco and Lister indicate that risk identification, analysis and management may not be practiced for several reasons. Among those are:

- If the project sponsors or funders are aware of the real risks they will not want to undertake the project, and we want to do the project.
- Customers like to have certainty about time and cost objectives, and are impatient at being told of the essential uncertainty in achieving key objectives.
- Given the competition for jobs, each competitor will try to avoid being the only one telling the truth because the job will surely be awarded to others who are almost certainly lying about their ability to meet the customer's time and cost objectives.
- There is no reliable data about project risk so the exercise is futile in any case.

DELIBERATELY UNDERSTATED COST ESTIMATES

Flyvbjerg and associates have documented the overruns in public transportation projects and have come to a disturbing conclusion – the project sponsors are giving out unrealistically low cost estimates on purpose. This explains the large and persistent project cost overruns summarized in the opening paragraphs of this chapter.

Of course some technical issues such as imperfect techniques, inadequate data, honest mistakes, inherent problems in predicting the future, lack of experience on the part of forecasters may be present. However, these do not account for the majority of the overrun/underestimate problem. The authors concluded that there was a large degree of deliberate under-estimating designed to make public transportation sector projects appear (to the public and other decision-makers) to be less costly than honest estimating would reveal, the idea being that the projects would be more likely to be approved for execution.

Various parties – including sponsors, construction companies and engineering companies – benefit from pushing the projects forward according to the authors. "We conclude that the cost estimates used in public debates, media coverage, and decision-making for transportation infrastructure development are highly, systematically, and significantly deceptive" (Flyvbjerg et al. 2002).

DEATH MARCH IT PROJECTS

Yourdon has characterized "death march" IT projects in several ways. Perhaps "the schedule has been compressed to less than half the amount of time estimated by a rational estimating process (or) ... the staff has been reduced to less than half the number of people that would normally be assigned to a project of this size and scope, (or) the budget and associated resources have been cut in half, (or) the functionality, features, performance requirements or other technical aspects of the project are twice what they would be under normal circumstances." In some cases each of these events has happened on a project (Yourdon 1997) While the scoping ("half," " twice") in the quotation above may be a bit extreme, projects in all industries but particularly in IT may have these characteristics in part.

Another way to describe the death-march project is that it is a violation of the Triple Constraint from the beginning.

Figure 1.1   The triple constraint of project management

Requiring too much high-quality scope to be delivered within too little time and with too little budget is a frequent finding (or at least a frequent opinion of the project team) leading to projects doomed to fail in one if not all of these dimensions. Yourdon says that "an unbiased, objective risk assessment … determines that the likelihood of failure is > 50 percent."[3] Yourdon suggests several causes of these "death march" projects (Yourdon 1997):

- politics, including bureaucratic struggles, within the performing company
- naïve promises made by marketing, senior executives, naïve project managers, and so on
- naïve optimism of youth ("we can do it over the weekend")
- start-up mentality of fledgling, entrepreneurial companies
- the "Marine Corps" mentality that *real* programmers don't need sleep ("that's what nights and weekends are for")
- intense competition caused by globalization of markets
- intense competition caused by the appearance of new technologies
- intense pressure caused by unexpected government regulations
- unexpected and/or unplanned crises.

One might suggest that these factors are not exclusive to the IT industry. People from industries other than IT – such as aerospace and defense, construction, and oil and gas – may recognize these as factors in their own project experience.

Project Risk Defined and Discussed

There is another cause for concern about the project cost estimate (and the schedule) – that the data available at a point in time when the estimate is made are immature and

---

3   In this author's experience the likelihood of success for the original schedule can be much less than 50 percent – even less than 1 percent – and that of cost success can be less as well, although with the addition of a contingency reserve of cost it is less likely that cost success is in such jeopardy.

incomplete, so even unbiased estimates have a wide error band around them. Estimators recognize the degree of estimating error associated with each class of estimate or estimate made during a specific phase of the project.

There are several definitions of project risk, but one of the most widely used definitions comes from the Project Management Institute: "Project risk is an uncertain event or condition that, if it occurs, has a positive or a negative effect on at least one project objective, such as time, cost, scope or quality" (PMI 2008).

The Association for Project Management (APM, based in the United Kingdom) distinguishes different levels for which risk is defined:

- "A risk event is an uncertain event or set of circumstances that, should it occur, will have an effect on achievement of one or more of the project's objectives.
- "The term 'project risk' is used to describe the joint effect of risk events and other sources of uncertainty."
- "Project risk is the exposure of stakeholders to the consequences of variations in outcome" (APM 2004).

The APM definition of "risk event" is similar to the PMI definition of project risk. In fact, the distinction that APM makes between the individual risk events and risk to the overall project objectives is extremely useful. Distinguishing the individual risk events from the overall project risk driven by those risks is the distinction between qualitative risk analysis and quantitative risk analysis that is used in the Guide to the Project Management Body of Knowledge (PMBOK®) Guide (PMI 2008).[4] In fact, the mapping of individual risk events to the overall project risk is the rationale for the use of Monte Carlo simulation, used in this book, to develop overall project risk statements from the specific individual risk events at the detailed level.

We should notice a few concepts in the basic definitions from PMI and APM:

1. Risk events are uncertain. They may or may not occur on any specific project. Their probability of occurring on the project is one of the main measures characterizing the risk event.
2. Risks are only important if they affect a project objective such as time, cost, scope or quality. In practice the impact of a risk (if it occurs) on an objective can be uncertain and be represented by a range of values.
3. Risks, if they occur, can have a positive or negative impact on an objective. This is the inclusiveness of the definition of "risk events," that they can represent opportunities to improve the project plan or threats to achieving that plan (Hillson 2004).
4. Overall project risk can potentially be influenced by many risks, causing the project to overrun (possibly to underrun) its total project objectives. Only using tools such as Monte Carlo simulation to consider all risks simultaneously can we estimate the risk to important total project objectives?

We also need to be able to take account of risks that will certainly occur but have an uncertain impact. In point number 2 above, we agree that a risk event may have

---

4   Later, in Chapter 6 we will show how to use quantitative risk analysis to prioritize individual risk events more accurately than possible with usual qualitative techniques.

potentially different impacts on project components such as activity durations or line item costs. This uncertain impact is actually a different uncertainty from the risk event's basic uncertainty of occurring at all. But what about those influences on a project's cost or schedule that come from an event or condition that will definitely occur on the project but which has an uncertain impact? Examples could include:

- Uncertainty in labor productivity. We know that there will be some level of labor productivity but we do not know what that level will be. Hence, we know that there is uncertainty in the level of labor productivity that will influence the cost and schedule. Is the uncertain level of labor productivity a risk even if it is 100 percent certain that labor productivity will differ from the level assumed in making the cost estimate?
- Uncertainty in raw materials prices. Again, there will be a level of prices for different raw materials that is set in the marketplace, but we know that raw materials prices will not be as expected when the estimate is made.
- Uncertainty in estimation of costs occurs in part because of immaturity of project data. At every project milestone except financial completion we are uncertain about costs and should admit that the estimate is not without its uncertainty range. Some estimating firms and customers have their own rules, such as; "At this stage gate we have a Class 3 estimate. The usual range on that is from + 20 percent to –10 percent (these uncertainty ranges need not be symmetrical, given the experience of cost growth)."

We need to provide a cost risk methodology that allows us to include the influence of risks that may or may not occur (risk events) and those that will definitely occur but with uncertain impacts. These influences are referenced in the PRAM Guide as follows: "Project risk therefore results largely from the accumulation of a number of individual risk events, *together with other sources of uncertainty to the project as a whole, such as variability and ambiguity (emphasis added)*" (APM 2004). The PRAM Guide agrees that sources of uncertainty such as variability and ambiguity, which are not exactly risk events, must nonetheless be included in an analysis of overall project risk of cost and schedule.

In a more recent publication produced by many of the PRAM Guide authors and others including this author, the uncertainties and ambiguities have been promoted to the status of risk, if not exactly yet risk events: " ... some risks concern variability of effect rather than whether or not an effect will occur. All variability risks are of this nature, as are many ambiguity risks" (Hopkinson 2008). An example of a variability risk is given as that of exchange rate risks on cost. An ambiguity risk example is given of an increase in software requirements that is expected to happen (100 percent probability) but with different possible impacts (between 3 and 5 people).

Whether or not the definition of "risk" includes factors that are confidently expected but have an uncertain impact, it is agreed that those uncertainties and ambiguities must be included in determining overall project cost or schedule risk. Any quantitative risk analysis methodology must be able to handle this class of risks while also handling risks that have an uncertain likelihood of occurring.

It is a short step to generalize the definition of project risk to include:

- risk events that may or may not occur but if they do occur they might have uncertain impacts, and

- risks that will occur but have uncertain impacts.

In Chapter 6 we introduce the Risk Driver approach to quantitative cost risk analysis and in Chapters 8 to 10 to integrated cost and schedule risk analysis. This method has been designed to handle these different types of risks.

Project Risk Tends to Cause Projects to Overrun Time and Cost Objectives

We define project risk to include both threats to the project objectives and opportunities to improve on those objectives. It is true, however, that there are more ways for things to go wrong on the project than to go better than planned (going *right* would be executing the project just as planned or better). For instance there may be a physically determined minimum amount of time that an activity can take (it certainly cannot take negative days) but there is literally no limit on the maximum amount of time an activity can take, specifically the activity could never complete. There may be various institutional and competitive limits to how little a piece of equipment may cost, or how little labor will work for, but there may be forces such as shortages that would add serious amounts to the cost of labor and equipment.

It is likely that as the profession of project risk management becomes more familiar with the concept of uncertainties that can improve the project we will find more of these opportunities when we conduct a risk analysis. It takes creativity to introduce the concept of opportunities to a project team and to encourage their thinking in that direction.

However at this point most risks, whether highly likely or not so likely, are thought of as making the project activities take longer or cost more than planned. As mentioned above, this phenomenon is due both to risks' impact being asymmetric toward overruns and the project plan being optimistic from the outset. In some risk analyses most of the risks are stated in ways that cannot help the project so it would be illogical for them to contain any element of opportunities. Some examples of these risks might be:

- We have a difficult time attracting or retaining good engineers. (We have assumed a full complement of experienced qualified engineers in developing our plan.)
- Equipment suppliers are busier than usual. (We know that the typical fabrication and deliver duration is 16 months so that is included in our schedule.)
- Line pipe suppliers may take longer than the contract to deliver sufficient pipe. (We took them at their word that they could do this in 12 months but nobody really believes that they can do this.)
- The project is large so there may be fewer bidders, reducing competition and increasing the bid prices. (We assumed that the bid prices would be held in line because of competition, but the bid packages are larger than most companies want to handle.)

It would be surprising that people interviewed for risk data would describe any improvement in the project schedule or cost estimate from risks stated as these are. Of course the risks could be re-stated in a more even-handed or symmetrical statement, but because of the assumptions made in the schedule or cost these risks are usually considered to be threats. While the methodology needs to accommodate opportunities, experience shows that threats outweigh opportunities at this point in project risk management history. Maybe in the future opportunities will be more routinely identified and advantage will be taken of them.

Summary

We conduct cost risk analysis on projects because projects frequently overrun and project participants usually do not recognize their exposure to cost overruns without examining the risks. There are many examples of dramatic project overruns from industries as diverse as public transportation and IT and, in the author's experience, in oil and gas, aerospace/defense and construction projects. All project managers have experience with projects large and small overrunning their budgets. Can we learn about the extent of these potential overruns early enough to take mitigation measures? Project schedule and cost risk analysis helps us do that.

Cost risk analysis provides answers to three questions that are critically important in helping projects succeed: (1) how likely are we to finish on budget, (2) how much cost contingency reserve do we need to add to the risk-free estimate, and (3) which risks are most important so we can develop risk mitigation strategies? Cost risk analysis is related to schedule risk so later in this book (in Chapters 8 to 10) we will integrate both cost and schedule risk analysis.

Cost overruns occur even though estimators use many time-tested approaches to developing the estimates. Historical experience and data, parametric analysis, engineering bottom-up analysis, labor/equipment/materials market analysis, information from potential suppliers and contractors and finally signed contracts are used in developing the estimates. Contingency reserves based on historical or the estimating organization's practices are included. Still, projects overrun their estimates even when the estimated contingency is included.

Why do projects overrun so frequently? The corporate culture and pressure from owners and competition favors optimistic estimates. Often the estimate assumes that the project will go smoothly and that there will be no external problems, change orders or institutional delays that could affect the cost. Aggressive estimates help management get the project approved, help contractors win bids and help project managers look good, at least until the overrun becomes obvious. Organizations often avoid discussing risk since that will raise unpopular issues, question judgments, challenge decisions and estimates that have already been made and advertised to others. The project teams may be truly optimistic and avoid the possibility that problems may arise. "We will not fail that test" is often heard, except the reason the test is required is that the product may not pass. Estimators may list the optimistic assumptions made but they are easily forgotten since it is the bottom line estimate that people remember and are reluctant to change.

Project risk analysis opens the discussion about the factors that can influence the final project cost. Risks include uncertain events or conditions that if they occur will affect the project's objectives for better or worse (opportunities or threats). Other uncertainties and ambiguities (such as uncertain levels of labor productivity or inaccurate cost information at an early estimate) may be 100 percent likely to occur but still have uncertain impacts, and these are also included. The risks that are identified are often threats that make the project overrun their cost and schedule objectives or underrun their scope or quality objectives, although opportunities are to be sought during interviews with the project participants.

The chapters of this book discuss how to quantify the project risks that affect cost components and how to use Monte Carlo simulation to derive overall project cost risk from those individual risks and risks on individual cost components. We will show traditional or conventional risk analysis using 3-point estimates that are applied to specific line items of cost. In Chapter 6 we introduce an approach to cost risk, the Risk Driver approach, that starts with the prioritized list of risks rather than with their effect on specific cost components. In Chapters 8 to 10 we present integrated cost and schedule risk analysis. Integrating cost and schedule risk analyses is important since a longer schedule can increase project cost, and the threat of a longer project implies that additional cost contingency (as well as schedule contingency) reserves will be needed. We will demonstrate that integrating cost and schedule risk analysis provides the most accurate information about cost risk and reveals the most important risks that affect cost, since some schedule risks have significant impact on costs. The most effective mitigation of both schedule and cost risk comes from identifying both cost – and schedule-type risks to the project and mitigating those that are highest priority.

References

APM (2004). *Project Risk Analysis and Management Guide (PRAM Guide)*. Buckinghamshire, UK, Association for Project Management Publishing Ltd.

DeMarco, T. and Lister, T. (2003). *Waltzing with Bears, Managing Risk on Software Projects*. Dorset House Publishing.

Flyvbjerg, B., Holm, M.S., and Buhl, Søren (2002). "Underestimating Costs in Public Works Projects, Error or Lie?" Journal of the American Planning Association, vol. 68, (No. 3).

Hillson, D. (2004). *Effective Opportunity Management for Projects: Exploiting Positive Risk*. New York, Marcel Dekker, Inc.

Hopkinson, M. et al. (2008). *Prioritising Project Risks – A Short Guide to Useful Techniques*. Association for Project Management.

Hulett, D. (2009). *Practical Schedule Risk Analysis*. Farnham, England, Gower Publishing.

PMI (2008). *A Guide to the Project Management Body of Knowledge*. Newtown Square, PA, Project Management Institute.

Wikipedia (2009). "Cost Overrun."

Yourdon, E. (1997). *Death March, The Complete Software Developer's Guide to Surviving "Mission Impossible" Projects*. Prentice Hall PTR.

2 *Cost Risk Analysis Basics: The Three-Point Estimate and an Analytic Solution, the Method of Moments*

Introduction

Traditional deterministic cost estimating produces specific values for each of the cost elements of the project.[1] Traditionally these estimates are then summed to determine how much the project will cost, without contingency. A contingency reserve is then added using the methods of the estimator. This process is good as far as it goes.

The problem with this approach is that it does not go far enough in estimating how much the project will cost. In specific terms, each of the deterministic element costs is only an estimate for that line item that will be performed in the future. The project element may cost more or less than the estimate. The disparity between the estimate and the actual cost (for each line item) may result from estimating error, ambiguity and risks that impact that element, influencing its ultimate cost.

We have to get over the notion that we *know* how much each project element will cost. The deterministic estimate, even if it is provided without bias and objectively is based on evidence, is just the beginning of cost estimating. Cost risk analysis is the continuation and conclusion of cost estimation.

Most cost estimators recognize the uncertainty of their estimates and usually believe that the overall project will cost more than the sum of the individual project line items as estimated. (Has anyone seen a negative cost contingency reserve indicating that the sum of the line-item estimates is too high?) Most cost estimates include a contingency reserve "below the line" to pad the estimate for factors such as estimating uncertainty, ambiguity and project risk events. Some cost estimates even include contingency "padding" in the costs of individual elements. The adequacy of these contingency reserves, given the specific risks associated with a given project, is the issue that cost risk analysis addresses.[2]

---

1   Project elements could include procured items, construction of specific project elements, installation and commissioning or testing, programming of a specific software element, fabrication of a component, engineering, and spread (level of effort) costs such as project management or quality control.

2   Since adding contingency reserves to cost estimates is common, and is usually required, the risk analysis is re-analyzing the specific risks to develop a realistic contingency reserve that is appropriate to the specific project. In scheduling it is uncommon to find a contingency reserve of time included in the schedule, so a schedule risk analysis is analyzing the risks to the schedule often for the first time. For the cost contingency result of a risk analysis we have something in the standard cost estimate to compare, but in the schedule risk analysis there is usually no time contingency in the original schedule for comparison purposes.

Most estimators do not conduct cost risk analyses, instead they use standard contingency factors that may or may not be adequate for the risks in any specific project. Cost risk analysis is designed to determine the most appropriate level of contingency reserve given the level of risk in the project and the degree of cost certainty the stakeholders want to provide. Also, cost risk analysis can identify the main risks to cost so that risk mitigation actions can be considered and planned. The appropriate contingency reserve usually differs from the reserve included in the traditional cost estimating process, which is often a rule-of-thumb figure.

Since the cost risk analysis calculates the cost contingency reserve afresh, we need to start that analysis with an estimate that has no contingency reserve, either below the line or embedded in individual project element estimates. For this purpose the individual cost elements need to be stripped of any padding or contingency that has been added during the traditional estimating process and, of course, we need to ignore the below-the-line contingency that has been added by the estimators. At the end of the risk analysis we will compare our recommended contingency reserve with that of the traditional estimators to see if they agree.

Building Blocks: The Typical 3-point Estimate Represents Cost Risk for a Project Cost Element

The traditional way to represent cost risk is to place uncertainty on the estimate for the cost of each project element.[3] This means that each cost line item is taken as possibly uncertain and the cost estimate is better thought of as a probability distribution rather than a single-point deterministic estimate. Of course, not all line items are uncertain, but the best assumption is that the cost estimators do not know the future with certainty. Probability distributions such as those we show below are better representations about the cost of a project *ex ante* than are single-point estimates.

The probability distribution of possible costs needs to encompass all of the possible costs of project line items.

- The optimistic (lowest) cost represents the extreme low cost, the least the project element might cost if only the opportunities (risks that, if they occur, would tend to reduce the cost of the element) are present, if that is possible on the line item. The balance of the uncertainties for this optimistic estimate may be for higher cost rather than higher cost. We all know that there could be good luck as well, and let us incorporate some good luck to construct the optimistic cost estimate for each project line item cost. Of course there is an absolute lower bound for the optimistic estimate – the line item cannot cost less than nothing.
- The pessimistic (highest) cost represents the extreme highest cost, the most the project element might cost if the threat risks were operating, in addition to any bad luck, (if that is appropriate) on the project element being estimated. For the pessimistic estimate we have to be expansive in considering the impact of project threat-type risks. It is easy and common for people to minimize the possible problems

---

3   Some of the most important risks to project cost are risks to the project schedule, which cause resources to work longer and hence increase cost. We introduce integration of cost and schedule risk analysis in Chapters 8 to 10.

in completing the work within the cost estimate, since they realize that working on the basis of a possible overrun is unpopular and may cause them to be looked on as "not a team player." Experience tells us that the pessimistic estimate representing the most the project element might cost is often under-estimated.

- The pessimistic estimate should be considered for the scope of work represented in the project element's line item. Some pessimistic events should not be allowed to influence the duration range of the cost element. For instance, if there is a 3-week test, the pessimistic estimate might easily conclude that in the worst case the test might take 6 weeks and the pessimistic cost should be consistent with a 6-week duration. But, what if the article (for example, aerospace component, pipeline integrity) fails the test? Test failure is a discrete risk event, not an extension of the cost of the test itself, with its own probability and impact on cost and should not be included in the pessimistic cost estimate.

- The most likely estimate is the one that falls typically somewhere between the optimistic and pessimistic estimates for the project element and that is considered more likely to occur than any other cost. It is most likely, that is the "mode," of a probability distribution as distinct from the "median" (the 50–50 point where half of the probability fall above and half below) and the "mean" (the weighted average cost). The important thing to realize is that this estimate is not necessarily the value for that project element that appears in the deterministic cost estimate. Although it is tempting to assume that the estimator was directed to put in the most likely estimate for each project element line item and was not pressured to change the estimate for any reason, the reality is that many line-item estimates are either old and overtaken by events or biased, usually lower than objectively determined most likely cost in order to win the bid or to make the project approvable.

The most likely value need not be equal to the value in the estimate, and any data collection exercise that forces the most likely value to equal the estimate is probably biased.

The Probability Distribution using the 3-point Estimates

Now that we recognize the reality that each project element cost is uncertain, we also conclude that the best way to represent the cost of any element is with a probability distribution. The way we talk about uncertainty and estimate the input data to achieve output results is by the use of simple statistics, and the probability distribution is a basic element of the statistics we use.

The probability distribution representing the alternative costs of a project cost element can take several forms. The uncertainty in costs that an element might take reflects all of the risks that could impinge on that project element. Figure 2.1 shows a typical project element's cost represented as a triangular distribution based on a 3-point estimate.

The probability distribution of possible costs for the project element, say construction direct labor, shown in Figure 2.1, has some characteristics that are common in the collection of risk analysis data:

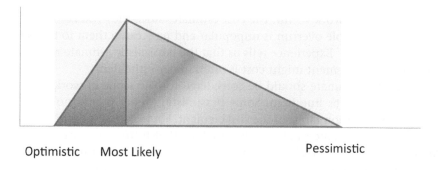

Optimistic   Most Likely   Pessimistic

Figure 2.1   Typical project element cost risk 2-point estimate with triangular distribution

- The distribution has 100 percent of the probability between the optimistic and pessimistic extremes. In this representation there is no possibility that the cost will exceed the pessimistic value or be less than the optimistic value.
- The distribution has a value between the two extremes that is more likely than any other. This is called the "most likely" but it need not be equal to the value in the cost estimate nor is it necessarily equidistant from the optimistic and pessimistic values.
- The probability that any cost value will occur on the project is represented by the height of the probability distribution at that point. In this representation we see the standard attribute that the probability is greatest around the most likely and tapers off as the values get close to the extreme values. We also see that in this case there is more probability that the element's cost will exceed the most likely cost than that it will be lower than that value.
- The triangular distribution can be asymmetrical, a very valuable characteristic since most cost risk phenomena are asymmetrical. That means if there are more reasons for the cost to be "higher than the most likely" than to be lower, the triangular distribution accommodates asymmetry by putting more probability (area under the curve) to the right of the most likely value than to its left. Of course, the triangular distribution does not need to be asymmetrical, and in fact the most likely can be closer to either extreme (optimistic or pessimistic).

The 3-point estimate has the benefit that it can be collected easily from project participants who are used to thinking in terms of estimates that are based on assumptions. The triangular probability distribution in Figure 2.1 is a common choice for a risk analysis because it has the right characteristics and it is fully described by the 3-point estimate – give any of the risk analysis Monte Carlo simulation software programs the same three points and they will each describe the same triangular distribution.

While triangular is a common choice we should note that this distribution is not found in nature so it may not be a choice for all. There are some other probability distributions that are commonly used.

- The Beta distribution. In statistics the Beta distribution is not specified by a 3-point estimate. Usually the Beta is described with minimum and maximum values and two "shape parameters" that describe where the most probable point is in the range and how "tall and narrow" or "short and fat" the distribution is. The problem with using the Beta distribution in this form is that we cannot collect data on the two shape parameters because interviewees will not know about them, what they mean or how to specify the parameters in use by the software.

• Recently several software developers have developed a "BetaPERT" distribution that has the shape of a Beta distribution but can be described by the 3-point estimate. To do this, the software has a built-in constraint around the "shape parameters." Commonly, this constraint is on the sum of those parameters. The greater the sum of the two shape parameters becomes, the more "tall and skinny" is the BetaPERT distribution. The benefit of the BetaPERT is that it looks more graceful and may have a long tail in the pessimistic direction, reflecting our common sense that there are some risks that make the costs large, even if those risks are not very likely

The BetaPERT distribution is more graceful and its distribution is aesthetically appealing, plus the Beta distribution appears in nature whereas the triangular distribution does not.

The triangular and BetaPERT distributions for the same 3-point estimate ($50 – $100 – $200) are compared in Figure 2.2 below.[4] Notice that the Triangular has more probability out toward the pessimistic tail of the distribution than the comparable BetaPERT does. Often professional project risk analysts will choose the triangular distribution since:

• It is perfectly described by the 3-point estimates.
• The "fat tail" toward the pessimistic estimate may tend to offset to some extent (this is admittedly an *ad hoc* rationale) the interviewees' inability or unwillingness to state their true pessimistic estimate, often understanding the corporate culture's unhappiness with bad news no matter how honest or accurate it is.

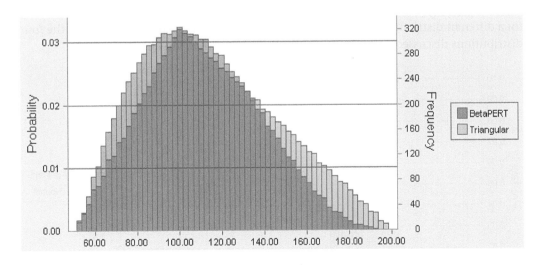

Figure 2.2   Asymmetrical triangular and BetaPERT distributions for 50–100–200

---

4   The software used here is Crystal Ball, a Microsoft Excel add-in, developed by Decisioneering which has been acquired by Oracle.

There are other probability distributions that are sometimes used:

- The uniform distribution is used when there is not much information about the risks and a guess can be made only about the best and worst case. In using this probability distribution the assumption is that there is no information that any one value is more likely than any other, so the values all have the same probability of occurring.
- The normal or Gaussian distribution, often called the "bell curve." This distribution must be symmetrical around a value that is at once the mean, median and mode. In application the software packages may record:
  - The optimistic and pessimistic values but ignore any value entered in the most likely column. Instead of using a value supplied as the most likely, the software positions the normal distribution's mean equidistant from the optimistic and pessimistic values.
  - The mean and a standard deviation. Unfortunately, it is difficult if not impossible to collect data on the concept of a standard deviation from most of the project personnel interviewed to collect the data.

In project risk analysis, where there is often asymmetry (more probability for overruns than underruns is common) the normal distribution and the uniform may not be applicable. Figure 2.3 shows a uniform distribution between 50 and 200, and a normal with 100 as the mean and a standard deviation of 10.

Which probability distribution is used depends on the shape of the uncertainty of the cost for each line item. It is possible and may be desirable to use different distributions for different circumstances. For instance, if the interviewees indicate that the pessimistic estimate is quite high, relative to the most likely and the low, but that it does not have much likelihood, a BetaPERT might be appropriate. Many times a risk analysis is conducted with only triangular distributions unless there are special circumstances that would call for a different distribution. Table 2.1 shows some of the important statistics from the four distributions discussed previously, so the user can see what the differences are.

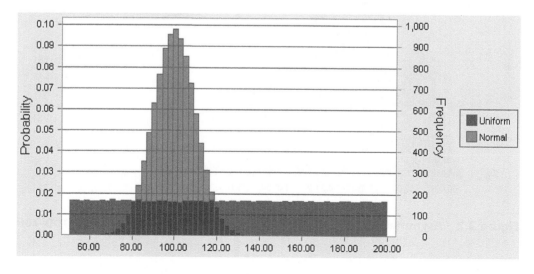

Figure 2.3   Symmetrical normal and uniform distributions on 50–100–200

Table 2.1   Comparison of four commonly used probability distributions using 50–100–200

Type	Mean	Median	Standard deviation
Triangular	116.7	113.4	31.2
BetaPERT	108.3	106.4	27.6
Uniform	125	125	43.3
Normal	100	100	User-defined

Notice from the table that the triangular has a mean and median that are further away from the most likely value of 100 than the BetaPERT and that the standard deviation is larger for the triangular. This is one reason triangular distributions are often used, that they convey a greater degree of uncertainty for the specific parameters and hence may offset the common tendency for interviewees to understate, for whatever reason, the true extreme ranges. Experience tells us that it is more important to get the extreme ranges and most likely values correct than to spend a lot of effort discussing the precise type of probability distribution to use, although the Monte Carlo simulation packages have multiple distributions available.

Combining the Project Elements' Probability Distributions to Find Total Project Cost Uncertainty

Once we have agreed that the cost of each project element in the project cost estimate is uncertain and we should use probability distributions to represent that uncertainty, we must recognize that we do not know the cost of the total project with certainty. In deterministic single-point estimating, summing the individual estimates of project element line item costs is commonly done, and it seems logical to add up the project elements' deterministic cost estimates to determine the overall project cost. However this is a dangerous practice and can lead to unwarranted confidence in a number that is probably not even the most likely total project cost, for two reasons:

- Experience shows that the most likely cost of any project element may not be the value found in the cost estimate. It is common for the cost estimate to be old, inaccurate, a guess or even biased, usually toward the low side, so that the true most likely line item value could be different from the value in the estimate.
- Even if each project element estimate is a non-biased most likely value, statistics tells us that the sum of the most likely values is not necessarily even the most likely value of the sum of the project cost elements. A well-known presentation is titled "Do Not Sum Most Likely Cost Estimates. This presentation makes the point bluntly that the sum of the most likely estimates is not a reliable estimate and is usually not the mean, most likely or median value of the probability distribution of total project costs (Book 1994).

This finding is related to the shape of the probability distributions of the individual project element line item costs, which we have found from experience are not often symmetric around the most likely value. Asymmetry of the line item cost probability distributions causes the most likely costs to differ from the distributions' means. Because the line item most likely values are not necessarily, or even usually, the means of the line item probability distributions, the sum of the most likely values is invalidated as representative of any overall total value in particular.

There are statistically sound ways to combine the probability distributions of the individual project elements to derive information about the total project cost. The analytical way to combine probability distributions that actually works when the cost estimate is simply a summation of project element line item costs is called the Method of Moments (MOM). The most commonly used way that has more flexibility and power and gives the correct answer in most circumstances is Monte Carlo simulation.

In this book we will introduce the MOM, but focus on Monte Carlo simulation as the best practice in conducting project cost risk analyses.

An Analytical Solution to Finding Total Project Cost Risk: The Method of Moments

The Method of Moments (MOM) is sometimes called PERTCost, since it uses the statistical principles that support PERT. Interestingly, the MOM or PERT was first applied to project schedule risk where it does not give accurate results (Hulett 2009). Instead, MOM or PERT approaches apply only to simple summation models where the only operations are adding and subtracting of uncertain values that can be represented by probability distributions. In this situation, the MOM is often applicable to the analysis of cost risk where the model used is simply a spreadsheet summation of individual values (costs of project elements) without any multiplication or other mathematical manipulation.[5]

Let us take a simple example of a construction project starting with design, engineering and procurement of equipment and bulk materials, leading to the actual construction and commissioning of the system. This project could be a medium-sized refinery project, though in fact the methods shown here work on all projects as long as the model is strictly summation in structure.

Here in Table 2.2 is the initial cost estimate without contingency in the estimates or below the line of a hypothetical construction project.

The question that management often raises, and should raise if it wants to establish accurate project economics and a mature project risk management program focusing on risk mitigation for better results is "What do we think of the estimate of $1.64 billion? Will it be adequate to construct the scope of work we intend for this project?"

---

5   The MOM will not apply accurately, and is not recommended for, cost models that have multiplicative formulae such as "quantity multiplied by unit cost." Monte Carlo simulation works in that case, however, and is more robust and therefore the best practice standard approach. Simulation is discussed in the next section.

Table 2.2   Estimate of hypothetical construction project without contingency

Project element	Cost estimate (millions)
Preliminary engineering	40
Detailed engineering	100
Procurement of equipment	250
Procurement of materials	300
Construction	800
Commissioning	150
Total project estimate	1,640

The answer to this question should be "We won't know until we analyze the project risks." So let us assume that we have the go-ahead to conduct cost interviews to get 3-point estimates for each of the six project elements. Here are the results of those interviews:

Table 2.3   Project cost estimate with 3-point ranges of uncertainty

Project element	Optimistic	Most likely	Pessimistic
Preliminary engineering	30	40	75
Detailed engineering	90	100	200
Procurement of equipment	210	250	400
Procurement of materials	250	300	500
Construction	750	800	1,000
Commissioning	125	150	300
Total project estimate		1,640	

Three characteristics of the table should be noted:

- Remember that the most likely cost value may not be the value in the estimate. In our case the interviews revealed that the Most Likely cost is in fact the value in the cost estimate of Table 2.2. In other words, any results we derive from these risks will not be caused by the base estimated costs being optimistic vis a vis the most likely estimate.
- Notice that all of the 3-point estimates show somewhat more threat of overrun than opportunity for underrun. As previously mentioned, this is a standard finding in cost risk analysis, because there are many ways to overrun the estimate and few ways to underrun the same estimate.

- Finally, the uncertainty of each project element's cost is 100 percent likely. While the most likely value is the cost estimate, it is just one value with a small probability of actually occurring. In other words, cost estimates are always incorrect, we just do not know by how much.[6]

Suppose that, while you have been permitted to interview project participants, the IT department is dragging their feet on purchasing the Monte Carlo simulation software that you need to use the simulation method to turn these 3-point estimates into an estimate of the Total Project Cost Estimate. You have heard of an analytical solution that can be performed on a spreadsheet using standard statistical rules for combining distributions and standard statistical tables for calibrating the results. This analytical method, available to anyone with a spreadsheet program, is called the Method of Moments. The MOM provides statically correct combinations of uncertain variables that are summed to make a total, so it is just right for an analytical approach to project cost risk analysis.

The goal of the MOM (and of Monte Carlo simulation discussed in the next chapter) is to derive information about the probability distribution of the total project cost from the distributions of the individual line items. The overall total project cost probability distribution can be characterized by its "moments," (hence the "Method of Moments") the first two of which are the mean and the standard deviation.

- The mean of the total project cost probability distribution anchors that distribution along the X-axis.
- The standard deviation of the total project cost probability distribution tells us whether the distribution is "tall and skinny" (a small standard deviation – and hence the mean is an estimate that is close to accurate) or "short and fat" (a large standard deviation – hence the mean is still the mean but the actual cost might be far away in either direction from that mean).

How do we use the individual line item probability distributions to find out the mean and standard deviation of the total project cost estimate?

The mean of the overall total project cost distribution is found by summing the means of the individual project element costs:

Mean total project cost

=

Sum (project element cost distribution *means*)

Notice that we are not summing the most likely costs or the estimates (which, in this case are the same number line by line). Remember the values in Table 2.1. For each distribution the most likely was 100 but the mean for the particular triangle (50–100–200) is 116.7 and for the BetaPERT the mean is 108.3. The means differ from the most likely

---

6   In Chapter 6 the Risk Driver approach to cost risk analysis shows that we can incorporate risk events that have a chance to occur or not and if they occur to have an impact on the project element's cost, in our analysis. At this point there is nearly a 100 percent likelihood that the cost will differ from the estimated project element's cost.

because the 3-point estimate is skewed toward the pessimistic or threat side, as we point out an occurrence so common in project cost risk analysis that we use it throughout this example.

How do we compute the standard deviation of the total project cost distribution from the data given to us as 3-point estimates for each project element line item? The standard deviation of the total project cost distribution is the square root of the sum of the variances (not the sum of the standard deviations) of each uncertain project element line item's cost:

Standard Deviation of total project cost distribution

=

Square root (sum of the individual project element line item's *variances*)

These equations are easy enough to program into the spreadsheet while we are waiting for the Monte Carlo simulation software to arrive. What we now need to know is the equation for the mean and standard deviation of our chosen distributions, in this case the triangular but perhaps later the BetaPERT, given the 3-point data that we have collected. Here are those definitions

Table 2.4   Equations for mean and variance to use in MOM – triangular and BetaPERT

Mean	Variance
Triangular distribution (exact formulae)	
(L + ML+ H) /3	((H – ML)^2 + (H – ML) * (ML – L) + (ML – L)^2)/18
BetaPERT distribution (approximate formulae)	
(H + 4*ML + L)/6	((H – L)/6)^2

The Monte Carlo software has arrived but the IT department is examining it before installing it on your computer. Hence we get on with the work of using MOM. Table 2.5 shows how the means and variances are applied and the results attained:

Table 2.5   Using the MOM to derive the mean and standard deviation of total project cost. Estimate with 3-point range uncertainty extended to applying the MOM: triangular distributions

Project element	Optimistic	Most likely	Pessimistic	Mean	Variance
Preliminary engineering	30	40	75	48	88
Detailed engineering	90	100	200	130	611
Procurement of equipment	210	250	400	287	1583
Procurement of materials	250	300	500	350	2778
Construction	750	800	1000	850	2778
Commissioning	125	150	300	192	1458
Total project cost		1,640	**Mean =>**	**1,857**	9,296
			Standard deviation =>		**96.41**

Notice that the mean cost is $1,857 million whereas the sum of the most likely estimates is $1,640 million. The standard deviation is $96.4 million so we now have the first two moments of the total project cost distribution. However, which distribution shape should we assume for the total project cost? The Central Limit Theorem in statistics indicates that if you have "enough" uncertain variables added together the shape of the resulting distribution is close to the normal or Gaussian. Putting aside whether six elements is "enough" under this definition, the shape of the distribution with a mean value of 1,875 and a standard deviation of 96.4 is best captured by the normal distribution. Such a distribution is shown in Figure 2.4 below:

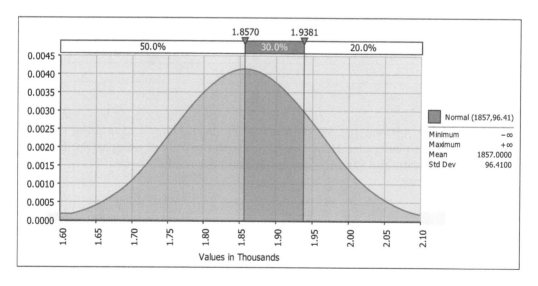

Figure 2.4   Normal distribution with MOM results, highlighting the 80th percentile[1]

---

1   This image was created in @RISK for Excel from Palisade Corporation.

The 80th percentile that is highlighted indicates that there is an 80 percent likelihood that this project, with the risks we have put into the spreadsheet model and solved using MOM, will cost $1,938 million or less. Why do we emphasize the 80th percentile? Admittedly it is not a recognized international best practice standard. Though a number of risk management professionals recommend the 80th percentile to their clients, some organizations have officially chosen other values such as 50 percent, 65 percent, 70 percent or even 90 percent for their decision-making. The higher the percentile chosen the more conservative the company wants to be about dealing with project risk. Using the 80th percentile as our target, the contingency reserve needed is calculated to be ($1,938 – $1,640 million) $298 million or about 18 percent of the base estimate of $1.640 million.

Suppose we have identified the 80th percentile, or "P-80," as our target. Using the MOM we only know the mean and standard deviation of this probability distribution, so how do we get the value for P-80? Using a table of the normal distribution, which can be found in any statistics texts or created in Microsoft Excel,[7] we find that the value that provides an 80 percent confidence level is the mean ($1,857) plus 84 percent of a standard deviation ($96.4 X.84 = $81 million) or $1,938 million.

It must be emphasized that project cost estimates usually have contingency reserves added below the line, and perhaps that value might be around 12 percent for $1,837 million cost including estimated contingency. Experience indicates that the mean value, in this case $1,857, is often pretty close to the estimator-furnished cost including contingency, indicating that whatever the estimator does is an approximation of the P-50, not the P-80. Hence, one benefit of using the Method of Moments is to be able to choose the level of certainty desired and compute the contingency to that level, even if it is not the mean value.

Why would we suggest a value of 80 percent which requires more contingency reserve and erodes project economics? If we adopt a budget that covers 80 percent rather than just 50 percent of the risks we know about, then we are in a better position to handle the risks we do not now know about, the unknown-unknowns that will be uncovered at a later stage of project execution.

Summary of Risk Building Blocks and Analytical Solution

The most important attitude adjustment needed when addressing the uncertainty in project cost estimates is to give up the conviction that the project cost estimate gives the correct result. In fact, since we do not know what will happen in the future, the estimate is just an educated guess. Many cost estimators do not ever understand that their well-prepared and well-documented cost estimate is actually only the beginning of project cost analysis. The balance of the story has to do with looking at the uncertainties and risks that could affect the cost of project element line items in actuality, given the current plan and the risks we can identify and quantify.

Often the project team or project manager is attached to the estimate, either because:

---

7   A table of the normal standard distribution is provided in Appendix A. A Table of the right half of the normal distribution in terms of any distribution's mean and standard deviation is provided in Appendix A. Find the percent of a standard deviation that provides an 80 percent likelihood of success.

- It is a political estimate already approved by upper management and there will be personal consequences if we admit there may be something wrong with it.
- The entire career and exposure to project cost estimating up to now has not included risk analysis, so why start now?
- Finding different (usually higher and sometimes dramatically so) costs will be embarrassing and might be put off until later.

However, we push ahead by interviewing project participants and others as well as reviewing history for similar project experiences, a step that the project manager may not have done in adopting the cost estimate. We develop for each project element line item cost a 3-point estimate:

- optimistic or lowest cost, usually with some benefits from finding opportunities (risks that reduce costs)
- most likely cost which may or may not be the same value that is in the cost estimate
- pessimistic or highest cost, often quite a bit higher than the most likely if we are honest, since there are many ways for a project to overrun a cost estimate.

With these 3-point estimates we can represent each project element's cost as a probability distribution rather than a single, deterministic number. The language of probability and the rules of statistics come into play when we realize that we are dealing with uncertainty.

Admitting that the line items are uncertain and that they should be described by probability distributions requires us to allow that the estimate of total project cost is also uncertain and represented by a probability distribution as well. Once we have 3-point estimates for each project element's cost we need to find a way to combine the probability distributions to derive the probability distribution of the total project's cost. The main best practice tool is Monte Carlo simulation, which will be covered in Chapter 3. In this chapter we introduce the Method of Moments or PERT Cost that will serve until the specialized simulation software has been purchased, received and checked out by the organization's IT department.

The Method of Moments or MOM uses the means and variances of the line items to compute the mean and standard deviation of the total project cost.

- Line item means are added to derive the mean of the total project cost. Notice that we do not add up the cost estimates or most likely values, since their sum does not correspond to any particular value in the total project cost distribution, following statistical rules.
- Line item variances are added and the square root of that number is computed to determine the standard deviation of the total project cost probability distribution.
- With the mean and standard deviation of the total project cost probability distribution and knowing that its shape tends toward the normal or Gaussian distribution with more and more line item distributions, we know a lot about total project cost risk. For instance we can calculate the 80th percentile cost.

The contingency reserves provided by cost estimating engineering companies usually are not based on thorough cost risk analyses and may in fact be estimates of the P-50, a fairly aggressive and risky value if experience can be relied upon. Using the MOM analytical approach, based on statistical rules and proven hypotheses as well as interviewed 3-point estimate data, we can do better than that.

References

Book, S. (1994). *Do Not Sum "Most Likely" Cost Estimates*. El Segundo, CA, The Aerospace Corporation.

Hulett, D. (2009). *Practical Project Schedule Risk Analysis*. Farnham, England, Gower Publishing.

Appendix A
Table of the Standard Normal Distribution Function

Sigma	Cum. Prob.	Sigma	Cum. Prob.	Sigma	Cum. Prob.	Sigma	Cum. Prob.	Sigma	Cum. Prob.
0.00	0.500	0.60	0.726	1.20	0.885	1.80	0.964	2.40	0.992
0.01	0.504	0.61	0.729	1.21	0.887	1.81	0.965	2.41	0.992
0.02	0.508	0.62	0.732	1.22	0.889	1.82	0.966	2.42	0.992
0.03	0.512	0.63	0.736	1.23	0.891	1.83	0.966	2.43	0.993
0.04	0.516	0.64	0.739	1.24	0.893	1.84	0.967	2.44	0.993
0.05	0.520	0.65	0.742	1.25	0.894	1.85	0.968	2.45	0.993
0.06	0.524	0.66	0.745	1.26	0.896	1.86	0.969	2.46	0.993
0.07	0.528	0.67	0.749	1.27	0.898	1.87	0.969	2.47	0.993
0.08	0.532	0.68	0.752	1.28	0.900	1.88	0.970	2.48	0.993
0.09	0.536	0.69	0.755	1.29	0.901	1.89	0.971	2.49	0.994
0.10	0.540	0.70	0.758	1.30	0.903	1.90	0.971	2.50	0.994
0.11	0.544	0.71	0.761	1.31	0.905	1.91	0.972	2.52	0.994
0.12	0.548	0.72	0.764	1.32	0.907	1.92	0.973	2.54	0.995
0.13	0.552	0.73	0.767	1.33	0.908	1.93	0.973	2.56	0.995
0.14	0.556	0.74	0.770	1.34	0.910	1.94	0.974	2.58	0.995
0.15	0.560	0.75	0.773	1.35	0.912	1.95	0.974	2.60	0.995
0.16	0.564	0.76	0.776	1.36	0.913	1.96	0.975	2.62	0.996
0.17	0.568	0.77	0.779	1.37	0.915	1.97	0.976	2.64	0.996
0.18	0.571	0.78	0.782	1.38	0.916	1.98	0.976	2.66	0.996
0.19	0.575	0.79	0.785	1.39	0.918	1.99	0.977	2.68	0.996
0.20	0.579	0.80	0.788	1.40	0.919	2.00	0.977	2.70	0.997
0.21	0.583	0.81	0.791	1.41	0.921	2.01	0.978	2.72	0.997
0.22	0.587	0.82	0.794	1.42	0.922	2.02	0.978	2.74	0.997

Sigma	Cum. Prob.	Sigma	Cum. Prob.	Sigma	Cum. Prob.	Sigma	Cum. Prob.	Sigma	Cum. Prob.
0.23	0.591	0.83	0.797	1.43	0.924	2.03	0.979	2.76	0.997
0.24	0.595	0.84	0.800	1.44	0.925	2.04	0.979	2.78	0.997
0.25	0.599	0.85	0.802	1.45	0.927	2.05	0.980	2.80	0.997
0.26	0.603	0.86	0.805	1.46	0.928	2.06	0.980	2.82	0.998
0.27	0.606	0.87	0.808	1.47	0.929	2.07	0.981	2.84	0.998
0.28	0.610	0.88	0.811	1.48	0.931	2.08	0.981	2.86	0.998
0.29	0.614	0.89	0.813	1.49	0.932	2.09	0.982	2.88	0.998
0.30	0.618	0.90	0.816	1.50	0.933	2.10	0.982	2.90	0.998
0.31	0.622	0.91	0.819	1.51	0.935	2.11	0.983	2.92	0.998
0.32	0.626	0.92	0.821	1.52	0.936	2.12	0.983	2.94	0.998
0.33	0.629	0.93	0.824	1.53	0.937	2.13	0.983	2.96	0.999
0.34	0.633	0.94	0.826	1.54	0.938	2.14	0.984	2.98	0.999
0.35	0.637	0.95	0.829	1.55	0.939	2.15	0.984	3.00	0.999
0.36	0.641	0.96	0.832	1.56	0.941	2.16	0.985	3.05	0.999
0.37	0.644	0.97	0.834	1.57	0.942	2.17	0.985	3.10	0.999
0.38	0.648	0.98	0.837	1.58	0.943	2.18	0.985	3.15	0.999
0.39	0.652	0.99	0.839	1.59	0.944	2.19	0.986	3.20	0.999
0.40	0.655	1.00	0.841	1.60	0.945	2.20	0.986	3.25	0.999
0.41	0.659	1.01	0.844	1.61	0.946	2.21	0.986	3.30	1.000
0.42	0.663	1.02	0.846	1.62	0.947	2.22	0.987	3.35	1.000
0.43	0.666	1.03	0.849	1.63	0.949	2.23	0.987	3.40	1.000
0.44	0.670	1.04	0.851	1.64	0.950	2.24	0.988	3.45	1.000
0.45	0.674	1.05	0.853	1.65	0.951	2.25	0.988	3.50	1.000
0.46	0.677	1.06	0.855	1.66	0.952	2.26	0.988	3.55	1.000
0.47	0.681	1.07	0.858	1.67	0.953	2.27	0.988	3.60	1.000
0.48	0.684	1.08	0.860	1.68	0.954	2.28	0.989	3.65	1.000

Sigma	Cum. Prob.	Sigma	Cum. Prob.	Sigma	Cum. Prob.	Sigma	Cum. Prob.	Sigma	Cum. Prob.
0.49	0.688	1.09	0.862	1.69	0.955	2.29	0.989	3.70	1.000
0.50	0.692	1.10	0.864	1.70	0.955	2.30	0.989	3.75	1.000
0.51	0.695	1.11	0.867	1.71	0.956	2.31	0.990	3.80	1.000
0.52	0.699	1.12	0.869	1.72	0.957	2.32	0.990	3.85	1.000
0.53	0.702	1.13	0.871	1.73	0.958	2.33	0.990	3.90	1.000
0.54	0.705	1.14	0.873	1.74	0.959	2.34	0.990	3.95	1.000
0.55	0.709	1.15	0.875	1.75	0.960	2.35	0.991	4.00	1.000
0.56	0.712	1.16	0.877	1.76	0.961	2.36	0.991		
0.57	0.716	1.17	0.879	1.77	0.962	2.37	0.991		
0.58	0.719	1.18	0.881	1.78	0.963	2.38	0.991		
0.59	0.722	1.19	0.883	1.79	0.963	2.39	0.992		

CHAPTER 3

What is Monte Carlo Simulation and How Does it Apply to Cost Risk Analysis?

Introduction

Project cost estimates provide single-point values that are represented by the engineering estimators as the basis for the cost of each project element. The estimator then sums those elements to calculate a number that is represented to the customer as the total cost of the project without contingency reserve. A contingency reserve is then added below the line and the total including contingency reserve is represented as "what the project will cost." This number is used in promoting the project and calculating project economics, in talking with financial sources and even government agencies.

In Chapter 2 we have been challenged to see the reality, which is that nobody knows with certainty the cost of any project element or of the entire project with or without contingency reserve. The costs of individual items are subject to all sorts of influences including bias or underestimating; risks from technical, external, organizational or even project management sources; uncertainties concerning the maturity of the data used in making the estimate or the appropriateness of the past completed projects that have been used for comparison purposes; and other sources that are essentially variable at the time the estimate is made.

In light of the uncertainty in the project estimate, we need a better way to estimate project costs. We have seen that the best way to think of project cost estimates is as probabilistic statements about future cost-related events. The project element costs are best represented by probability distributions with a range of possible values from optimistic (low) to pessimistic (high) with, usually, some value that is more likely than any of the rest (most likely). It is up to the project team, often with reference to engineering calculations, past projects and input from others in management or consultants, to describe the probability distribution of project element line item costs.

The problem we faced in the last chapter was that it is impossible to sum up probability distributions or shapes. We know how to add single numbers to get an accurate total down a column of numbers, but the line items are no longer single numbers. What do we do? How do we get a handle on the total project cost, which must also be a probability distribution if its input components are distributions?

We have heard of Monte Carlo simulation but unfortunately it requires specialized software that we do not yet have (it's coming, just a few more days). So, in Chapter 2 we introduced an analytic method called the Method of Moments that has correct statistical rules that allow us to define the mean and standard deviation of the total project cost distribution.[1] As a way to sum up probability distributions, the MOM has its limitations, including:

- It can only be used on simple summation-type models. If there is any detail to the project cost estimate that uses other arithmetical operations such as multiplication of quantity times unit cost, and you have uncertainty about quantity (material take-offs are not always accurate) and unit cost (market cost of raw materials, labor or even equipment are volatile), the MOM cannot be used ahead of a multiplication.
- The MOM assumes a type of probability distribution for the total project cost estimate. We assumed that the total project cost distribution was normal, relying on the Central Limit Theorem, but we really do not have enough project elements to invoke the result that the sum distribution is close to the normal. Still, we used the normal distribution assumption, knowing it was not exactly correct, and derived values for the total cost such as its distribution's mean, standard deviation and 80th percentile.

We are told that the Monte Carlo simulation software will be installed tomorrow morning. We will be happy with that, since it does not have the limitations of the MOM. And we can use the simulation results to see how accurate our MOM results were.

What is Monte Carlo Simulation?

There are several ways to describe Monte Carlo simulation.

- We often like to make estimates by referring to many similar projects and their results. Unfortunately we do not have many similar projects, so Monte Carlo simulation creates a virtual population of projects that are just like the one under analysis, down to its structure, estimate and project risks. We can learn something from this population of projects that can provide intelligence about this project.
- While there are many projects created by Monte Carlo simulation we do not know which one is ours, so we have to rely on summary statistics from this virtual population of projects like ours. Summary statistics such as the mean cost, costs at any percentile, and other characteristics will help us understand our specific project.

Monte Carlo simulation starts with the cost or schedule model of the project, so it is based in project management discipline, methodology and essential documents. Monte Carlo simulation also recognizes the uncertainty that we have put into the model for those elements' costs that we do not know with clarity. The cost model with the line items used in this chapter is shown in Table 3.1.

---

1   There are more than two "moments" that describe probability distributions shapes, including skewness, and the like. In project risk analysis we need to deal only with the first two moments, the mean and the standard deviation of variance.

Table 3.1   Estimate with 3-point ranges representing cost risk

Project element	Optimistic	Most likely	Pessimistic
Preliminary engineering	30	40	75
Detailed engineering	90	100	200
Procurement of equipment	210	250	400
Procurement of materials	250	300	500
Construction	750	800	1000
Commissioning	125	150	300
Total project cost triangular		1,640	

- Monte Carlo recognizes the distributions that we have put into the cost model. It knows the shape of those distributions and the parameters (3-point estimates) because we have specified those.
- Monte Carlo "runs" or "iterates" the project multiple times, creating often thousands of projects that could represent our own. For each iteration Monte Carlo selects at random a cost for each project element and calculates the total cost of the project for that iteration by summing those elements. Each of these iterations represents a possible project since it creates a different possible project every time by taking its costs from the cost probability distributions specified by the analyst.
- The way Monte Carlo selects the costs at random for each cost element and for each iteration is to use the cumulative distribution implied by the 3-point estimate and the distribution chosen (triangular in this case) for each of the uncertain project element input distributions. For each iteration and for each project element the simulation software selects at random a number from 0 to 1.0 using the computer's random number generator. This value is placed along the Y-axis of the project element's cumulative distribution. (In our case with the six project elements shown in Table 3.1 there are six random numbers are selected and used for each iteration.) This random number is translated into a specific cost by the cumulative distribution derived from the 3-point estimate of that project element, and that cost value is used for that element in that iteration. This process is illustrated in Figures 3.1 and 3.2.

The triangular probability distribution function for Construction shown in Figure 3.1 can be converted to a cumulative distribution shown in Figure 3.2. The cumulative distribution function is used to translate the random numbers between 0.0 and 1.0 to cost values such as $877.5 million that corresponds to a randomly chosen Y-axis value of .7.

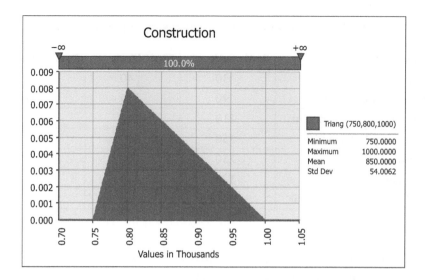

Figure 3.1   Triangular distribution for construction (750, 800, 1000)

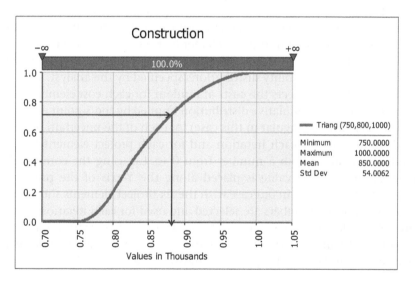

Figure 3.2   How Monte Carlo simulation selects a cost value for a specific iteration[2]

- Because the simulation software uses the cumulative distribution from the analyst's 3-point estimate and choice of distribution shape, the entire project element cost distribution is reflected in the random costs selected for each iteration and each cost during the simulation. Notice that the cumulative distribution is relatively steep around the most likely value (800 in Table 3.1 because we chose the construction project element). For the iteration shown, the random number selected was .7 and the

---

Construction cost used for that iteration is about 877.5 million. Each of the uncertain cost elements has a random number selected and a translation using this method on the element's specific cumulative distribution for each of the iterations. For each iteration the values selected at random are considered to be known with certainty.

- Because we do not know the costs with certainty, we have to admit that the first iteration, using randomly selected costs, might not represent our project. Hence we want to conduct (find the cost of) another project that might be our project, by selecting some other project element costs. In fact we want to calculate many project costs that may be our project, in the sense that they have the same project elements and the same probability distributions for each element's cost. Table 3.1 above shows the estimate and the 3-point ranges derived mainly from interviewing the project team and others. Note that the Optimistic and Pessimistic columns are not totaled. It would be practically impossible for all of the project elements to be optimistic or pessimistic together.

Table 3.2 below shows the resulting cost estimate and the first five iterations.

Table 3.2   Compare the estimate to five randomly selected iterations in Monte Carlo

Project element	Estimate	Iteration 1	Iteration 2	Iteration 3	Iteration 4	Iteration 5
Preliminary engineering	40	68	51	55	32	58
Detailed engineering	100	116	148	103	120	99
Procurement of equipment	250	265	300	311	321	220
Procurement of materials	300	390	324	380	285	346
Construction	800	909	819	796	912	873
Commissioning	150	213	173	181	264	186
Total project estimate	1,640	1,961	1,815	1,826	1,934	1,782

Notice that a different value is chosen *in each iteration* for *each* line item, and that the project estimates derived from those iterations are different as a result. Of course it could be that in 10,000 iterations we might get repeats in inputs and certainly in outputs, but the process is random.

Technical Aspects of Monte Carlo Simulations

There are a few technical aspects of the practice of Monte Carlo simulation that all practitioners should know. For instance:

- Why do we usually select the Latin Hypercube sampling approach? "Monte Carlo" technically refers to the way that the random numbers are selected to support the calculations. Monte Carlo data selection is strictly random, so one value in a series might be close to or far away from the previous value in the same series.

What is used nowadays is the Latin Hypercube method of random data selection. Latin Hypercube is a stratified approach to selecting the random numbers for the calculations wherein the selection is more likely to match the input distribution, particularly in selections representing values in the tails of the distributions. (See Vose 1966 pp. 42–5 for a discussion.) We get more accuracy for the same number of iterations or we can get the same accuracy with fewer iterations compared to strictly random Monte Carlo data selection. Anyone who has Latin Hypercube sampling available in the simulation software will choose to use it over purely random Monte Carlo sampling.

- How many iterations are required for accurate results? This question is always subject to discussion among professionals. The more iterations are performed the more accuracy is produced, but with diminishing returns. Usually analysts want to perform 5,000–10,000 iterations for accuracy, particularly for the final report runs, but in some cases the results from 5,000 iterations are not materially different from those produced by 2,000 iterations. In project risk analysis, unlike some of the natural sciences, the input data are usually derived from interviews of knowledgeable project participants using a combination of their expert judgment along with some historical data. It would be unhelpful to insist on many thousands of iterations to polish the last few decimal places on an analysis where (1) the input data are not precise, and (2) the main message is produced with fewer iterations. Clearly 100 iterations will not do, and a 1,000-iteration simulation is marginal. You may use fewer iterations for draft or provisional simulations to save computer time while reserving the large-sample simulations for final results. Happily, most of the computers are fast and most of the software is optimized for simulation speed.[3]
- What is the "seed value" that starts off the selection of random numbers that are applied? The seed value is the value that initializes the random number sequences generated by the computer's random number generator. If the seed value does not change from one simulation to the next, precisely the same series of random numbers will be chosen and applied in the second simulation as in the first. This is useful if one is trying to measure the difference on the results caused by a new assumption (for example, different 3-point estimate or a BetaPERT versus a triangular distribution). Any difference between the results will be the result of the assumption change and will not, in addition, differ because the random numbers have changed between simulations. To evaluate whether the selection of random numbers makes a difference in the results, an analyst might re-run the same simulation with a different seed value. Notice that the effect of the seed value is less if the number of iterations increases.

---

3   The simulations in this chapter were conducted with 10,000 iterations and each simulation took less than 5 seconds. Of course the spreadsheet has been kept small to be used for illustrative purposes, but even larger spreadsheets simulate rapidly.

Results from Monte Carlo Simulation

The simulation produces a very large sample of projects, any one of which could be our project. Any one of the iterations generated by the simulation could be our project because they have the same basis and were generated to include the same risks as ours does. However, there is no telling which of the large sample of projects produced by the simulation is ours. We have to use the statistical properties of the Monte Carlo results as a guide to understanding our project.

The 10,000 iterations of the entire project using the 3-point estimates we gathered produces a histogram, namely the probability distribution of possible results for our project. The results are shown below in Figure 3.3.

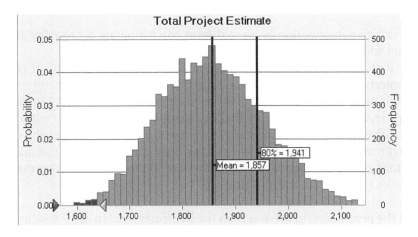

Figure 3.3   Histogram of the total project estimate using 10,000 iterations

What can we say about the project from this histogram?

- The estimate of $1,640 (see Table 3.1) is not the most likely cost. The most likely total cost from the histogram is about $1,857 billion which is also the mean of the distribution.
- The range of the distribution falls between $1.566 billion and over $2.270 billion, a difference of about $700 million.[4] This indicates that, with the current plan and without further risk mitigation there is a wide range of possible values.
- The four columns on the far left-hand side of the histogram are shaded, indicating the probability that the project will come in at or under the total project estimate (without contingency) of $1.640 billion. In cost estimating this may be understood and the reason that the owner demands the project estimators to include in addition

---

4   Note that the sums of the optimistic and pessimistic values in Table 3.1 would have been $1,455 and $2,475 respectively, outside of the lowest and highest values out of 10,000 generated by the simulation. The simulation results differ because there is cancelling out in each iteration – where one cost element is high in its range another may be low, moderate or high in its own range. The elements' costs are considered to be independent of one another and there is no correlation between costs in this example. This is why summing those columns in Table 3.1 is not professional and not advised.

an estimated contingency reserve. However, these estimated contingencies may not be based on anything solid or related to the project under analysis.

● There is a marker at the 80th percentile point. The value is $1,941 million. This means that there is an 80 percent chance that this plan, with these risks unmitigated, will cost $1,941 million or less. Project risk analysts often highlight the 80th percentile since it is useful to get ahead of the risks we know about (known unknowns) so that the new risks (unknown unknowns) can be addressed from a position of some strength. However, some companies or government agencies focus on the 50th percentile (called P-50), although others target the P-65, P-70 or even P-90 and are somewhat conservative.

The histogram also has its corresponding cumulative distribution shown in Figure 3.4.

● The cumulative distribution is created from the histogram by moving from left to right and adding the height of each vertical bar as you come to it.
● Clearly it starts at zero percent and accumulates until 100 percent of the possible total project cost values have been accounted for. There is no probability below the minimum value ($1,566 million) or above the maximum value ($2,270 million).
● Its shape represents the height of the histogram as you move from left to right. For instance, the cumulative distribution curve has a rather low slope at the ends where the height of the histogram bars are low but quite a steep slope in the middle where the histogram bars are high. The cumulative distribution, which makes the percentile costs easier to read is shown in Figure 3.4.

Notice that the percentiles up the Y-axis on the left correspond to the P-x values discussed above where "x" represents any value of interest. For instance, clearly the P-80 horizontal line intersects the cumulative distribution at $1,941 million. This cumulative distribution provides much of the analytic information from the simulation. A table of values using the percentiles and their corresponding values is shown below in Table 3.3.

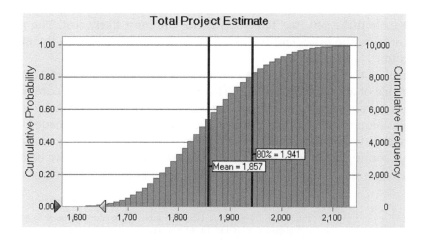

Figure 3.4   Cumulative distribution of total project costs

Table 3.3   Dollar values by percentile for total project cost from the simulation

Percentile	Forecast values
0%	1,566
10%	1,732
20%	1,770
30%	1,800
40%	1,828
50%	1,853
60%	1,878
70%	1,907
80%	1,941
90%	1,987
100%	2,270

The dollar values and their associated percentiles are interpreted as follows: "Given the project plan, cost estimate and risks as stated, the cost of the project has an X percent chance of costing $Y or less," where X is the Percentile and Y is the Forecast Value that corresponds to that percentile as shown in Table 3.3. It is the "or less" part of this statement that is seen most clearly in the cumulative distribution of Figure 3.4. Focus on the 80th percentile, or the "P-80." Notice that in the table the value is $1,941 million. The cumulative distribution also shows that there is 80 percent of the total probability distribution to the left of $1,941 million.

Creating the Project Cost Contingency Reserve

The result of a project risk analysis leads to a recommended contingency reserve, or rather to several alternative reserves from which the project stakeholders can choose based on their desire for cost certainty. The amount of reserve needed if the current project plan is to be followed depends on the stakeholders' tolerance for project cost risk or their risk aversion. The risk analyst produces the table shown below as Table 3.4, and the project owners or contractor (depending on who is commissioning the cost risk analysis) will apply their own desired level of certainty. Since we have emphasized the P-80 we are perhaps representing a fairly conservative organization. The table indicates that the total value of the project at the P-80 is $1,941 million (we have shown this previously in the figures). Comparing that value to the estimate without contingency of $1,640 million we have a $301 million contingency reserve, which is calculated as 18 percent over the contingency-free estimate.

Table 3.4   Calculating the cost contingency reserve using risk analysis and the project owner's risk tolerance

Total project estimate		Contingency reserve	
Percentile	Forecast	Dollar	Percent
0%	1,566	−74	−5%
10%	1,732	92	6%
20%	1,770	130	8%
30%	1,800	160	10%
40%	1,828	188	11%
50%	1,853	213	13%
60%	1,878	238	15%
70%	1,907	267	16%
80%	1,941	301	18%
90%	1,987	347	21%
100%	2,270	630	38%

Most project cost estimates constructed by engineering firms include a contingency reserve. Experience tells us that those reserves estimated by the engineering firms are frequently close to the P-50 value that results from a Monte Carlo simulation exercise. This observation does not imply that the estimators have conducted a Monte Carlo simulation and chosen the P-50 value. It is more likely that the multiplicative values that are used by the standard contingency calculations represent average risks found over many prior projects, so the results may confirm those values.[5] One benefit of a Monte Carlo simulation is that the project owner has several values, graduated as to the degree of certainty they provide, to choose from and that the client knows that the values reflect the project cost risks directly.

Comparison of the Method of Moments and Simulation Approaches

Let us see how close our MOM results from Chapter 2 were to the Monte Carlo simulation results. Remember, Monte Carlo does not assume anything about the shape of the total project estimate probability distribution, whereas our MOM assumption, based on the Central Limit Theorem, was that this distribution was normal. The comparison is shown in Table 3.5.

---

5   Of course, when the standard contingency calculation has been overridden by the application of political pressure, it becomes essentially unusable.

Table 3.5   Similar results in this case using MOM and Monte Carlo simulation

	Mean	Sigma	80th Percentile
Method of Moments	1,857	96.4	1,938
Monte Carlo Simulation	1,857	96	1,941

In this case the results are similar. The P-80 values are within 1 percent of each other. Of course this result does not mean that the Method of Moments is equal to simulation. We have seen that the assumption of a normal total cost distribution is close in this case.

The main difference between the MOM and simulation approaches lies in the limitations of applying the MOM which are discussed in Chapter 2. MOM is applicable only to simple summation models where uncertain values are either added or subtracted. Monte Carlo simulation does not suffer from that limitation. We could correctly apply Monte Carlo simulation to values that are multiplied, divided or raised to some power, whereas in these situations the MOM is not applicable. Simulation is simply more powerful and flexible than MOM. Admittedly, MOM can be applied on a common spreadsheet platform whereas simulation requires specialized software. Happily simulation software is available that is not expensive and that adds-in to the commonly available spreadsheet.[6]

Sensitivity Analysis – Most Important Risk Elements

Suppose the project manager finds that the results of the risk analysis, say at the P-80 level, raises the cost to a value that is too high. Perhaps the contractor conducts the risk analysis and decides that they cannot bid successfully if they need to add $301 million or 18 percent to their base estimate. Of course this begs the question: "If the P-80 is a company-standard risk tolerance threshold for this type of project at this time in the business cycle, perhaps you should not wish to win the bid at some lower number." It may be unwise to select a lower contingency reserve.

The contractor may very much want to bid the project but still adhere to the company policy of bidding at the P-80 level. Another question they might have is: "Which of the uncertain project elements is most important in determining the uncertainty of the total project cost?" This question often leads the project team to a focused risk mitigation exercise that results in adjusting the project plan to one that has less risk of overrunning the base estimate. Of course risk mitigation usually costs money, so the project manager must accept paying actual dollars to mitigate risks that might not happen. This is often a tough choice to make and many project managers avoid changing the plan, preferring instead to "cross their fingers" and hope the risks will not occur. Cross-your-fingers project management does not seem to be an enlightened approach.

One analytical tool that helps understand the relative importance of the different risks is the sensitivity analysis. This analysis correlates the input uncertainties, in this case

---

6   Two popular simulation software packages that add in to Microsoft Excel are Crystal Ball from Oracle and @RISK from Palisade Corporation. Each of these is used in this book. There are other simulation tools as well, several of them simulating project schedules.

the uncertain project element costs, with the uncertain total project cost estimate. The sensitivity analysis presents the uncertain project elements in order of their correlation to the total cost, highest correlation on the top of the chart, in order to prioritize the risky elements. The basis of the usefulness of this tool is that:

*   While correlation between two uncertain variables does not necessarily imply causality, in this case causality can be assumed since the project's cost elements drive the total project cost, not vice versa.
*   The closer the variation in the two types of uncertain variables is, as shown by the coefficient of correlation between them, the more closely the project element line item input drives or determines the total project cost output. It follows that if you want to reduce the uncertainty of the overall total project cost, it would be useful to focus your efforts on those uncertain project elements that cause the project cost to be uncertain.

Examining Figure 3.5 it seems that uncertainty in the cost of construction and in the cost of procured materials are the most important in determining uncertainty in total project costs. It seems logical that controlling the uncertainty in the project components at the top of the sensitivity chart will be most effective in controlling total project costs. The prioritization of project elements does not mean that the mitigation of the risks on construction and procured materials will be easy or even feasible. The project manager will also want to consider the ease and cost of risk mitigation compared to the effectiveness in reducing the risk in total project cost before enacting risk mitigation.

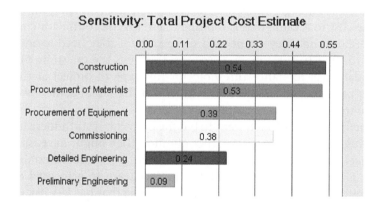

Figure 3.5   Sensitivity chart – values represent correlation. Compare the results using triangular and BetaPERT distributions

Effect of the Choice of Probability Distribution on the Results

Earlier in the last chapter we saw that two alternative distributions have the attractive property that they can be asymmetrical and specified fully by the 3-point estimates. These are the Triangular and the BetaPERT distributions. We showed, using the measures of the mean and standard deviation, that the triangular distribution exhibits more uncertainty than the BetaPERT for the same 3-point estimate. Let us look at the practical impact of the choice of one or the other of these two distributions on the total cost results distributions.

In Figure 3.6 the two distributions are overlaid on each other. The broader distribution reflects the use of the triangular input distribution for all project elements while the taller but narrower uses only BetaPERT in each example the 3-point estimates are the same.

Notice that the mean using triangular distributions is the same as before (MOM and simulation) at $1,857 million while if the BetaPERT were used (we could get something close to this in MOM as well) the mean is $1,748 million, at least $100 million less risky. This serious difference is simply the result of a choice of probability distributions, since the model and seed values are the same. The difference is shown also at the P-80 where triangular distributions result in $1,941 million and BetaPERT in $1,814 (or $127 million less). Again, the BetaPERT distribution exhibits less risk, equivalent to more certainty about its mean value than does the triangular. The lesson to be learned here is that the choice of distribution types makes a difference. Many risk analysts use the Triangular distribution routinely, moving to another distribution only if the description of the risk clearly rules out the Triangular.

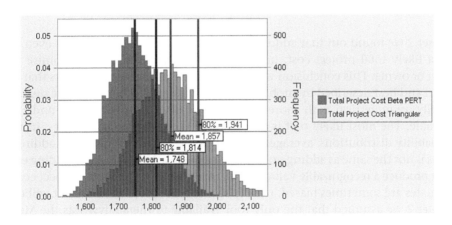

Figure 3.6   Comparison of triangular and BetaPERT distribution result histogram

The percentile results are compared in Table 3.6, with the P-80 results highlighted.

Table 3.6   Comparison of triangular and BetaPERT distribution results percentiles

Percentile	BetaPERT	Triangular
0%	1,523	1,566
10%	1,651	1,733
20%	1,680	1,771
30%	1,704	1,802
40%	1,725	1,828
50%	1,745	1,854
60%	1,765	1,879
70%	1,788	1,907
80%	**1,814**	**1,941**
90%	1,852	1,986
100%	2,076	2,292

Summary

In Chapter 2 we found out that adding the project cost estimates does not even produce the most likely total project cost, much less will it be a safe cost to promise to some customer or owner. This conclusion was caused by the project element costs that were (1) uncertain and best described by probability distributions and that (2) those distributions are usually asymmetrical with more likelihood of overrunning than of underrunning the estimate. The most likely cost is not even the cost estimate in all cases. In this case the probability distributions' averages differ from the project estimates, so adding up the estimates is not the same as adding up averages or means. Another reason adding estimates does not produce a recognizable value (mean, most likely) for the total project cost is that the estimates are sometimes biased, usually to make the project look like it will cost less. In Chapter 2 we assumed that the only tool available to the analyst was the Method of Moments (MOM), an analytical tool that is only applicable to simple summation models without any arithmetic operations other than adding and subtracting.

In this chapter we introduced the much more flexible, powerful and generally accepted best practice tool of Monte Carlo simulation. This tool requires specialized but available software that is worth the wait. For instance, Monte Carlo simulation can be applied appropriately to many different mathematical operations such as multiplication, division, exponentiation, net present value, and so on.

We discussed the notion of randomness in the variables that are inputs to the cost estimate, and how simulation represents that randomness using the computer's random number generator. The input probability distributions translate the random values into costs that can be used, in each iteration, to represent a combination of possible input costs and hence possible total cost outcomes for our project. Since we do not know which iteration represents our project we need to iterate many times (10,000 iterations was used to create the graphs and table values of this chapter). We illustrated how iterations come about by showing a few iteration results. The simulation created cost results for a synthetic but large population of projects just like ours in every respect (same input variables, same cost estimates and same risks represented by 3-point estimates and triangular distributions). We learn about our project by examining the statistical characteristics of the many possible projects it could become.

The results from the simulation are histograms, cumulative distributions, tables of costs and percentiles and sensitivity charts. The histogram indicates the overall shape and range of possible costs, and identifies the most likely or mode of the total project cost distribution. Typically the mode or most likely total cost is greater than the sum of the project elements' costs. This finding is perhaps the basis for the traditional cost estimator's creation of a contingency reserve – he knows that typically engineering estimates are exceeded in practice.

The cumulative distribution and its associated table of values shows probabilities of the total cost being equal or less than certain values (called percentiles). The interpretation of this information is that, with the project plan and risks as we know them, the percentile is the probability that the project will cost the associated value, or less.

Since we care more about cost overruns than underruns, it is useful to look at the probability that the value will be overrun, so a P-80 value of $1,941 million has a 20 percent (100 percent – 80 percent) of being overrun. Experience shows that many organizations take a conservative approach, so they select target values of P-60 up to P-90. This represents (1) the realization that the penalties for overrunning exceed the benefits of underrunning, and (2) the fact that the analysis cannot include the risks that are unknown, which will likely push the project cost higher when they are revealed. If the project owner's or bidding contractor's risk tolerance to determine the appropriate percentile were P-80, the cumulative distribution determines the appropriate contingency reserve, in our case $301 million or 18 percent.

We showed that, in this simple model, the results from the Monte Carlo simulation and the MOM of Chapter 2 were very close to one another. This does not support using the MOM in any exercise other than the limited simple summation model, however, and simulation is the best practice approach to project cost risk analysis.

We examined the sensitivity analysis and showed how a statistical measure of correlation, together with our knowledge that project element costs drive total project costs, lead to our ability to prioritize the risks for possible risk mitigation exercises.

Finally we illustrated the importance of the selection of the input distribution types by comparing the results using (1) the triangular distributions for the uncertain project element cost inputs with (2) those that would result if we had used the BetaPERT distribution, the other obvious choice of potentially asymmetrical distributions that can be described by a 3-point estimate. Since the BetaPERT shows more certainty in the cost estimate than the triangle for the same 3-point estimate, we are not surprised that the results show more certainty in total project cost risk using BetaPERT. This exercise does not lead to a choice of one distribution over the other. Rather, the input distribution shape needs to reflect the facts of the risks as revealed by risk interviews and other analyses. The results will follow the input assumptions.

References

Vose, D. (2008). *Quantitative Risk Analysis, A Guide to Monte Carlo Simulation Modelling.* John Wiley & Sons, Ltd.

4 *Collecting High-Quality Data on Cost Risk Methods and Challenges*[1]

Introduction

The quality of the cost risk analysis depends to a large extent on the quality of the risk data used in the analysis. It is arguable that collecting data on 3-point estimates should be easier than agreeing on a single-point estimate, since the estimator is encouraged to express his uncertainty rather than suppress it. This should make it easier to collect risk data than to make the single-point estimates of cost. Surely the greatest amount of time in any risk analysis exercise is spent gathering good-quality data which in turn underpins good-quality results and provides credibility for the exercise with the organization.

On one level, risk analysis is no different from any other planning or analysis function (such as estimating) that requires people to quantify their judgments about things that may happen in the future. In another, risk analysis seems to differ in character from, say, project scheduling or cost estimating, since it asks those involved to admit and calibrate their uncertainty about those estimates. It is puzzling that people seem to be more comfortable making single-point estimates of activity durations that they will take responsibility for, rather than providing an estimate within an uncertain range. However, experience shows that many people have very little experience or feel uncomfortable expressing the degree of their uncertainty, so collecting quantified or calibrated risk information is a challenge.

Collecting data about project risk can be difficult. Some organizations avoid project risk analysis entirely because they believe the data collection is so problematic as to be no better than a guess. Other people use the problems associated with collecting risk data and the paucity of risk databases on which to draw as their rationale for avoiding risk analysis when, in fact, they are simply uncomfortable about considering the risk on their project in a quantitative way. Because the risk data are difficult to collect, you need to be both diligent and persistent in your efforts to gather the data and circumspect about their accuracy. Still, experience tells us that valuable and accurate results can be generated in project risk analysis.

---

1   This chapter is taken largely from Chapter 5 of *Practical Schedule Risk Analysis*, David Hulett, Gower Publishing, 2009, since the data quality issues in schedule and cost risk are much the same.

Types of Risk Data Needed

Risk analysis explores uncertainty in important project metrics. The main data that help in quantifying the schedule risk include the following:

- In cost risk analysis, the main issue is uncertainty in the project element line item cost (See Chapter 2). This uncertainty is represented by the 3-point estimate of cost for each risky project cost element.
- Coefficients of correlation between project element line item costs (see Chapter 5) are often calibrated.
- If the Risk Drivers approach is used (see Chapter 6), the individual risks are characterized by both their probability of occurring on this project and their impact range (a 3-point estimate of impacts) if they do occur.
- If there is a discontinuous event such as failing a qualifying test, the recovery from that event may cause cost elements to occur that are not in the original estimate. While this discrete risk is not used in cost risk as much as in schedule risk, if it were estimated the recovery work would have a probability and an impact if it were to occur.

These are the main types of risk data needed for mainstream schedule risk analysis.

The impact ranges are often misinterpreted by interviewees, particularly by those interviewees who are inexperienced in the risk analysis process. The inexperienced interviewee will often focus on estimating error alone, stipulating that the risk is "plus 10 percent and minus 5 percent." In contrast to the strictly estimating error that comes from a lack of mature data from which to make the estimate, the 3-point estimate needs to reflect also uncertainty based on risk events and other uncertainties. The 3-point estimate needs to reflect the very-most pessimistic cost, the very-most optimistic cost and the most likely cost considering all the risks that may have an influence on the project element.

Risk impact range estimating often starts with the line item cost estimate. Estimates of cost have at least three types of uncertainties that must be included when considering how the project plan could be affected:[2]

- Estimating uncertainty or error. This type of uncertainty is well-known and discussed in estimating class. Estimating error is 100 percent likely (until financial completion) and arises if there is a lack of definition of the work or some uncertainty in the input data needed to make the estimation. Estimating error is larger in the early versus later phases of the project. For instance, conceptual estimates are often subject to wide ranges, say +50 percent and −30 percent, whereas definitive estimates are narrower, for example, +20 percent and −10 percent, since the latter have the benefit of ongoing detailed engineering, data from vendors and information from prospective prime contractors. Ultimately, before the project execution, the owners' estimators have bids from contractors and some contractual basis of estimate. Even at that point, the actual costs may be thought of as within a range of +10 percent and −5 percent from the estimate. Those interviewees, who do not understand that we

---

2   Using the Risk Drivers approach, which is introduced in Chapter 6 the separate impacts of uncertainties and of risk events can be represented with their own probability and 3-point estimate of impact.

need to look at risk-based uncertainty as well, may respond with simply estimating error.

- Uncertainty based on risks. These errors typically involve risks that are discrete, with a probability of occurring that may be less than 100 percent and an impact range that may drive the actual line item cost away from the estimate if the risk occurs. The impact of these discrete risks, should they happen, is often not symmetrical because risks in project management are dominated by threats to the project that will be more likely to cause overruns than underruns if they occur. (Of course the opportunities that are found will determine the optimistic values in the 3-point estimates, so opportunities are not unimportant. A risk range that includes both opportunity and threat possibilities is usually skewed more toward bad results than toward the good results, however.)
- Uncertainty based on ambiguities. Some project cost risk is based on uncertainty in numbers that are always present but with uncertain impacts. Labor productivity assumption in construction projects is one such. There is always an estimated productivity underlying the cost estimate so its chance of occurring is 100 percent. However, the productivity assumption is usually uncertain which leads to productivity-influenced costs that can be higher or lower than the base estimate. These uncertainties are often not included in the definition of risk, as in "risk events," but they must be included in the analysis of cost risk.

We have to be clear in collecting data that all three types of risk impact ranges are needed. Some inexperienced interviewees will provide estimating error only, either under the impression that it is what we are asking or because they do not have the experience or the confidence to provide risk impact ranges as well. With experience, interviewees tend to become more inclusive and their risk data becomes more useful.

Some Considerations that Make Gathering Risk Data Difficult

Several factors contribute to making the gathering or generating of project risk data more difficult than the gathering of traditional project management data (such as single-point estimates of schedule durations and project element costs) or other data used to build up the project plan. These factors can be classified into those that relate to individuals and those that relate to the cultural environment within which the risk analyses are conducted.

REASONS THAT ARE BASED ON THE INDIVIDUAL

Risk data are inherently different from standard project planning data since they explore the limits of our uncertainty. While it seems counterintuitive, it appears to be easier for people to be definite about a single number, say the cost of a project element, than to express a range within which that duration will probably fall. This is true even if they know the number is likely to be wrong. Exploring the degree of uncertainty makes people uneasy because:

- The very act of supplying risk data impugns the basis of our plan itself. Describing a range of values is tantamount to admitting that the interviewee does not know the answer. Most engineers are very influential in developing project plans and estimates, by dint of their professional credibility. They have a preference in favor of precision and against ambiguity, even when their own history provides examples where the exact estimates have been repeatedly proven wrong. Individually, they like to be definite, and suggesting that a value is correct only within a range runs counter to their training and mindset.
- Uncertainty concepts such as the most pessimistic, most optimistic and even the most likely costs are new to them. For some reason, many people find that making a set of assumptions for a single-point deterministic estimate is easier than making a set of assumptions for the pessimistic or optimistic values, even if the link between assumptions and the single-point estimates is vague or untested.
- Some other risk concepts are just plain new to team members. For instance, in many cases, they have not been asked to estimate the probability that a risk will occur. The question comes to them without any context which makes them uncomfortable about making an estimate. Calibrating the correlation between two activity durations is even more unfamiliar and puzzling to most.
- Interviewees know that projects could proceed differently from the plan but each individual has a limited set of experiences from which to draw. Team members typically find it difficult to generalize from a subset of experiences to the broader concepts.
- Interviewees do not have training or mentoring in specifying the optimistic and pessimistic extremes that could happen to change the activity durations. In specific they are not accustomed to considering the extreme pessimistic or extreme optimistic case, preferring to discuss the P-10 and P-90 (10th and 90th percentile) values. Their training usually involves how to make single-point deterministic estimates without any uncertainty (representing unreasonable hope in the face of uncertain reality). Even accepted "fudge factors" or contingency reserve estimates are prescribed by management or their profession as exact percentages of specific line items or summary lines.

Individuals typically develop risk data by using their expert judgment. It is well documented that most people rely on heuristics or rules of thumb when using their expert judgment to develop these data. If heuristics were perfect, the data would be very good. However, we describe below some well-known biases associated with the use of heuristics that are documented in the literature and in practice. These are generally classified as "cognitive biases."

These reasons that come from the individuals' own background or mindset can be overcome in most cases by positive experience, expert facilitation, repetition of good practices and encouragement from management. Positive feedback and encouragement when they first encounter these new concepts will help them overcome the resistance they initially feel. However, the organization may not always be supportive of the risk analysis exercise.

REASONS CAUSED BY THE ORGANIZATIONAL CULTURE

Organizational culture tends to set up penalties for those who contradict the corporate position. These penalties often establish an atmosphere where "motivational bias" occurs. Even discussing project risk may have unfavorable implications for the individual, since risk usually has negative implications for the organization. Those who provide risk data may be punished or otherwise made to feel uncomfortable or "not a team player":

- The organization may have made representations to the public, lenders or government agencies based on a specific number. For instance, suppose a company applies for and receives a project development loan for $100 million dollars based on a cost estimate and schedule for the project. If the risk analysis calls into question the cost and schedule that were used as the basis for the loan, there will be resistance and reluctance even to consider analyzing the risk. If the risk analysis is conducted the organization will exert pressure to make sure "there is no risk in our plan." If the risk analysis shows there is substantial risk it is likely to be thrown away and those involved may be punished. It is easier for the organization to avoid conducting the risk analysis at all.
- Management or customers may have decided that a project will finish on a certain day and that its cost will be a certain amount. Contemplating a risk analysis is not comfortable for the team because it may challenge management's target milestones.
- Any manager, team member or other subject matter expert (SME) who is asked about the risk in the project is being asked, essentially, to challenge the very basis of the project plan and the basis of estimate (BOE) that results in the cost estimate. The implications of any honest risk analysis are unlikely to make the project look better than planned, and most people do not look forward to being part of that analysis.
- There may be an atmosphere that is hostile to project risk analysis because it is new or unconventional. It may even be deemed to be too difficult for the organization to perform, even if the organization is made up of true "rocket scientists." Perhaps risk analysis is not part of the traditional project management suite of tools.[3] Often organizations do not want to look into risk. Anyone within the organization who raises the specter that risk may occur and jeopardize the plans may be ostracized or punished in other ways. The term "shoot the messenger" is common for the way these people are treated by a hostile corporate culture.

These organizational culture issues can trump any individual's desire to conduct risk analysis. Major David Christensen reviewed the Navy's A-12 acquisition program, which was cancelled in 1991 because of cost overruns and concluded: "Expert judgment must not be impaired by a culture that suppresses truth ... In short, a so-called "shoot the messenger" culture will absolutely destroy responsible decision-making by biasing the database of the analysis of it" (Christensen 1993).[4]

---

3   Craig Peterson, then President of the Project Management Institute's Risk Management Specific Interest Group has often said that the Risk Management chapter of the PMI's PMBOK® Guide would be only one page with: "This Page Left Intentionally Blank" if it only reflected current practice at most companies.

4   The earned value data had been projecting significant cost overruns for some time before cancellation of the A-12 project. The corporate culture of the contractors and the Navy overrode those forecasts for months.

The organization may be worse than unaware of project risk analysis; it may actually be hostile to the concept. A hostile culture may be way beyond a simple lack of maturity in risk management. Aversion to project risk management is often strongest in middle management who are trying to make the project look good to management and other stakeholders. Sometimes top management understands that there is risk and would like to know that the project manager is aware of it and doing something about it, although in other organizations the top management may also be opposed to risk analysis.

All of the training, software, risk management handbooks and desire to examine risk can be thwarted by a hostile corporate culture. Sometimes, even in the face of a competent risk analysis, management says: "I am not giving up on my numbers."

It may be necessary to engage an independent expert from outside the organization to conduct the risk analysis. Somebody who gets a salary from the organization may not be willing to go up against his own organization and risk his career. An outside independent expert will be hired for a specific risk analysis engagement and can often do that job honestly, even enhancing his or her future or reputation. If a champion hires a consultant and supports them in the face of the corporate culture the job can be done with honesty and integrity. The expert does not depend on the organization for a large part of their income and gets hired in part based on their integrity and honesty as well as their expertise.

The good news is that actively hostile corporate cultures are encountered less frequently as time goes on. There are several factors that make the environment more conducive to risk analysis:

- Experience with risk analysis. Sometimes just having someone in the organization, the "champion," conduct risk analysis and derive benefits will serve as an inducement and cover for others to follow.
- Some organizations are adopting procedures and publishing handbooks for the conduct of project risk management. This often includes quantitative risk analysis, although quantitative risk analysis is not usually the first discipline likely to be included.
- Customers are demanding risk analysis for reluctant contractors. The problem with this approach is that the contractors have most of the information and the customers do not have their own experts ready to step in with the data to validate contractors' results.
- For government agencies involved in acquisition of major systems or products, Government agencies such as the Office of Management and Budget and the Government Accountability office in the USA have required risk analysis. (US GAO 2007, US GAO 2009 and US OMB 2006) The Department of Defense issues Data Item Descriptions (DIDs) that include the requirement for a schedule risk assessment (OUSD(AT&L)ARA/AM(SO) 2005).

Developing Risk Data from Expert Judgment Poses Challenges

Those attempting to develop plans for a project tend to be more comfortable if they have historical data that can be applied reliably to estimate future activities. They are comforted if there is a project that is recent and relevant to the one being planned. People are comfortable using historical data, perhaps adjusted for size, technical difficulty, weight or complexity, to help estimate future work. Even building up a detailed engineering estimate from scratch is made more credible if there is a database from which to draw in making estimates.

Unfortunately, most risk data are not available from historical databases, industry studies or recent and relevant projects. Of course, in many cases, a contractor will be familiar with many of the specific activities in any project, on which they are bidding (or they would not propose on the work). Of course, even historical data may be wrong as applied to a specific project:

* New projects frequently differ from prior ones, making estimating cost tricky even for semi-familiar work. In development projects, where much is new, most project managers feel very uncertain about any schedule or cost estimate. For development projects many contractors prefer to contract on a time-and-materials basis rather than fixed price basis, in recognition of the impact of uncertain new activities and unknown risks on any plan or schedule.
* Many estimates are compiled before all information is available. These estimates become well established. "New information" or "more detail" impact the evolving project cost estimate as the planning for the project proceeds. New information usually leads to an increase in the work from that estimated at a higher or strategic level, meaning that activities will end up more expensive than initially scheduled. The early estimates become "engraved in stone" and later differences, even if well documented, meet with resistance.[5]
* Since "hope springs eternal," many contractors will hope/believe/claim that their performance on a new project will be better than it has ever been because of "learning." Usually learning comes from frequent repetition of the same task where new ideas and techniques can be developed and adopted. Having done a project or two does not constitute "frequent repetition of the same task."

The project estimate may be developed according to the customers' or other stakeholders' desires even if those desires are unlikely to be met in practice. These estimates are biased and may be fraudulent, but they may also be adopted and defended by management. No wonder costs are exceeded in these cases.[6]

For these reasons, at least, data in the cost estimate are likely to be biased in the optimistic direction and the reality may be quite different. Cost risk analysis is conducted to improve the understanding of the project costs and to improve the estimate by considering uncertainty and risk.

---

5   On one project the new estimate was about 25 percent over the early estimate and it took many briefings before the concept of a new estimate based on a risk analysis was accepted.

6   See Flyvbjerg, B., Holm, M.S., and Buhl, Søren (2002) for some examples of optimistic estimating in public transportation projects.

Estimating Cost Risk using Judgment and Heuristics and the Biases that can Occur[7]

When people are asked about the probability that something will occur or the range of impacts that might occur they often turn to heuristics or rules of thumb in building their answers. Research and experience has indicated that these heuristics can cause or at least seem to be connected with some well-known biases that should concern risk interviewers. The biases tell us what to look for and, potentially, what type of questions we need to ask or adjustments we need to make to the data. Project risk analysis data collection is based on expert judgment and is subject to biases of representativeness, availability and adjustment and anchoring.

Representativeness Bias

Representativeness involves evaluating the probability or impact of an event by referring to another similar event. This is not in itself a bad thing to do – in fact we hope to have some comparable activities to use in judging the project we are now analyzing. There are some representativeness biases to consider, however.

Insensitivity to the prior probability of outcomes can apply when project leaders claim that their project is representative of successful projects even though there is a preponderance of failed projects in the company, industry or in their own past. These leaders discount or ignore the probability that this project may overrun in common with most of their earlier projects and believe (or at least claim to believe) that nothing bad will happen on their project even though it has happened on others. Examples might include:

*   Many project managers indicate that "this time there will be no design changes" even though in every other project design changes were common, costly and time-consuming. Given the large number of projects where design changes occur it may make sense to say that the commitment to avoiding design changes is actually counterproductive.
*   The tendency of early estimates of cost and schedule to grow as more information becomes available and more detail is worked out. Even though the large majority of projects experience cost and schedule growth, a project manager may claim that it will not happen on his project. The prior probability of cost growth is ignored when the current project is your own.

Incorrectly weighing the influence on the project of prior probabilities and current events is fairly common and may be considered as an example of "denial."

Insensitivity to sample size is a very common bias observed during risk interviews. When asked about the probability of a risk's affect on a specific activity or about the range of a specific activity's risk from pessimistic to optimistic, many team members

---

7   A classic article by pioneers in this discipline is Amos Tversky and Daniel Kahneman, (1974). This section is based on that article. A recent compendium of more recent articles is Gilovich, T., Griffin, D., and Kahneman, D., (2002), which is an edited compendium of articles in this discipline.

will apply the range based on the average over many different projects or from a large sample of activities. Using these ranges for an individual project element cost produces risk probabilities that are much too low for the probability or impact ranges that are too narrow when applied to specific project elements. This is true since, in Monte Carlo simulation, we apply the extreme possible 3-point estimates, not the averages for entire phases or projects, to the individual project element costs. It seems to be difficult for most interviewees to realize the width of the risk impact ranges that can occur on individual project element costs or durations. Wide ranges on individual risks will, when combined with the ranges on all project element costs, lead to moderate ranges for the phase or the entire project due to offsetting overruns in some areas with moderate costs or even underruns on others. This occurs in projects and in Monte Carlo simulation. Starting with narrow ranges for individual activities will result in underestimating the overall project cost risk. One way to address this phenomenon is found in a later section of this chapter entitled "A Suggestion to Address Narrow Ranges Provided During the Interview."

The illusion of validity occurs when people predict the outcome that is most representative of the inputs with little or no regard for the factors that limit predictive accuracy. Unwarranted confidence may be placed in the validity of the project plan in the face of evidence of serious project risks. This confidence is the continual reliance on planning as a success indicator despite repeated demonstrations of its inadequacy. This illusion persists even among experienced project managers, attesting to its strength.

The availability bias occurs when people assess the frequency of an event by the ease with which an historical precedent can be brought to mind. Risk data interviewees come into the interview with their own experiences and, when asked to quantify a probability or an impact range, they rely on their own memory for relevant comparisons. It is good to refer to your own experience or that of others, but in doing so some of the events brought out for comparison have more importance or impact on the answers than they warrant. These are the historical events that are easy to remember, perhaps because they were dramatic, made an impression at the time or had an impact on the individual themselves.

Availability risk occurs when a past experience used as a benchmark is affected by factors other than its frequency or probability, notably the familiarity of a particular event or the dramatic impact the reference event has on the interviewee which may make a relatively unlikely or dissimilar event come to mind. If this happens, the assessment of risk on the current project may be biased in the direction suggested by the unlikely but dramatic or familiar event.

An example of the availability bias is a failure of a project component on a prior project. Suppose the interviewee was involved in a prior project where their assigned component failed and he was held up to criticism. Any project that uses that component might go to this person as a subject matter expert, and their initial assessment as an interviewee is that the component is very likely to fail. The interviewee is likely to insist that the probability is high for failure on the current project in the face of argument from others. This is one bias that may lead to an overestimate of project risk as shown in Figure 4.1.

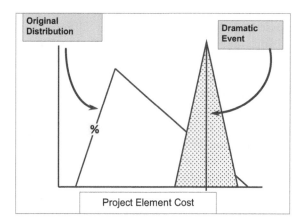

Figure 4.1   Availability bias can lead to an overestimate of risk adjusting and anchoring bias

Adjustment and Anchoring Bias

Anchoring is experienced when people start from initial values that are taken as a basis from which a value to be estimated can be adjusted. The initial value takes on an unjustified significance and the adjustment to represent the value – for instance, the optimistic and pessimistic extreme costs – is often insufficient. Research shows that the anchor need not even be a valid point of reference to cause underestimation of the extremes. As with other heuristics, adjusting from a starting point is probably a good approach when estimating values using expert judgment. However, there is evidence that people tend to make insufficient adjustments when doing so. In the risk arena this leads to underestimation of project risk.

In project risk analysis a common example is the estimation of optimistic and pessimistic extreme impact ranges on a project element cost. The interviewee often starts with the estimate as a basis and adjusts from there to arrive at the extreme impact ranges. If the interviewee has been responsible for making the schedule estimate, that estimate has additional influence in pulling the adjusted extreme optimistic or pessimistic ranges back toward the estimate. Figure 4.2 illustrates the underestimation of duration risk that often occurs in these interviews.

A further example of adjusting and anchoring is the estimation of the probability of a threat event, which is a risk with negative consequences. The technique of Risk Drivers (see Chapter 6), which is used to represent uncertain risk events requires estimates of probability of occurring. In normal planning and estimating practice it is unusual to incorporate the risk of failing the test into the baseline schedule so the implicit assumption is that the probability of failure is zero. The anchor, therefore, is a probability of zero percent.

If the adjusting and anchoring bias is in play, the interviewee estimates the risk's probability of occurring on this project by adjusting from zero. While the probability of failing a test may be substantial, the interviewee often underestimates the probability of the event. (The fact that the event represents bad news for the project is another motivation to keep the estimate of probability low: that is a motivational bias.)

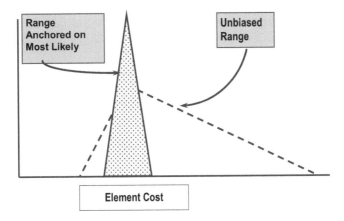

Figure 4.2   Picture of adjusting and anchoring bias producing narrow risk ranges

Tversky and Kahneman report on some research indicating that people overestimate the probability of "conjunctive events" as part of the adjustment and anchoring bias. A conjunctive event occurs if some event, such as finishing an activity within the cost estimate, must happen over and over again for all project elements to produce a successful project. Put another way, our unit of observation is the project element and if any project element overruns its estimate the line item and hence the project will be overrun.

In risk interviews we often hear "Everything has to go right for this schedule to be successful." That statement indicates that the project elements are aggressively estimated and the speaker actually expects one or more line items to exceed their estimate. Even though the probability of any one activity's exceeding its estimate may be low, with enough activities, the probability that at least one activity overruns may be large.

Tversky and Kahneman say "The successful completion of an undertaking, such as the development of a new product, typically has a conjunctive character: for the undertaking to succeed each of a series of events must occur. Even when each of these events is very likely the overall probability of success can be quite low if the number of events is large. The general tendency to overestimate the probability of conjunctive events leads to unwarranted optimism in the evaluation of the likelihood that a plan will succeed or that a project will be completed on time ... Because of anchoring people tend to underestimate the probabilities of failure in complex systems."[8]

Using New Information to Modify Prior Judgment

The project team may be given new information that conflicts with their prior assessment about the project. New risks appear as the project progresses and these often conflict with the initial assessment that the project is on-budget. How should this new information change the prior assessment of the project's risk? There are three general positions that you can take:

---

8   Tversky and Kahneman, ibid., 1129.

- The new information is the only thing that matters. Prior judgment has been shown to be wrong by more current events and should be abandoned. This is thought of as a "panic mode" response.
- The new information is considered to be irrelevant since the project was approved based on the initial judgment. This response is similar to the "see no evil, hear no evil, speak no evil" mentality.
- The new information is given its due influence on the estimate, along with the prior assessment that was made with the same care and attention based on information available at the time. This response is generally the measured and mature response.

As a common example, suppose a project is viewed to be low risk and is approved on that basis. Subsequently, some problems arise that were not anticipated. The project manager needs to evaluate those new events and see what they represent for the project at hand. The common interpretations of this event include:

- These specific problems observed represent a failed project with cost/schedule/quality problems. While this interpretation conflicts with the low-risk project as earlier assessed, it is a common reaction to problems that arise. Many people respond most strongly to the last person to leave the office.
- These specific problems represent only the types of issues all successful projects experience and do not change the earlier assessment of a low-risk project. This represents ignoring more recent information because admitting its importance would require adjusting the prior assessment, increasing the budget and perhaps even cancelling the project.
- Each of these interpretations by itself is probably wrong, and a proper blending of the two would be the right approach. Current pessimistic events might cause the prudent project manager to adjust his prior assessment that the project is going to be successful, leading him to change the position and shape of the probability distribution to something between the original assessment and the new data.

The proper weighting of the two factors, (1) the prior expectation and (2) the new information, is derived from Bayes' theorems (Wikipedia 2010). It is beyond the scope of this book (Barclay 1977). Figure 4.3 indicates how new information, when added to the original distribution, might lead to a revised distribution of risk impacts on activity durations.

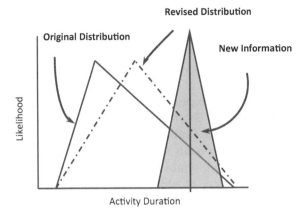

Figure 4.3   Adjustment of prior assessment about the project because of recent information

The Risk Interview: Collecting High-quality Risk Data

Exercising skill and experience in organizing and conducting the risk interview can contribute to the success of the risk data gathering exercise and hence enhance the credibility of the risk analysis. There are several aspects to the risk interview. These are particularly important issues for those organizations and individuals that have low risk management maturity levels and are inexperienced in risk analysis.

Whom to Interview?

Risk data are generally best collected in an interview session with people who are knowledgeable about the project or some aspect of it. Subject matter experts, or SMEs, have experience in the industry of the project, its geographic location, the markets in which its equipment/material/labor will be purchased, the regulatory environment surrounding the project, the technologies in use, the performing organizations and the customer or sponsor organization.[9]

In many cases the SMEs are members of the project team and its management, contractors or advisors. Collecting data from the team members has benefits and draw backs:

- On the one hand team members are most familiar with the project and have been intimately involved with the issues, assumptions, options and information about the project.
- On the other hand, the team members are often too close to the project and may be biased. They have made the decisions and estimates themselves and may be suffering from some of the biases discussed above, particularly the anchoring and adjusting

---

9   Some risk analysts prefer to collect risk data in workshops with many attendees. One serious problem with this approach is that strong personalities or high-ranking attendees may dominate the workshop and intimidate others who have information to contribute. There is no way for the facilitator to correct for this except to ask the dominating persons to leave the room, a hard thing to do.

bias. In addition, since any negative news about the project could get it cancelled there is a motivational bias toward making the project look good. In general, the higher in the project hierarchy the interviewee is the more likely it is to get data that is biased toward making the project look less risky than it is.

Sometimes SMEs who are not on the project team itself but have relevant experience can provide less-biased information. Often these people are from the same performing or owner organization and therefore confidential information needed for the analysis can be revealed to them. These non-team SMEs are generally supportive of the project and organization while they are more removed from the specific implications of the risk results than are project team members. In addition to bringing a new set of experiences to the interview, these non-team SMEs have less stake in the success of the project and may be more objective than project team leaders.

Organizational Issues Affecting the Quality of Risk Data Collection

There is an organizational issue that can affect the quality of the risk data collected. If the risk analyst reports to the manager of the project that is being evaluated that project manager may bring pressure to bear, directly or indirectly, to make the risk analysis results favorable to the project. Project managers may want to avoid the risk analysis entirely or, failing that, to make the results validate the approved project plan for the benefit of the organization's management or the customer.

- The project manager wants to go about the business of managing the project without having to adjust the plan or explain to management why it is risky and what he or she will do to mitigate the risk.
- Often project managers claim or actually believe that they can recover successfully from any overrun. The project manager wants to report good news to the organization and project stakeholders and hopes to be left alone. "Just leave me alone and let me build my bridge (refinery, software project, satellite payload or building)."
- Risk analyses conducted by project managers are often a "whitewash" of the project. These self-serving analyses are worse than not worth the effort – very little effort may have gone into these analyses – because they are misleading.
- Organizations that close their eyes to risk in order to emphasize how good the project plan is will lose the opportunity to deal with risks. They are using "project management by crossing your fingers," a generally losing approach.

An organizational arrangement that ensures the risk analyst does not report to the project manager can enhance the quality and credibility of the risk data gathering and hence the risk analyses. In some companies the risk analyst is organizationally located in the project management office (PMO) or in centralized corporate engineering function. From that vantage point the analyst reports to a risk officer or risk board rather than to the manager of the project under analysis. Of course it is necessary to present the analysis results to the project manager before submitting it in final form so that any errors can be corrected and the project manager is warned about the results. But, the analyst should be protected from repercussions at the hands of the project manager if he indicates the project will not finish on budget or on schedule.

A number of organizations will hire an outside consultant expert in project risk analysis to conduct the risk analysis. External consultants can be more objective than those who derive their livelihood from the project organization. Since that consultant does not derive much of their income from one company, they will leave at the end of the engagement whatever the results, and their reputation relies on their objectivity. Still, external risk experts sometimes face serious pressure from the project management hierarchy, including actual lying in the interviews, to make the project risk look minimal.

Project risk management maturity (see section, Risk Management Maturity of the Organization) of the organization may be indicated in part by the degree to which the risk analysis function is independent of the project under review. In some very risk-mature organizations where risk analysis is standard practice and people are experienced in participating, organizational separation may not be necessary. However, in any organization the independence of the risk analysis, and specifically risk data gathering, can remove a barrier to effectiveness.

Conducting the Risk Interview

Interviews to elicit project risk analysis data are of at least five kinds, usually tailored to the role of the SME interviewee. Not all risk analysis exercises will have each type of interview represented:

- Detailed information is being sought about risks or cost elements from people with specialized knowledge. These interviews are often focused on specific areas of the project such as procurement, design, construction, permitting or commissioning. The interviews may include one or a few individuals who are involved in or at least knowledgeable about those elements of the project.
- Summary or overview information is collected often from the project manager or others in the organization with a broad scope of responsibilities. These interviews may be most successful with the Risk Driver approach (see Chapter 6) where the basic building blocks are Risk Register risks. Many of the risk register risks are broad, high-level risks that can profitably be discussed from the "30,000 feet" perspective.
- Background information may be contributed by some interviewees. These interviews are not always intended to be limited to background knowledge but may result from scheduling an interview with someone who is not particularly familiar with the project. Information of a general nature can be helpful, but it is important to quantify the data on project element cost risk or risk register risks. Under expert questioning, someone who begins the interview saying he or she does not believe they can help is soon able to quantify the data.
- Confirmatory information can be gathered by interviewing more than one person about each risk or project element cost. The benefit of having several experts quantify risks' probability and impact is that people will have different perspectives or opinions that have some benefit. This type of interview gives the risk analyst confirmation of data already gathered or may raise alternative diagnoses leading to further questions.

The drawback to having several opinions about the same Risk Drivers, for instance, is that the analyst needs to be able to choose from them or in some way synthesize the data used for the analysis by combining the data.

- Independent information is sometimes collected from people not on the project or even not in the organization who are knowledgeable in the type of project, region of the world, technology, supplier and labor markets or regulatory situation. Participant experts from outside the organization will either sign a non-disclosure agreement (NDA) or may not be given proprietary information.

During the interview the interviewees are encouraged to bring with them any documentation that will help. Those who bring in actual records from recent, relevant projects usually contribute better information because they can refer to real data. As an example, data on real projects may be the antidote to belief in excessively optimistic plans. Of course historical data has a downside since it is really just one instance of the work under investigation and may not be representative of the true risk of the current project.

In many interviews the interviewee has no hard-copy data to use as a reference and all of the heuristics and their biases discussed above can color the answers. The interviewer needs to be alert to the biases of the interviewees.

Risk interviews are more productive if the interviewees look at the risks and write down their preliminary probabilities and impact ranges in advance of the interview. Sometimes teams can prepare the data together, benefiting from discussion among them. These interviewees or teams should bring to the interview filled-in tables of probabilities and impact ranges. Experience shows that the estimates of probability may be too low and of risk impact ranges too narrow, but it is very helpful for interviewees to have considered risk and prepared responses in advance. One of the interviewer's main responsibilities is to recognize when the biases affect the responses. Interviewers probe and challenge the rationale of the interviewee to find out the full extent of the risks. The probabilities and impact ranges often change during the interview.

Strategies for Interviewing about Impact Ranges and Risk Probability

A useful technique for exploring risk impact ranges is to address the pessimistic case first. Experience shows that the pessimistic project element cost is the more difficult for interviewees to quantify. We often ask the interviewee to first describe what events would lead to the worst-case scenario, then to estimate the value that it represents.

The pessimistic scenario may include several elements. The interviewer must be sure that the pessimistic cost value is at the edge of worst-case believability; that the elements making up the pessimistic scenario could all occur on one project. A useful device is to ask the interviewee to then make an estimate of the pessimistic case impact that reflects the scenario just described. Try to elicit the quantification of the pessimistic case where there is only 1 percent likelihood that the risk will be worse, since if you ask for a value that will never be exceeded the interviewee may spin some pretty bizarre stories that lead to values that are so extreme as to be useless in simulation.

The next step is to explore the optimistic scenario. Experience shows that people are rarely as aware of opportunities to improve the project plan as you would like them to be. A number of commentators have challenged the notion that project risk includes opportunities at all (Hulett, Hillson and Kohl 2002). The optimistic scenario should include consideration of as many opportunities as might conceivably happen together on the project. It is useful to build a description of the optimistic scenario before trying to quantify it.

Finally, for impact ranges we need to explore the most likely scenario. You may think that this scenario is, obviously, the budget or estimate number for the project element's cost. The most likely cost may not be the value in the estimate at all. In fact, in many cases the interviewee looks at the cost and designates it as the most optimistic value; perhaps because the estimating was optimistic to begin with or new data has surfaced that make the old estimate obsolete. If the plan value is optimistic, then in most cases, the most likely scenario is greater than that original value.

Before the interview it is good practice to brief the participants, perhaps all in one briefing, about the data needed, the importance of the data to the project cost risk analysis and of that analysis to the success of the project. If the Risk Drivers method is used, it is helpful to provide the prospective interviewee with a form containing the risk events that have already been identified, usually in the Risk Register, that will be filled in with probability and impact data during the interview. The interviewee is encouraged to make a stab at filling out the form before entering the interview and to bring the document with them.

Structure of the Risk Interview

The risk interview normally begins with an introduction during which the interviewee is prepared for a productive discussion. This introductory period has several purposes:

- To overcome the interviewee's resistance to the process or reluctance to be interviewed. Sometimes the interviewee will be unfamiliar with risk interviews and may be suspicious about the process, unsure of and generally resistant to providing risk data. The risk analyst needs to answer the questions patiently and to reassure the interviewee of the process while nonetheless persisting to obtain the data. In addition, the interviewee should be made aware that they need to overcome any resistance or objections they may have; the interview will take place. Interviewees need to participate willingly but may not always approach the process with an open mind.
- To answer questions about concepts. The initial questionnaire will often ask for probability and/or impact ranges, and the interviewee may well not understand what is needed. Concepts that seem to be clear to the interviewee are not always those used in the risk analysis.
- To ensure that enough time is available for the interview. It is easy to assume that the interview should take only 30 minutes or an hour. Experience tells us that risk interviews can take 2 hours or more if the interviewee has a lot of risks to discuss, or is resistant to the process itself. Lengthy interviews can be 2–3 hours and on very rare occasions have lasted half- to all-day. It is best to prepare the interviewee for a realistic interview time.

- To complete the risk interview in one session. It will be very difficult to get the interviewee or team back for a continuation session. We find that the inconvenience of the interview is less if it is allowed to go on until concluded. Do not be surprised if the interview runs over the initial allotted time. On occasion the interviewee becomes so involved or intrigued with the subject that the session lasts longer than it needs to, but in this case good quality data are usually received and the interviewee emerges enthusiastic about the process.
- To inform the interviewee that, while all interviewees will be included on a list in the final report, specific responses will be confidential and will not be attributed to individuals. Close the door to the interview room. The promise of anonymity is important to establish the atmosphere of confidence necessary between the interviewee and interviewer. It will help many interviewees to speak freely and honestly, knowing that there will be no repercussions for honest opinions. The risk interviewer should keep notes for the documentation, but those notes are not made available to the project manager or anyone else in authority over the interviewee.
- To emphasize the need to look for opportunity-type risks. This emphasis on opportunities is not simply to please the project manager. Rather, opportunities will not be recognized even when they are present unless they are emphasized, because most people are used to thinking that risk is a threat to the project's objectives. If we do not look for opportunities we will certainly miss them and lose the chance to act on them, helping the plan.

Risk interviews will often start very slowly, particularly if the interviewees are inexperienced in the process. The introductory period can take half an hour or more. The interviewee may take stock after the first half hour and conclude that, since no data have yet been collected, the interview will take all day. Even after the introduction, when risks are first discussed in substance, deciding on a value for the probability or impact range of a risk can take some time. It is not unusual that, at the end of an hour, only two or three elements of risk data are collected. At this point an interviewee may again become discouraged since the progress extrapolates to a very long interview. However, participants should take heart! There are several reasons why the interview tends to proceed faster as it goes along:

- The introductory period is behind you and does not have to be repeated.
- The risk concepts become clearer. Even interviewees who have never participated in the risk interview will become more comfortable with the concepts as they go along.
- When some risks have been successfully calibrated, succeeding risks may be easier to deal with. For instance, later risks may be very similar to risks calibrated previously. Alternatively, risks encountered later in the interview may be calibrated as being more likely or having wider impact ranges. Reference to risks that have been discussed earlier makes collecting data on later risks easier.
- It is not uncommon for people who have been resistant to the entire risk analysis process to become enthusiastic and to buy into the process as it goes along. They may become more comfortable deciding on numbers for the risk probability and impact ranges as the interview proceeds.

- Some interviewees who enter the room believing that they can contribute nothing, and certainly cannot "put numbers" to the risks may find out, with a little expert coaching by the facilitator, that risk calibration is easier than they thought.

As the risk interview progresses most interviewees becomes more adept at answering the questions. It is not uncommon for people who are new to risk interviewing to become adept within the space of their first interview. If interviewees have been involved in risk interviewing on other projects the interview will proceed more quickly.

At the end of the interview the risk analyst-interviewer needs to document the data collected. It is difficult to wade through notes that are several days old to try to remember what a specific interviewee said. Recording the results, including the data and their rationale, in a simple database by entering the data on the interview form and showing it to all using a projector and screen during the interview will help the interviewer document the interview.

The Risk Workshop

Risk ranges may be developed in workshops with 10–25 participants as an alternative to interviews with one or just a few participants. Workshops can provide a good environment for sharing information and encouraging cross-disciplinary discussion. Risk data gathered in a workshop has the potential for greater accuracy because of the shared contributions.

The workshop usually starts with a preliminary discussion of the process that will occur including the type of data needed by the end of the day. From preliminary work, a list of relevant "candidate risks" should have been developed. The objectives of the workshop are to:

- Review the candidate risks. Make sure they are stated correctly, with a cause, a risk and an impact on some project objective. This is harder than it seems and can benefit from an assertive facilitator.
- Add any new risks that are not on the list. No initial list will be complete and new risks can be added during discussion by the group.
- Eliminate any risks that do not apply to the project at hand. They may have been included from an earlier project or an out-of-date plan.
- Consolidate synonymous risks.
- Calibrate the 3-point estimate of costs or risks' probability of occurring and impact ranges if they do occur. Identify which activities in the project schedule these risks will affect.

There are some concerns about the workshop method of collecting risk data.

- Often there will be several different subjects to discuss in the workshop, or there may be many risks to consider and calibrate. Some participants will have more narrow focus or interest and only contribute to specific risk discussions. This concern can be mitigated by separating the workshop participants into smaller working groups, each led by a facilitator, with assigned risks to review. The risks can be a sampling of all risks in the list, so they cover many areas (engineering, construction, procurement, planning, financing, decision-making, commissioning, environmental permitting and the like) or they can be segregated by subject matter area and assigned to those experts competent in the appropriate area. In either approach the participants are assigned to sub-groups. You will often need more than one expert facilitator to handle the different groups.

- A serious concern about the workshop approach to gathering risk data and that is the possibility for intimidation. Workshop attendance often includes people at different grade levels in the organization. Sometimes the SMEs will be in the same workshop with their supervisors, the project manager and team leaders, thus representing three or more hierarchical levels within the organization. The facilitator can insist that during the workshop there is no hierarchy and that everyone's voice is equal, all can contribute with valuable information, but this may not be credible to the attendees. Those at the lower levels of the organization may not be willing to say anything that could anger or contradict the position of their supervisor or the project manager for fear of being criticized or ostracized. The intimidation effect is greater in hierarchical cultures. It takes a strong person at a lower level to introduce a threat-type risk into a workshop that includes their team leader, the project manager or other stakeholders. This is why the guarantee of anonymity in the interview is so important, and one reason why some risk analysts prefer interviews over workshops.

Frame of Reference for the Risk Analysis

A project risk analysis needs to have a frame of reference that must be agreed before the interview or workshop starts to deal with the substance. The frame of reference sets the boundaries to define which risks will be considered and which will not. The basis can depend on the perspective from which the analysis is conducted. The perspective will differ depending on whether the analysis is being conducted for the owner or a contractor, for instance:

- Whether a risk of change orders represents a fundamental change to a project or a risk to the same project depends on whether the analysis is being done from the owner's or contractor's side. The owner is likely to consider change orders to be part of the project and thus the risk of change orders needs to be included for the owner. The contractor will be paid for change orders so contractors will only wish to analyze risk associated with the contracted work while changes would be part of a different analysis.
- Risks over which the project manager has no control are nevertheless still live project risks. If an interviewee says: "We cannot do anything about it, so it is not a risk," then this is incorrect. It could be argued that any risk that cannot be affected by the project team is more of a risk to the project than a risk that can be mitigated. Even if the project manager or owner cannot do anything about the risk he or she can position the project so that the risk, if it happens, has a smaller impact than if the project were unprepared.

Risk Management Maturity of the Organization[10]

The initial success of the project risk analysis depends on the risk-maturity of the organization within which it is conducted. Several aspects of risk management maturity are important:

- People and resources must be available in sufficient quantity and trained to do the risk analysis. They should be expert in the field of risk analysis and have mastery of the tools including the people skills of the interview, project management experience, software skills to analyze the data and communication skills to present the results.
- Practices and standards must include project risk management as a "best practice" that is expected to occur on all important projects. Risk management must be considered to be part of a successful project and its results must be incorporated into each decision node or stage gate review. Risk management that is considered an "add-on" will be less successful than if it is mandated as routine practice.
- Leadership must be alert to the benefits of project risk management and supportive of it, rather than be hostile or indifferent to it. Leadership should model risk management and be seen to use the results to choose between projects and make project success more likely.
- The mindset of the organization must favor discovering the reality of the risks rather than hiding risk. Honesty and objectivity must be rewarded, not punished by the organization.
- The organizational structure must be conducive to risk analysis. Risk data collection must be protected from the motivational biases that are common when project managers control the process and its results.
- There needs to be a network of risk management professionals who will both support each other and promote a dynamic and progressive view of best practices within the organization. On occasion, outside expert consultants are important members of this network.

A Suggestion to Address Narrow Ranges Provided During the Interview

The bias of adjustment and anchoring leads to optimistic and particularly pessimistic impact ranges that are too narrow and probabilities that are too low. Representative bias will encourage participants to take the impact ranges that apply to the entire project estimate and assign those averages to individual cost elements, instead of applying the extremes needed to represent the risk of the individual plan elements, again resulting in narrow ranges at the overall project risk level.

We want to know the so-called "outliers" to calculate the impact range of a single project element cost or a risk, in other words, the very best and the very worst values that may occur. Yet we may be given a narrow range during the risk interview. Team members have described a serious risk but then quantified its impact as only –10 percent or +20 percent on the project element's cost or schedule. It appears to the interviewer that the

---

10   This section draws from Salim and Hulett, 2008.

range provided is too narrow given the risk description just provided. The interviewer becomes concerned that the interviewee is biased. Even under questioning by the interviewer, the interviewee may continue to insist on the narrow ranges given. What should the experienced interviewer do in this case?

The Problem when the Activity Ranges are Too Narrow

A practical example will serve to illustrate the problem with developing overly narrow ranges on a specific project schedule.

The first problem is that interviewees incorrectly ascribe their range for the total to its constituent parts. Consider a $100 thousand project element for which it is agreed that the worst case is $160 thousand and the best case is $80 thousand. (The most likely may or may not be the $100 thousand estimate.) Now consider that this project element is made up of 10 project sub-elements estimated to cost $10 thousand each. Interviewees often try to apply the overall risk range (80 percent to 160 percent) on each of these project sub-elements, confusing the cost impact range that was appropriate for the entire project element with the range that would be required for the sub-elements. Simulating the 10 sub-elements using 80 percent and 160 percent ranges for each individual sub-element provides the project element result of from $92 thousand to $125 thousand, much narrower than originally estimated. This result is shown in Figure 4.4.

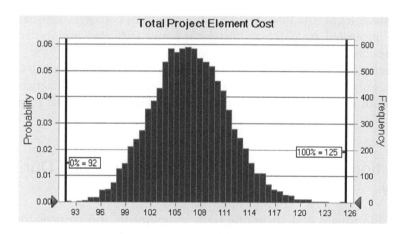

Figure 4.4   Project element cost is too narrow if the 10 sub-elements have a range of from $8 to $16 thousand[11]

The cost range on the entire project element of $92 thousand to 125 thousand is much narrower than the range of $80 thousand to $160 thousand which was initially judged a sufficient range for the element as a whole. Why is that? It is because if the project elements' cost uncertainty values are independent there is a lot of cancelling out – some

---

11   These figures were created by Crystal Ball, a program that simulates models created in Microsoft Excel. Crystal Ball, created by Decisioneering, is now owned by Oracle.

elements' costs will be high in their ranges while others may be low, moderate or high in their own ranges – so these high, moderate and low values cancel each other out as the cost elements are summed to compute the total element cost.[12] There is no chance, in the simulation or in a real project, of getting a project element cost range from 80 percent to 160 percent if the individual activities only have those same percentage ranges.

Applying to the component costs the percentage range that is appropriate for the entire cost element is a special case of individuals' generally underestimating the range on the cost of the 10 sub-elements because they do not appreciate the implication of a sample size of just one. You may wish to illustrate this error to the interviewees by showing them the ranges that would have to be applied to the 10 individual sub-elements that, when simulated, result in the 80 percent and 160 percent impact range for the entire project element (of which they constitute the components). Individual sub-element ranges, using triangular distributions, with an estimated cost of $10 thousand, must be expanded to $4.4 thousand minimum to $20.7 thousand maximum. In other words, instead of the 80 percent and 160 percent ranges on individual sub-element costs we would need ranges of 44 percent to 207 percent to get the total project element cost result of 80 percent to 160 percent expected. See Figure 4.5.

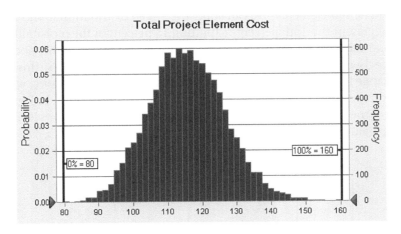

Figure 4.5   Result of path made up of 10 activities with range of $4.4 and $20.7 thousand

In the interviews interviewees typically reject realistically wide cost uncertainty ranges as being too extreme. They do not appreciate that a sample of one activity can have, *indeed must have*, a wider range than that for entire Project Element in order to get the results previously assessed.

When interviewees assert a range of 80 percent and 160 percent for the individual sub-elements, but we know that individual sub-elements' impact ranges should be 44 percent and 207 percent, how can we correct their input for the sample-size bias? There is

---

12   We have assumed that these project elements' costs are independent. An alternative assumption could be that they are correlated. The difference is between a correlation coefficient of 0.0 for independent and a coefficient close to 1.0 for perfect positive correlation. See Chapter 5, Correlation.

a correction factor available in most Monte Carlo simulation software that can be applied when we believe the ranges are narrower than they should be because of a bias.

The Trigen Function

The triangular distribution, which is often used in cost risk analysis, has a first cousin distribution, the "Trigen" function. Short for "triangle generation," this Trigen function reinterprets the values given in the interviews as something less than the extreme optimistic and pessimistic values, and it generates a new triangular distribution with wider ranges. This reinterpretation involves the analyst's determining what those extreme values actually mean to the interviewees and putting that specification into the software.

We have just seen that the insensitivity to sample size and the adjusting and anchoring biases can lead people to understate the ranges on individual activities. If we suspect that this bias has occurred, we can reinterpret the values as representing distribution points that are other than the most optimistic (0 percent) and the most pessimistic (100 percent). In the current case the interviewees have provided values of 8 days and 16 days on the individual sub-elements. We can apply the Trigen distribution to those values and make them represent the 15th percentile (putting 15 percent of the probability below the low value) and the 85th percentile (putting 15 percent of the probability above the high value) of a revised triangular distribution. As Figure 4.6 below shows, this adjustment widens the range to $4 thousand optimistic and $21 thousand pessimistic, which are the values that caused the total project element results shown previously in Figure 4.5. The comparison of the input values of the triangular and the Trigen functions is shown below, where the "parameters" used were 15 percent and 85 percent.[13]

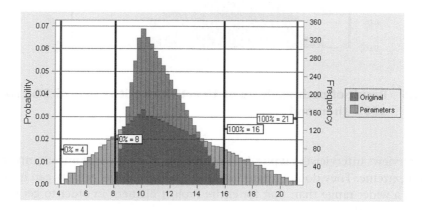

Figure 4.6   Comparing the triangle with the Trigen with the extreme values interpreted as P-15 and P-85 parameters

---

13   The analyst can put different parameters into the software and generate different (wider) triangles. A common situation occurs when the interviewees state that their numbers are "the P-10 and P-90 values." The analyst will use 10 percent and 90 percent for the parameters and the Trigen function will extend the triangle's optimistic and pessimistic tails out so that there is 10 percent probability below the value called the "P-10" and 10 percent probability above the value called the "P-90" value by the interviewees.

At the end of one 2-hour risk interview, the interviewees left the room saying: "So, those are the P-10 and P-90 estimates, correct?" Of course we had to expand the triangle using the Trigen function.[14]

Summary

The quality of the risk data determines the success and credibility of the cost risk analysis. Gathering risk data is the most important activity in a risk analysis exercise. Data gathering takes more time and requires more understanding and sophistication on the part of the risk analyst than does the risk modelling.

Risk data are gathered from people usually in interviews or workshops. The risk analyst/interviewer must understand the dynamics of those environments, the pressures from the organization and the individual motivational and cognitive biases that often occur, particularly when interviewing people new to the practice of risk analysis.

The chapter covered the types of risk data needed. Risk probability and impact ranges are the most common data but other data such as correlation coefficients are needed as well. We are interested in data that encompasses three types of uncertainty, estimating error and ambiguity that have 100 percent likelihood of occurring but uncertain impacts and uncertainty caused by discrete risk events that have probability less than 100 percent as well as uncertain impacts.

Some problems in collecting risk data arise from the individual and others from the organizational environment within which the people providing the data operate.

The corporate or organizational culture is often hostile, or at best indifferent, to conducting project risk analysis. People who talk about project risk, even in workshops scheduled for that purpose, may be punished for offering their honest assessment of risk. We have discussed organizational risk management maturity as it applies to making the people comfortable and giving them the tools for realistic risk assessments. We also recommend assuring interviewees of the confidentiality of their inputs, providing cover for them to discuss risk honestly and realistically.

Individuals experience difficulty in providing risk data because the concepts may be new to them. They may have limited or no experience or training in providing risk data and lack access to databases than might help. Individuals providing data about uncertainty ranges and probability typically rely on heuristics or rules of thumb to calibrate their judgment. While heuristics can help people make useful estimates of risk concepts, some well-known biases exist that mostly lead to underestimating uncertainty through project risk parameters.

- The representativeness class of bias includes being insensitive to historical probabilities or experiences, which means not applying the bulk of history when discussing uncertainty in a single project. Included here also is insensitivity to sample size, which in this context implies that people tend to use data that may be appropriate for many projects at an overall level to apply to individual project elements; it is difficult for interviewees to imagine the high probabilities and wide ranges that would be appropriate for specific activities. Also there is the illusion of validity or

---

14   The same correction factor also works well with the BetaPERT distribution.

unwarranted confidence that occurs when using this heuristic. All of these can lead to underestimating project risk.

- Availability bias leads people to estimate the risk of a project based on the past events that are most easily brought to mind. It becomes clear when conducting interviews that past events that were both dramatic and personal to the interviewee are often problems that affected that person. This risk can lead to over-estimating? or under-estimating risk.

- A specific case of the availability bias might lead to an over-reaction to events that are dramatic and very current. Many people will react to the last information they are given and perhaps throw out earlier project assessments, however well considered. A rational approach would be to combine the prior and current information correctly for a revised estimate of risk.

- Adjusting and anchoring leads to SMEs providing risk impact ranges that are too narrow and probability of the risks that are too low for the risks they are describing. Their estimates are based on inadequate or small adjustments made from the anchor of values in the baseline cost estimate. We have explored a useful way to adjust the risk ranges provided, using the Trigen function, and given only one example where the interview ranges are reinterpreted to represent the 15th and 85th percentiles, to offset this underestimation if it is perceived.

Risk interviews may be conducted for the purpose of collecting detailed or high-level summary data, for confirmation of data by getting second opinions, or for getting information from sources independent of the project or for background data. The interview itself is described.

The interview for people without experience in risk analysis usually includes an introduction to familiarize the interviewee with the process and answer questions. The facilitator asks the interviewee to describe pessimistic cases before calibrating them, since that is the most difficult value in the impact range for most people. The interview may start slowly if the interviewee is new to the process, but it will pick up speed as it goes along. However, interviews can take on average 1–3 hours, and may even take longer, depending on the interviewee and the amount of data required.

Interviews proceed smoother if the interviewee is provided a format for the required information and prepares for the interview by writing down the information in advance. Interviewees should be expecting challenges from the facilitator, however, particularly about low probabilities and narrow impact ranges. This is not because the facilitator wants to show more risk than there is, but rather in recognition of the biases associated with the heuristics many people rely on to form their data.

The interviewee needs to understand the frame of reference for the risk analysis. The analysis is concerned with all risks that can affect the project. This includes technical, organizational, external and even project management risks, whether the organization can do anything about them or not. Whether change orders are included depends on the perspective of the client – the owner would consider change orders that ensure the project will achieve its original objectives to be project risks but the contractor will consider them as constituting new work for which additional money and time will be allotted. The argument that "we cannot do anything about it anyway" does not disqualify a risk from being included in the analysis.

Risk data are sometimes collected in a risk workshop. The workshop has some benefits in gathering a number of people's views at once. There is synergy between the participants that can uncover new risks and considerations about risk calibration that is absent in one-on-one interviews. One problem with the workshop is the lack of anonymity and the possibility of pressure on participants from their peers or supervisors to minimize the risks or to consider some risks "out of scope." In the interview the facilitator can promise anonymity, which usually helps participants talk honestly about project risk.

Collecting realistic data about project risk is more challenging and important than learning about the Monte Carlo software or statistical theory. A successful risk analyst or facilitator will combine understanding of the possible biases with a way to interact with the interviewees to get the data.

References

Barclay, S. (1977). *Handbook for Decision Analysis*. Defense Advanced Research Projects Agency.

Christensen, D. (1993). "The Estimate of Completion Problem: A Preview of Three Studies." *Project Management Journal*: 37–42.

OUSD (ATandL) ARA/AM(SO) (2005). Integrated Master Schedule (IMS) Data Item Description. Defense.

Tversky, A. and Kahneman, D. (1974). "Judgment under Uncertainty: Heuristics and Biases." *Science* 185: 1124–31.

Flyvbjerg, B., Holm, M.S., and Buhl, Søren (2002). "Underestimating Costs in Public Works Projects, Error or Lie?" *Journal of the American Planning Association*, vol. 68, (No. 3).

Gilovich, T., Griffin, D., and Kahneman, D. (2002). *Heuristics and Biases, The Psychology of Intuitive Judgment*. Cambridge University Press.

Hulett, D.T. (2009). *Practical Schedule Risk Analysis*. Farnham, England, Gower Publishing.

Hulett, D.T., Hillson, D.A. and Kohl, R. (2002). "Defining Risk: A Debate." *Cutter IT Journal*, vol. 15 (No. 2), February, 4–10.

Salim, Y. and Hulett, D., Hulett and Associates, LLC (2008). "Assessing Project Risk Management Maturity in a Large Energy Company," © Project Management Institute, presented at the Asia-Pacific PMI Congress, Sydney, Australia, March.

Tversky, A. and Kahneman, D. (1974). "Heuristics and Biases," *Science*, 185, 1124–31.

US GAO (2009). *Cost Estimating and Assessment Guide*, GAP-09–3SP.

US GAO (2007). *Cost Estimating Guide*, GAO-07–1134SP.

US OMB (2006) *Capital Programming Guide*, Supplement to the Office of Management and Budget Circular A–11, Part 7: Planning, Budgeting and Acquisition of Capital Assets.

Wikipedia (2010). Bayes' Theorem, January.

5 Correlation Between Project Element Costs Reflects Common Risk Drivers and Implies More Cost Risk at the Project Level[1]

Introduction

In cost risk analysis we do not believe that all project element costs will be at their most pessimistic or most optimistic durations in the same project. Such extreme scenarios would just be unrealistic. In the simulations shown in previous chapters we have assumed that project elements' costs vary within their own probability distributions but independent of each other. That means that some costs will be high in their distribution while others may be low, moderate or high in theirs. Because of this independence between project element costs there is substantial cancelling out when the costs are added up in any iteration (or any project). This cancelling out of high costs for some project elements by other elements with costs that are not necessarily also high in the same project or iteration of a simulation keeps the total project cost from being extremely high or low.

For some project elements this assumption of independence between costs may not be correct. This chapter examines the way to handle the situation when two or more project elements' costs might "move together," that is when they may systematically be high or low in their respective probability distributions together, either in a project or in an iteration. This phenomenon of high costs occurring together and low costs occurring together is called "positive correlation."[2]

What would happen if many project elements were to overrun their estimated costs together on our project? That event could cause very large overruns of the total project budget. This is because the overruns on the project elements' costs are summed down the column, and high costs in one correlated project element reinforce high cost of other project elements. Of course, if the project elements' costs were systematically low in their

---

1   Some parts of this chapter are based on Chapter 10 of David T. Hulett, *Practical Schedule Risk Analysis*, Gower Publishing Ltd., 2009.

2   There is also negative correlation in which high costs of one project element tend to coincide with low costs of another element. We do not see negative correlation much in project risk analysis.

probability distribution together the total project cost could be lower than expected because they would reinforce each others' optimistic costs.

Each risk analyst, and indeed each project manager, should ask:

- Is correlation between project elements' costs possible on my project? Yes, correlation is fairly common in project management.
- What would cause project elements to overrun or underrun their costs together? Project elements' costs that are affected by the same risks would be correlated.
- What would be the impact of strong correlation of costs on my target total project percentile, say the P-80? The P-80 cost would be larger with correlation than if there were no correlation simply because correlated durations reinforce each other as they are added down the cost estimate column. Correlation between project elements' costs will spread the tails (both high and low tails) compared to the total cost distribution associated with project elements that are independent.

This chapter examines the assumption of independence between project element costs and introduces the concept and implications of correlation between those costs. It turns out that correlation is fairly common and that its presence affects the results, particularly the upper and lower percentile results.

Correlation Concepts

HOW DOES CORRELATION ARISE?

If project element costs are correlated it would be unlikely to see high costs on one element combined with low costs on another. That would be an inconsistent scenario for a project with correlated costs. Implementing correlation during simulation between the project element costs that are affected by the same risks ensures that we do not have any iteration that represents an inconsistent scenario. Suppose that we may encounter high costs for raw steel in the world marketplace. We believe that if that happened we would experience higher than expected cost for all items that contain significant amounts of steel such as structural steel, steel pressure vessels, piping and other project equipment. During simulation we should not produce any iteration (scenario) that assumes the cost of structural steel is high but that of piping or vessels is low. We believe the project element costs would all be influenced by the "uncertainty in steel price" in the same direction in any project, so that an iteration in which costs go different ways from their means would be inconsistent with our assumption that they all move together.

The problem of creating inconsistent scenarios during simulation arises from a purely random selection of costs. Selecting the costs at random will probably yield some iterations in which one or another of these project elements had costs that were higher than their means while the others are below their means. In other words, a purely random selection of costs from input probability distributions would produce a scenario that is inconsistent with the observation that steel prices affect several project elements simultaneously. Examining and implementing correlation is intended to ensure that each iteration specifies an internally consistent scenario, one that could possibly be our project.

Correlation is caused by a risk's affecting two project elements on the same project. An example would be the same Risk Event, perhaps uncertainty about the complexity of a software development project, affecting the cost of software coding and testing. If the risk occurs on a project and software coding is more difficult than assumed when the estimates were originally made, both coding and testing will cost more than expected. These element costs would then exhibit correlation. Examples of such risks and their impact on multiple activities could include:

- Poor labor productivity would affect the cost of all construction activities in the same project.
- Technology difficulties would affect many design, fabrication and testing activities similarly.
- If management imposed optimistic bias on the basic cost estimate; for instance to make it appear to be less expensive so the project will be approved, most if not all of the project elements that had their cost estimates reduced might overrun their cost estimates together.

The mechanism of how correlation arises in project management is shown in Figure 5.1. Suppose the "Risk Event," say the assumption of reusing prior software, is incorrect causing more new software both to be created and to be tested than assumed in the original cost estimate. If this risk event occurs on the project it occurs on each of the two project elements, Software Coding and Software testing. As stated it would cause additional hours of both coding and testing, leading to additional cost on each of those project element line items. Their costs would be higher than originally estimated, together. Of course, if the risk event did not occur, it would not occur for each of the project elements and their costs would not be affected, at least by this common risk.

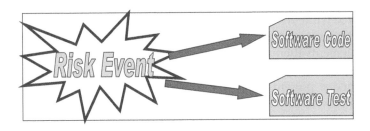

Figure 5.1   One risk driving two activities causing their costs to be correlated

IS CORRELATION THE SAME AS CAUSALITY?

Correlation does not imply causality. If the increase in one project element causes the cost of another to vary, the relationship is causal and can be modelled in the spreadsheet that contains the cost estimate. For instance, suppose that the cost of a subcontract and management of the same subcontract have both been estimated and appear on separate lines in the cost estimate. Often subcontract management is estimated as some percentage (say, 15 percent) of the value of the subcontract itself. Now suppose that the subcontract is more expensive because it is more complicated and takes longer than first estimated. It is reasonable that subcontract management will also cost more than originally estimated. However, these two project elements are causally related and correlation need not be applied – the cost of subcontract management can be modelled to be always a certain percentage of the subcontract since the direction of causality is known.[3]

Calibrating Correlation

Correlation is defined between two uncertain project elements. While many elements' costs may be correlated, the correlation is defined between them in pair-wise fashion.

The degree of correlation is measured by a "correlation coefficient." The correlation coefficient can be any value between –1.0 and +1.0.

- Positive correlation exists if, when one project element's cost is above its expected value the cost of the correlated element tends to be above its own expected value.[4] Project element costs that are positively correlated can be expected to be higher or lower than their respective means together on any project, probably because they are influenced by a common risk or set of risks. If projects experience positive correlation among some project elements then a Monte Carlo simulation's data inputs should be correlated in the simulation software. Positive correlation is fairly common in project risk analysis and has been a driving force in the development of cost risk analysis practices over the years.
- Negative correlation exists when one project element is above its expected value and the correlated element's cost will tend to be below its own expected value. Negative correlation is not common in project management. Negative correlation may occur when scope of work is re-assigned from one WBS category or activity to another; if the work is moved out of one project element that element's cost will be lower than expected while the cost of the element to which the work is transferred will be higher by the same amount. Again, if there is negative correlation between the costs of project elements then a simulation of the project should have cost inputs that are negatively correlated.
- Independence is present when the cost of one project element is not related to that of another element's cost, even though both are uncertain. We have assumed independence in earlier chapters in this book.

The strength of correlation between activity durations is determined by the strength of the common risks in driving the project elements' costs and is reflected in the size of the correlation coefficient. Taking positive correlation, the closer to a coefficient of +1.0 the closer to perfect correlation is between the two project elements and the more predictable it is that their costs will "move together." With perfect positive correlation, the correlation coefficient is +1.0. The correlated elements' costs move in lock-step, and in this rare case

---

3   Causality going the opposite direction would be illogical – subcontract management will not drive the cost of the subcontract.

4   Each of these project elements will be varying within their own probability distribution so the fluctuation in cost of one project element is generally not the same as that for the other correlated element of the pair even if correlation is perfect (coefficient of 1.0).

if one element's cost is at its maximum (or minimum) point the other will also be at its maximum (or minimum) point. The requirement that all project elements have perfect positive correlation is the only condition for which it makes sense to add up the columns of optimistic and pessimistic costs.[5]

There are three conditions that affect the degree of correlation between different project elements' costs:

- Risk must be common to both project elements. If the risk occurs on a project it will influence the cost of (at least) those two elements.
- The risks must be influential in determining the project elements' costs. For instance, if the risk affects strongly one element's cost but only weakly affects another element's cost, then correlation may be present but may not be strong.
- The risks that have a large variability can exert a large influence on the project. The impact of a risk that has small variability is unlikely to affect significantly the activities that it influences even if it is common to the two project elements and helps to drive their cost.

What determines the strength of correlation? The degree of correlation depends on the risks that are present and that affect the costs as well as other risks that may be present but are not common to the two activities. Take the situation where there is one risk that is common to two activities and other risks are absent, causing perfect correlation (within rounding error) between the costs of a pair of project elements. This situation is shown in Figure 5.2:[6]

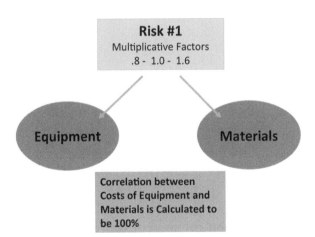

Figure 5.2   Perfect positive correlation

---

5   In the most recent PMBOK® Guide (Project Management Institute 2008) the mistake was made to add up the low and high extreme ranges of project cost estimates for all three project elements shown in Figure 11.13. In earlier editions the temptation was avoided, and we have also not summed those columns in Figure 3.1.

6   In these examples the risk was assigned and a simulation of 10,000 iterations was run. The resulting 10,000 pairs of costs were saved to Microsoft Excel and its correlation function calculated the correlation coefficient between the two project element's costs. In other words, we are creating correlation, not assuming correlation, with these experiments.

Perfect positive correlation is shown in the scatter diagram for the costs of Equipment and Materials. Figure 5.3 shows that these two are perfectly correlated, because there is only one risk driving both of them.

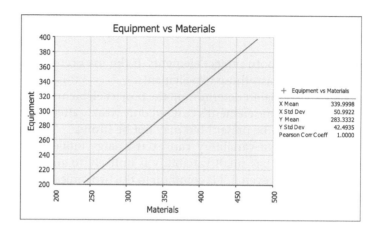

Figure 5.3   Perfect positive correlation scatter plot

The degree of correlation is reduced if there are other confounding risks that affect the activities but are not common to them. Figure 5.4 indicates that Risk 2 affects only equipment and Risk 3 affects only materials.

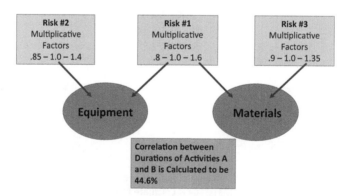

Figure 5.4   The presence of non-common or confounding risks reduces the degree of correlation

Because of the presence of Risk 2 that is specific to equipment and Risk 3 that is specific to materials, the correlation between equipment and materials caused by Risk 1 is weakened, even though Risk 1 is still common to the two project elements. Taking the 10,000 pairs of costs for the two project elements and calculating their correlation shows a correlation coefficient of 44.3 percent. The scatter diagram in Figure 5.5 shows that these element costs are no longer moving in lock step.

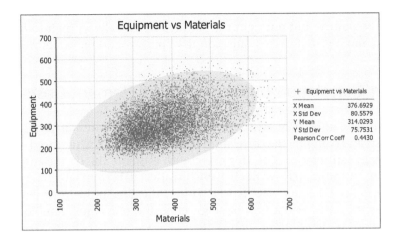

Figure 5.5   Correlation with common and confounding risks scatter plot

The identification and quantification of the risks, then assigning them to project elements, is the basis of the Risk Driver approach to project risk analysis that is described first in Chapter 6. The Risk Driver approach models how correlation arises rather than assumes a correlation coefficient between project element costs.

How Monte Carlo Simulation Software Uses the Correlation Coefficient

Unfortunately we do not know the correlation between two project elements' costs. The traditional approach to specifying project element cost correlation is to make an educated guess about the strength of the correlation between the two elements and input that correlation coefficient into the simulation software. If the costs of two project elements are thought to be correlated, the correlation coefficient must be determined by examining history or making judgmental estimates.[7] Correlation coefficients are then assigned to the pair of project elements' costs. After the pair of correlated element costs is identified we need to decide on an estimate of the correlation coefficient (from −1.0 to +1.0 but usually in project risk analysis positive correlation is believed, so the coefficient is usually between 0.0 and +1.0).

The Monte Carlo simulation software typically selects hundreds or thousands of values chosen at random for the costs of the project elements to be used in the iterations. If the elements are deemed to be correlated, the software then arranges the costs in correlated fashion by iteration before feeding them into the simulation. Hence, if two element's costs are positively correlated, the columns of numbers chosen initially at random by Monte Carlo or Latin Hypercube techniques are rearranged so that high values in one column are paired with high numbers in the column for the correlated element. If the correlation coefficient is thought to be high the pairings are tight, so high costs in one column are almost always paired with high costs in the paired column. If the correlation

---

7   In the next section we discuss how difficult choosing the coefficient may be.

is thought to be positive but not tight the pairings are not always high-to-high and low-to-low, but are more paired in that direction than purely random values would be.

Specifying Correlation between Project Element Costs

For those who are unfamiliar with correlation it might be useful to collect data on correlated costs and compute the correlation coefficients. Then, when faced with a specific project the team can refer back to this exercise to estimate the coefficients to assign in the simulation. Unfortunately we rarely have historical data from which we can compute actual correlation coefficients so we have to collect the data in the interviews with SMEs. In many cases the SMEs lack a firm basis for choosing one correlation coefficient over another and resort to descriptions such as "low," "moderate," or "high." For quantitative risk analysis these vague descriptors need to be translated into values, such as .25, .50 and .90 respectively. In some cases databases of many projects have been assembled; the US Air Force procurement data base is one example. Correlations can be calculated using the many projects in the USAF database. The next question would be whether correlation in the past projects can be reliably assumed for a new project.

Correlations and the Method of Moments

In Chapter 2 we assumed that the Monte Carlo simulation software had not arrived yet, or was hung-up in the IT department – in any case we did not have simulation capabilities so we used the Method of Moments to calculate the mean and standard deviation for the total project cost from the mean and variances (square of the standard deviation) of the project elements' costs. We did not introduce the concept of correlation and were implicitly assuming that the project elements' costs were independent, exhibiting correlation coefficients of 0.0.

It turns out that the presence or absence of correlation does not affect the mean of the total project cost distribution but it does affect the standard deviation. Remember the way we found the standard deviation of the total project cost by summing the variances of the project elements and taking the square root. That formula was incomplete, but we did not need to introduce correlation until now.

The complete formula for the standard deviation ("Sigma") of a 2-element summation problem including taking account of correlation is:

$Sigma_{TC}$ = Square Root (Variance$_1$+Variance$_2$+2*Rho*Sigma$_1$*Sigma$_2$)

Where: $Sigma_{TC}$ = Standard Deviation of Total Project Cost

Variance$_1$ and Variance2 = the variances of the costs of project elements 1 and 1

Sigma1 and Sigma2 = standard deviations of the cost of project elements 1 and 2

Rho = the correlation coefficient between the costs of project elements 1 and 2

The effect of correlation between element 1 and element 2 is in the term 2*Rho*Sigma₁*Sigma₂. Notice that if there is no correlation, Rho is zero (0) and the term disappears, so our ignoring it in the earlier discussion of MOM was the right thing to do. However, what is the impact of correlation using MOM?

Table 5.1 shows, for a 2-element cost estimate, the impact of correlation on the standard deviation, comparing the standard deviation (sigma) with correlation at zero and at .9 between the material and equipment project elements' costs. Notice that the mean of the sum of equipment and materials costs stays the same at $637 thousand but the standard deviation without correlation is $67.7 thousand, This value can be contrasted to the case assuming a high correlation of .9 that increases the standard deviation to $92.5 thousand. This means that the probability distribution that takes account of correlation is more widely spread than if the distributions are independent, all around the same mean value.

Table 5.1   Impact of correlation at 0.9 on the standard deviation of the total cost 2 elements using MOM

	Optimistic	Most Likely	Pessimistic	Mean	Variance	Sigma
Procurement of equipment	210	250	400	287	1,672	40.9
Procurement of materials	250	300	500	350	2,917	54.0
			Mean	637		
			Sum of variances		4,589	
			Sigma no correlation	**67.7**		
			Sum of variances and Rho term		8,564	
			Sigma Correlation = .9		92.5	

Correlations using Monte Carlo Simulation

Using simulation to replicate the same comparison that is shown in Table 5.1 using the MOM, we find the same results (with some rounding). Figure 5.6 shows the overlay of the two histograms. The one with no correlation is taller and thinner, whereas the one with correlation is shorter and broader. The means are the same and the standard deviations are close to the MOM results in Table 5.1 as shown in the table to the right of the graph in Figure 5.6.

Notice that the histogram with a high level (.90) of correlation has more optimistic values (lower costs) as well as more pessimistic values (higher costs). Notice also that the P-80 value has been affected. With correlation it is $721 thousand, but without correlation that value is about 88 percent likely. This result shows better in the comparison of the cumulative distributions in Figure 5.7. The steeper curve, equipment and material costs without correlation, shows less risk at the P-80.

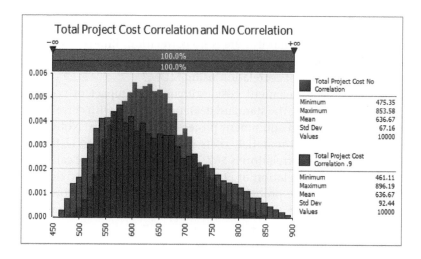

Figure 5.6   Histogram of equipment and materials cost with and without correlation @ .9

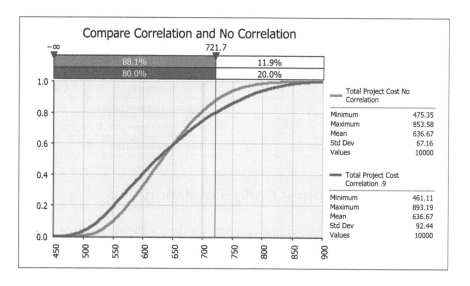

Figure 5.7   Cumulative distribution of cost with and without correlation @ .9

The Effect of Correlation on Total Project Cost Risk

Why should we care about whether our activities are correlated or not? The short answer is that correlation makes it more possible for very high and very low costs. We are sensitive to projects overrunning their cost estimates and we recommend establishing a contingency reserve to protect against that eventuality. Correlation increases the amount by which they could overrun at percentiles not close to the 50th percentile (shown in Figure 5.7), and hence also increases the cost contingency reserve needed. For this reason correlation must be examined and included in our analysis.

Let us return to the 6-element project cost estimate we have used in earlier chapters. Now we can examine the impact of correlation on the probability distribution of total project cost and on the contingency reserve of cost that we would need to hold to provide for a degree of certainty that the performing organization, or the customer, deems necessary. We will stay with P-80 as that level of certainty. We would like to show the comparison of histograms with and without correlation. To make the impact dramatic, we have constructed a correlation matrix with very high levels of correlation, 90 precent, shown in Figure 5.2.

In this simple example the correlation between all possible pairs of activities is equal at 90 percent, making this an example of very high but not perfect correlation. The correlation coefficients do not need to be all the same since, within limits that are described below, these correlation coefficients can take on different values if some pairs are more strongly correlated than others. Of course we may also expect that some activities are not correlated at all and that their correlation would show up in the matrix as zero. Notice that the correlation matrix is square and has the value 1.0 down the principal diagonal. That means that each element is perfectly correlated with itself, which is not surprising. We only need to fill out the lower-left portion of the correlation matrix since it is symmetrical. That means, if Commissioning is correlated .9 with Construction then Construction is correlated .9 with Commissioning and we need to show ".9" only once.

Table 5.2   Correlation matrix with high correlation between each pair of elements

	Preliminary engineering	Detailed engineering	Procurement of equipment	Procurement of materials	Construction	Commissioning
Preliminary engineering	1					
Detailed engineering	0.9	1				
Procurement of equipment	0.9	0.9	1			
Procurement of materials	0.9	0.9	0.9	1		
Construction	0.9	0.9	0.9	0.9	1	
Commissioning	0.9	0.9	0.9	0.9	0.9	1

The 6-project element cost estimate is simulated with these high correlation coefficients and generates the results shown in Figure 5.8 (histograms) and Figure 5.9 (cumulative distributions).

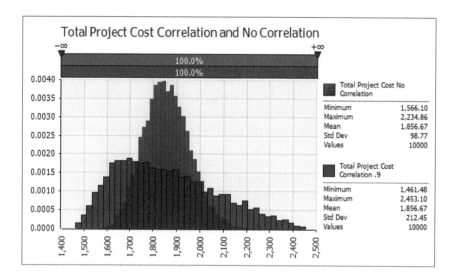

Figure 5.8   Effect of high correlation between elements' cost on total project cost risk – histograms

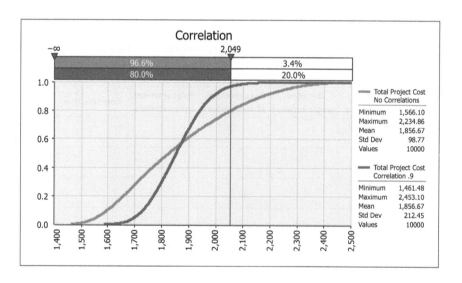

Figure 5.9   Effect of high correlation between elements' cost on total project cost risk – cumulative distributions

The summary statistics (see Table 5.3) show that:

• The P-80 is $2,049 thousand with correlation compared to $1,939 thousand without correlation. If we forgot correlation we would plan to hold a contingency reserve that is too small by $110 thousand.

- The probability of finishing on budget ($1,640 thousand) is about 15 percent with correlations but it is less than 5 percent without correlation. This indicates that considering correlation actually improves our chances of finishing on budget because it spreads the tails in both directions.
- The standard deviation with strong correlation is $212 thousand, which can be compared to $98 thousand without correlation.
- The mean cost is the same for the two scenarios.[8]

Table 5.3   Summary statistics from simulations with correlations @ .9 and without correlations

Statistic	No Correlation	Correlation @ .9
Minimum	1,566	1,461
Maximum	2,235	2,453
Mean	1,857	1,857
Std Deviation	99	212
10%	1,732	1,600
20%	1,771	1,659
30%	1,801	1,712
40%	1,827	1,768
50%	1,852	1,828
60%	1,879	1,891
70%	1,906	1,962
80%	1,939	2,049
90%	1,987	2,167
90%	2,165	1,985

These findings show that, with a simple cost estimate, correlations increase the spread of the distribution but do not change the mean value. If the organization cares about a high likelihood of achieving a date it might choose a P-80 or some other high percentile, and those are affected by correlation. If it estimates to the mean or even the P-50 correlation is not as important.

---

8   This finding differs from that in schedule risk analysis. The cost model we are using is a simple summation model where the mean is the same with or without correlation. In schedule risk analysis the schedule has a structure of paths, some of which are in parallel that merge at major milestones. This structure is the reason the Method of Moments does not work for schedules but does work for simple summation cost estimate risk analysis. See Appendix 1: The Problem with PERT in Hulett (2009).

Specifying Correlation Coefficients – the Possibility of an Inconsistent Correlation Matrix

In traditional cost risk analysis, the values of correlation coefficients are usually determined by individual SMEs meeting in interviews or risk workshops where they talk about risks and their impacts on the project schedule. It is rare that the participants in these meetings have historical data that can be used to compute the correlation coefficients. And yet, not having data does not mean that correlation is zero. The results above show that we should not ignore correlation. Even if they have no historical data the project participants need to become adept and comfortable estimating correlation coefficients using their expert judgment.

As mentioned previously, the teams look for:

- common risks driving the durations of pairs of project element costs
- risks that are important in determining those cost
- risks that show significant variability.

There are some difficulties in developing correlation coefficients using expert judgment, however.

- The team members are often unfamiliar with the concept of correlation.
- The calibration of correlation coefficients is difficult. For instance, what coefficient should be assigned when someone believes there is "strong" correlation between a pair of project element costs?
  - Could two people agree that correlation is "strong" but have a different coefficient in mind?
  - Could people argue about whether correlation is "strong" or "moderate" but have the same coefficient in mind?
  - How do people arrive at a value for a correlation coefficient in the absence of historical data?
  - How do correlation coefficients relate to each other in a system represented by the correlation coefficient matrix? Are there some combinations of correlation coefficients that are not possible in reality?

At the end of the day, the team members arrive at a set of pair-wise correlation coefficients. Some coefficients are high, some are low, some are zero and occasionally some may be negative. These are the best or at least the consensus values they have agreed to when considering the coefficients pair-wise. Of course, as project participants get more comfortable and experienced with risk concepts they will get better at specifying these numbers. At the outset, or with some team members new to the data generation process, accuracy with correlation coefficients may be difficult to achieve.

In some cases the pair-wise comparisons may appear to be reasonable when examined individually but may not be consistent when examined within the correlation matrix. At this point we realize that we have a "system of coefficients" that imposes its own discipline on the possible correlation coefficients, which is not present when the coefficients are considered individually.

Some correlation matrices are logically impossible to find in real life. For instance, even though project participants may settle on the correlation coefficient matrix shown in Table 5.4, it is impossible to imagine 100 projects, represented by 100 iterations in a simulation, each one on a line in a spreadsheet with costs of project elements A, B and C arrayed in columns where:

- the cost of project element A is strongly correlated with the cost of project element B with a coefficient of 90 percent
- the cost of project element A is strongly correlated with the cost of project element C with a coefficient of 90 percent
- and yet, the SMEs assess that the cost of project element B and the cost of project element C are only correlated 20 percent.

The team may agree on these correlation coefficients when they are discussed one pair at a time, but the coefficients have to be feasible as a system as shown below:

Table 5.4   An inconsistent correlation matrix

	Procurement of materials	Construction	Commissioning
Procurement of materials	1	0.9	0.9
Construction	0.9	1	0.2
Commissioning	0.9	0.2	1

The problem can be seen immediately once the coefficients are arrayed in the matrix. If procurement of materials and construction are strongly related, and procurement of materials and commissioning are also strongly related, then commissioning and construction must be at least correlated with moderate strength. A 20 percent correlation between commissioning and construction is too low and not consistent with the other two 90 percent correlation coefficients. The matrix is impossible – the coefficients are inconsistent within the system.[9] There are three different ways this coefficient matrix is impossible:

- the correlation of 20 percent between Construction and Commissioning is too low;
- the coefficients of 90 percent between the other two pairs are too high; or
- at least one of the high coefficients is too high and/or the low coefficient is too low.

In any case, this correlation matrix is not internally consistent. This set of correlation coefficients cannot happen on real projects. Yet the project team might have settled on these values when discussing correlations pair-wise. The system shows a problem that can occur with coefficients that are determined by expert judgment.

---

9   In statistical terms, this matrix is not positive semi-definite. See Risk Glossary Website (2010).

Happily there is a test for the correlation matrix internal inconsistency. Popularly known as the Eigenvalue Test, it is based on the characteristics that such a matrix (square, 1.0 down the principal or main diagonal and off-diagonal values that mirror each other) must have. The Eigenvalue Test shows that this matrix is a mathematical impossibility and hence is a real impossibility as well.

Simulation software that offers proper correlation also offers the Eigenvalue Test. It performs this test before it begins the simulation and alerts the user if the correlation coefficient matrix is inconsistent. Most software packages will offer to fix the correlation matrix by creating a new matrix that is as close as possible to the one specified but which just barely passes the Eigenvalue Test. These software packages will indicate to the user which fixes were made so the user can review them and determine if those changed coefficients are acceptable.

Different simulation software packages use different algorithms so the "repaired correlation matrix" may differ between software packages, but if correlation is required they will not perform the simulation until the correlation matrix is fixed.

One example of trying to use the correlation matrix in Table 5.4 is from @RISK from Palisade Corporation, a Microsoft Excel add-in often used for financial or cost risk analysis. Attempting to start the simulation returns the message shown in Figure 5.10. Choosing "OK" causes @RISK to change the matrix to one that is consistent. The original matrix and the corrected matrix are shown below in Table 5.5:

Figure 5.10 Example message warning of an inconsistent coefficient matrix (@RISK)

Table 5.5   Correcting an inconsistent correlation matrix by @Risk

This inconsistent correlation matrix			
	Procurement of materials	Construction	Commissioning
Procurement of materials	1	0.9	0.9
Construction	0.9	1	0.2
Commissioning	0.9	0.2	1
Has been changed by @RISK to			
	Procurement of materials	Construction	Commissioning
Procurement of materials	1	.765	.765
Construction	.765	1	.170
Commissioning	.765	.170	1

The only surprising correction is the reduction of the correlation between construction and commissioning, which was already too low to be consistent with the other two correlations, from 0.2 to 0.170. In fact, Crystal Ball, shown overleaf, analyzes this as an inconsistent correlation matrix.

Another example of providing the revised correlation matrix is Crystal Ball,[10] another Microsoft Excel simulation package. This software also tells the user what the resulting "near-by" matrix is that passes the Eigenvalue Test. Putting in the matrix shown above returns the following message (Figure 5.11) from Crystal Ball:

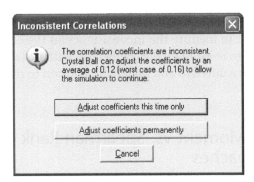

Figure 5.11 Message from failing the Eigenvalue Test (Crystal Ball)

Choosing "Adjust coefficients permanently" option allows the user to see the revised matrix. In this case the coefficients have been changed by that software as follows in Table 5.6.

Table 5.6   Correcting an inconsistent correlation matrix (by Crystal Ball)[11]

This inconsistent correlation matrix			
	Procurement of materials	**Construction**	**Commissioning**
Procurement of materials	1	0.9	0.9
Construction	0.9	1	0.2
Commissioning	0.9	0.2	1
Has been changed by Crystal Ball to			
	Procurement of materials	**Construction**	**Commissioning**
Procurement of materials	1	0.743	0.743
Construction	0.743	1	0.235
Commissioning	0.743	0.235	1

---

10   Crystal Ball is made and sold by Decisioneering, a unit of Oracle.

11   Different software uses different algorithms to find a nearby correlation matrix that passes the Eigenvalue Test. Some do not tell you what they did. Risk+, a risk simulation package for Microsoft Project schedules performs the Eigenvalue Test and offers to revise the correlation matrix to pass that test. The revised correlation matrix values can be printed out to a .csv file. Primavera Risk Analysis now has the Crystal Ball functionality.

Notice that the high-correlation values of .9 have been reduced to .743 and the low-correlation value of .2 has been increased to .235. This matrix passes the Eigenvalue Test, but it may not be agreeable to the project team.

Different software packages will implement their own algorithms that may result in a different corrected matrix. Using the revised matrix we can proceed with the simulation.[12]

Passing the Eigenvalue Test does not ensure that the correlation coefficients are correct. It just ensures that they are not mathematically impossible. This is a low threshold, but one that we should not trip over. When the software tells the user that the pair-wise correlation coefficients when put into the correlation coefficient matrix fail the Eigenvalue Test, it is best to identify the inconsistency in the correlation matrix and go back to the project team to re-estimate the coefficients with system integrity in mind. The team members may have a different and preferable solution to the one that the computer calculates.

Pearson Product Moment vs. Spearman Rank Order Correlation Approaches

There are two concepts of correlation that are in use with retail simulation software: the Spearman Rank Order approach and the Pearson Product Moment approach. The Pearson Product Moment approach is preferred but is rarely available. It preserves the linear relationship between variables when creating the correlated series. This means that it recognizes that 3 is 1.5 times larger than 2, not only that 3 > 2. This is the way we intuitively think about correlation. Using the Pearson approach the result of the simulation properly accounts for the amount of spread in the inputs and gives more accurate results than the Spearman method. Combining inputs using this approach will result in the proper degree of risk.

Most of the retail software that provides Monte Carlo simulation capabilities uses the Spearman Rank Order approach to correlation. The Spearman approach somewhat underestimates the effect of correlation on the result probability distribution – the resulting distribution is narrower than it should be. This is because the Spearman correlation only assures that the input values used in the simulation are rank ordered after conditioning. It preserves the monotonic order of values but does not preserve the linear relationship, the degree to which the outliers are away from the mean.

Risk+ from Deltek, a software product that simulates Microsoft Project schedules has an option to implement Pearson Product Moment correlation. The algorithm (Price 2002) is a sophisticated application including the Lurie-Goldberg transformation (Lurie and Goldberg 1998) that allows Pearson Product Moment approach to be used with distributions that are not Normal or Gaussian.

---

12   In discussions with John Neatrour in January 2010, I learned that it has been shown that the commonly used approach of Gaussian Elimination to correcting correlation matrices that are not positive semi-definite can cause false negative results in some circumstances. Although some analysts use Gauss Elimination to perform the test for positive semi-definiteness of Eigenvalues to weed out bad correlation matrices this practice is not well advised. Standard texts on numeric analysis such as Stoer and Bulirsch (1980) and Press, Vetterling, Teukolsky, and Flannery (2002) do not recommend Gauss Elimination for finding Eigenvalues of symmetric matrices. Instead Jacobi rotation and Cholesky decomposition are preferred because the pivoting problems that have to be dealt with to make Gauss Elimination stable do not appear.

Other software packages implement the Spearman approach. In practice the results from using the different approaches do not seem to be significantly different given the level of accuracy of the data. However, we should use a calculation method, Pearson if it available, which would be correct if the data were perfectly accurate.

Summary of Correlation in Project Schedule Risk Analysis

It is a fact of project life that risk is not always random. Sometimes risks can affect more than one project element's cost, and cause those affected costs to be high or low together. That means that on any project the elements' costs are expected to be large or small within their probability distributions together, and it is the "together" part of that sentence that indicates the presence of correlation. If they are large together there is a greater chance for serious cost overruns because the costs that are in the upper ranges of their probability distributions that occur on the same project reinforce each other, adding to the possibility of overrunning the project's cost estimate. Of course, in cost risk analysis there is a similar chance with correlated costs that total costs will be lower than expected.

Correlation is imposed on the randomized data used during Monte Carlo simulation so that each iteration will represent an internally consistent scenario.[13] If it is improbable that one project element cost is high while another is low (within their own risk ranges) because they are both influenced by the same risks, then they are correlated. If the cost inputs to the simulations were selected purely at random there will be no correlation between costs and some iterations would be internally inconsistent with the assumption of correlation. The total cost probability distribution would be too narrow and the stakeholders would be lulled into a false sense of low risk security.

Monte Carlo simulation software allows the user to specify correlation so that the inputs to the iterations will be high or low within their own probability distribution together as observed in real life or at least believed to be so by the project team.

Correlation expresses the way pairs of project elements' costs will be high or low together on the same project, representing positive correlation that can be strong or weak. (Of course we might have negative correlation, although that seems to be rare in project management.) We used Monte Carlo simulation with one common risk and with two risks that were not common to synthesize data for 10,000 projects (10,000 iterations). When we computed the correlation coefficient using a spreadsheet function we found a correlation coefficient that was below 45 percent. (This exercise represents the Risk Driver approach to modelling correlation.) Correlation occurs in different strengths and the project team will have to be alert to degrees of correlation.

The impact of correlation is to spread the tails of the total cost distribution and hence to increase the needed contingency reserve of cost if the organization targets a desired confidence level above the mean, say at the P-80 level. If the project costs are thought to be correlated the risk analyst needs to explore correlation to achieve an answer representative of the real project.

---

13   The Risk Driver approach introduced in Chapter 6 models the creation of correlation, eliminating the need to estimate correlation coefficients and the possibility of trying to impose an inconsistent correlation matrix on the simulation. This is just one of the benefits of the Risk Driver approach to project risk analysis.

Unfortunately most organizations do not have a number of projects from which they can compute correlation coefficients so they must estimate those coefficients using project teams' expert judgment. We saw that this expert judgment can cause inconsistent matrices of correlation coefficients. We introduced the Eigenvalue Test for inconsistent correlation matrices. If the correlation matrix fails this test (is not positive semi-definite), the simulation software uses an algorithm to find a nearby matrix that passes the test. Different software uses different algorithms and their results may be inconsistent with each other. Risk managers are encouraged to review these adjusted coefficients but to go back to the project team for confirmation and correction.

Finally we mentioned that we recommend using the Pearson Product Moment approach to correlation if it is available, indicating that it is preferable to the Spearman Rank Order approach. Pearson is a linear approach preserving both the rank order and the degree of difference from the mean, which is the preferred approach. Spearman preserves the rank order of values but not the linear relationship between variables. It is felt that Spearman underestimates the impact of correlation on the total project cost risk – the probability distribution of total project completion dates is too narrow under Spearman. Unfortunately Pearson product moment correlation is not offered on most simulation products. Fortunately, the differences of the results generated by the two different approaches are not large

Correlation is a fact of project life and the project manager who ignores its importance will underestimate the risk to the project schedule.

References

Hulett, D.T. (2009). *Practical Schedule Risk Analysis*. Farnham, England, Gower Publishing.

Lurie, P. and Goldberg, M. (1998). "An Approximate Method for Sampling Correlated Random Variables from Partially Specified Distributions." *Management Science* 44(2): 203–18.

Press, V. et al. (2002). *Numerical Recipes in C++*. Cambridge University Press.

Price, J. (2002). An Implementation of the Lurie-Goldberg Algorithm in Schedule Risk Analysis, Presented to the Space Systems Cost Analysis Group, Long Beach, CA.

Project Management Institute (2008). *Guide to the Project Management Body of Knowledge (PMBOK(R) Guide)*. 4th edition.

Risk Glossary Website (2010) (www.riskglossary.com/link/positive_definite_matrix.htm) accessed January 2010.

Stoer, J. and Bulirsch, R. (1980). *Introduction to Numerical Analysis*. Springer-Verlag.

6 Using Risk Register Risks to Drive the Cost Risk Analysis: The "Risk Driver" Method[1]

Introduction

TRADITIONAL COST RISK ANALYSIS

In the earlier chapters of this book risk to the project element cost is represented by applying 3-point (optimistic, most likely and pessimistic) estimates to the elements' line item costs, and choosing the correct probability distributions that indicate the relative likelihood of each of the many possible costs before Monte Carlo simulation. The 3-point duration estimate data are usually collected by interviewing experienced project personnel. During the interviews the discussion focuses on the activity being "risked" and the various risks that could cause its duration to be different from (perhaps shorter than or longer than) its duration in the schedule. The probability distribution generated during these interviews combines or summarizes – some would say confuses – all of the various risks that influence the activity's duration.

We have always known that there are some limitations to this approach:[2]

- There is no provision for specifying the probability the risk will occur on the project. The representation of project risks using only their uncertain impact on project element costs ignores the possibility that these risks may or may not occur on our project. This assumption misses one of the two well-documented dimensions of project risk events, the probability of occurring. One accepted definition of project risk is: "An uncertain event or condition that, if it occurs, has a positive or negative impact on at least one project objectives" (PMI 2008). Notice the words "uncertain" and "if it occurs" in the definition. Traditional quantitative risk analysis is sometimes criticized because it emphasizes impacts of risks on costs but ignores the probability that the risks themselves may or may not occur at all on this project.

---

1   This chapter is derived from Hulett, Hornbacher and Whitehead (2008) and Hulett (2009b). This chapter is also similar to Chapter 8 in Hulett (2009a) which introduces the risk driver method applied to schedule risk analysis.

2   These criticisms also apply to the standard schedule risk analysis approaches, which are based on the application of 3-point estimates to schedule activity durations.

- We cannot separately distinguish the impact of individual risks on total project cost. Suppose that the analyst wants to identify the most important risks to the cost estimate in order to guide risk mitigation. Because the 3-point estimates summarize or represent the impact on the element's cost of all the risks that are relevant, there is no way to distinguish the cost impact of one risk from that of the others. The traditional cost risk analysis uses measures of risk sensitivity such as tornado diagrams. In the traditional approach, these measures identify those project elements that have uncertain costs and are correlated with the total project cost, but they will not indicate which risks are crucial.
- Since the impact of a risk is not necessarily limited to one project element's cost (an additional important limitation of the traditional focus on individual project element costs is that it misses a risk's effects on several project cost elements), its complete impact on total project cost would not be felt by a measure that checks the correlation between individual cost elements and total cost.
- For risk mitigation we want to prioritize the risk's entire impact on the project, whether it is combined with other risks' impacts on specific project elements or spread out over several project elements. If several risks affect an element's cost uncertainty, we need to sort out the impact of each risk on the activity's 3-point impact estimate and have a way to account for a risks' impacting multiple project elements.
- Traditional analysis requires applying correlations directly to the uncertain cost probability distributions, and estimating correlation between cost elements is difficult. Correlation is often found between cost elements in project risk analysis, but specifying the strength of correlation is difficult in the absence of large databases of project actual costs. We often specify inconsistent correlation matrices because correlation coefficients are specified by interviewees using their judgment.

The focus of traditional cost risk analysis on the cost of individual line items rather than on the risks themselves is a serious limitation that the Risk Driver Approach is intended to remedy.

THE RISK DRIVER METHOD – SUMMARY

The Risk Driver method to conducting a cost risk analysis is an alternative to the traditional approach using 3-point estimates on project element costs. The "Risk Driver" approach starts with the risks that are typically prioritized in the Risk Register that is usually available. (The Risk Register starts with identified risks and then uses a qualitative risk analysis approach to prioritize them.) The Risk Driver approach drives the elements' cost risk directly from the risks themselves. It addresses the criticisms listed above.

In this approach:

- The risks are identified, generally from those risks that were judged to be high-risk in the qualitative analysis leading to the Risk Register's list of prioritized risks. Hence, the link from qualitative to quantitative risk is made explicit. This connection between qualitative and quantitative risk analysis has not always been as strong as it should have been when using the 3-point estimate approach to represent risks.

- The risk-data-gathering interviews focus on risks, not on the impacted project element costs. These interviews are generally conducted at a more summary level than those of traditional approach that drive down to individual project element costs. Hence the interviewee and interviewer are quantifying strategic risks that are often more important to the project than detailed technical risks. These interviews are generally shorter and more illuminating than those in the traditional approach that focus on the most detailed level cost elements one at a time.
- In Risk Driver interviews we interview for the probability that the risk may occur, the impact range if it were to occur and the project elements that it affects if it does occur. By including the probability that the risk occurs on the project, this differs from the traditional 3-point estimate approach that does not use directly the probability that a risk occurs. The Risk Driver interviews include both the probability and the impact, the two main dimensions of project risk events.
- The impact range of a risk is specified in multiplicative terms. Because of this, a risk may be applied to large and small project element costs with the same proportional impact. Probability distributions are assigned to each risk's impact range. Since the cost model resides in a spreadsheet, several probability distributions are available to the analyst.
- If several risks that affect one activity occur during an iteration, the multiplicative factors (chosen at random from the probability distribution of possible impact factors) of the risks are multiplied together for any iteration and applied (multiply) the cost of the project element's cost to determine the cost to be used during that iteration. If the risk does not occur for an iteration it is given a value of 1.0, so it has no effect on the multiplication of factors.
- The risks are assigned to the project elements that they affect, and may be assigned to several or many line items. This differs from the traditional 3-point estimate approach since the Risk Driver method captures all of the risks' impacts on all of the element costs they affect.
- Since risks are often assigned to multiple project element costs, those costs become correlated as the simulation proceeds. Thus, the Risk Driver method models the way correlation occurs rather than requiring the interviewees to estimate the correlation coefficients. There is no chance to get an invalid correlation coefficient matrix either, since correlation is derived consistently from the structure of the model. The Risk Driver method is based on the notion that the Risk Drivers are independent of one another. Thus risks are generally not correlated except for technical reasons.
- Project element costs may be affected by one or several risks. This is true with the traditional approach, but in the Risk Driver approach the influence of each risk is identified separately, not combined with others in a single 3-point estimate. The Risk Driver method derives the element cost probability distribution during the Monte Carlo simulation, based on the parameters of all risks assigned to the element cost. Using this method the interviewees do not have to do in their heads the complex calculations involving the probability and impact of multiple risks that contribute to the uncertainty in a project element's cost.
- The cost model is simulated using Monte Carlo methods. For each iteration during a Monte Carlo simulation (1) if the risk occurs for one activity it occurs for all that it is assigned to, and (2) if its impact is a strong threat (or opportunity) for one it is a strong threat (or opportunity) for all affected activities for that iteration.

- The usual results such as histograms and cumulative distributions (S-curves) are derived. However, the tornado or sensitivity charts now highlight the risks' correlation to total cost rather than the project elements' correlation because the risks are the uncertain variables identified by the simulation software as driving total project cost.
- As the risk mitigation is being planned, the probability and/or impact of the risk, or its assignments to various activities can be altered and the analysis re-run. The cost of the mitigation can be compared to the impact of reducing the risk to project cost for a benefit-cost analysis of risk mitigation. This will help make intelligent choices within a complex project of which risks to mitigate first. This impact can be calibrated at any particular percentile of total project cost.

The Risk Factors method can be implemented in Microsoft Excel using spreadsheet modelling and a simulation tool such as Crystal Ball from Oracle or @RISK from Palisade Corporation.

Source of the Project Risks used in the Risk Driver Method

Most projects have a Risk Register compiled before quantitative schedule risk analysis is conducted. The Risk Register includes identified risks that have been assessed and prioritized, using qualitative risk analysis methods, for their importance to the project. Historically Risk Registers contained only threats to the schedule, containing risks that, if they were to occur, would delay the project or increase its cost. These days Risk Registers also include opportunities – that is, an uncertain event or condition that if it occurs would have a positive impact on the project's cost objective. Typically the threats overwhelm the opportunities and a contingency reserve needs to be added to the risk-free estimate. However, the Risk Driver's approach allows both opportunities and threats.

Sometimes the Risk Register specifically identifies risks that are assessed to have an impact on the project's schedule, cost, scope and quality objectives considered separately. It is not only the influence of risks thought to be important on the project's cost estimate that we are concerned about in this chapter, since risks to schedule may be important for cost because for some time-dependent resources such as direct labor or level of effort (LOE) support labor, the longer the work takes the more it costs.[3] The Risk Register usually lists the probability that the risk will occur and, if it does occur, the impact on the project. To specify risks for the Risk Driver approach we start with the Risk Register information but we need to re-interview in order to quantify the risk parameters since the parameters used in qualitative risk analysis leading to the Risk Register are usually specified in terms that are too general to be used in quantitative risk analysis.

Since the Risk Register already exists it is most natural and powerful to use it as the basis of the Risk Driver method cost risk analysis. Doing so makes explicit the importance of the qualitative risk analysis process for the quantitative risk analysis process that helps compute the overall project schedule risk, the contingency required and its own prioritization of risks within the structure of the project schedule.

---

3   Chapters 7–10 introduce the integration of cost and schedule risk analysis that takes the full effect of schedule on cost into account.

The Risk Driver Method Applied to Project Cost Risk – Mechanics[4]

The Risk Driver method starts with a Risk Register. We will explain and demonstrate the method using:

- Individual risk applied to a single project element cost. These examples show how one element cost's risk reflects the application of one risk with different probability and impact assumptions.
- Individual risk with several risks applied.
- A simplified cost estimate for the development of a new refinery, with several risks applied to different project element costs.

Specify the Risk – an Uncertainty that is 100 percent Likely

The first example shows the impact of a single risk on a cost element whose estimate, without padding for risk, is $100. The first risk is 100 percent likely, so some might call it an uncertainty. The result, if this were the only risk on the project element's cost, is just like applying a 3-point estimate using traditional methods.

Consider the uncertainty that the Labor Rates (cost per hour) may differ from the rates assumed in creating the project cost estimate as shown in Table 6.1.

Table 6.1   Uncertainty: probability 100 percent likely with an impact range including opportunities and threats

Risk Driver	Probability	Risk factor		
		Optimistic	Most likely	Pessimistic
Labor rates may differ from assumed in the estimate	100%	0.90	1.05	1.20

Applying a risk with 100 percent probability of occurring may seem strange since a risk is "an uncertain event or condition." although it may still be projected to occur in the future. In the labor rate case the existence of the uncertainty is not uncertain but the impact is uncertain. In this instance some would be unhappy calling this a "risk" but would still require that we capture this uncertainty or ambiguity in our analysis.

It is a strength of the Risk Driver method that it can encompass risks with a 100 percent probability but uncertain impact as well as risks with probability of less than 100 percent and uncertain impact. In addition, risks with 100 percent certainty of occurring can be combined with risk events of less than 100 percent certainty in the same analysis as they affect the same or different project elements's cost. Also, the impact can be both

---

4   In this chapter we are using a cost and cost risk model developed in Microsoft Project and using @RISK from Palisade. The equivalent exercise can be successful using Crystal Ball from Oracle.

opportunities (factor < 1.0) and threat (factor > 1.0) in one Risk Driver, such as the one shown in Table 6.1 above. That uncertainty can have a positive or a negative impact on different iterations in the same simulation.

Let us assign the labor-rate risk to a particular project element with a cost estimated at $100. In a Monte Carlo simulation, the element to which the uncertainty "Labor Rates May Differ from Assumed in the Estimate," has the probability distribution in Figure 6.1.

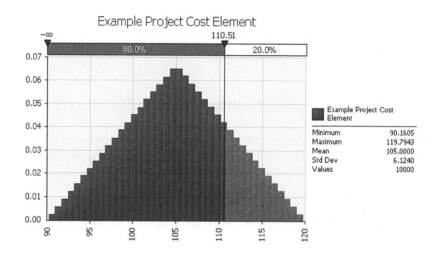

Figure 6.1   Example project element of $100 with labor rate uncertainty applied[5]

Notice that the range is from $90 to $120 and that the most likely cost is $105, reflecting the 3-point estimate applied to the Risk Driver. Notice that the probability distribution does not need to be centered on the cost in the estimate – in this case the most likely cost is 5 percent above that estimate. However, with a single uncertainty that is 100 percent likely, we do not see any difference between applying a 3-point estimate directly on the element cost or applying a multiplicative factor and assigning that factor to the element cost, except that we know which risk is responsible for this cost's uncertainty.

Specify the Risk – Multiple Uncertainties with 100 percent Likelihood

Consider applying more than one uncertainty to a project element's cost estimate. This is what we have done traditionally with 3-point estimates making mental calculations to pre-process the risk data and using our own judgment. Traditionally, when several uncertainties apply to a cost element we try to determine a 3-point estimate that combines the impacts of the risks or uncertainties (or both) that would have an impact on the cost

---

5   The figures in this chapter were generated using @RISK for Excel from Palisade Corporation.

estimate. In the Risk Driver approach we do not have to make assumptions about how the risks interact with each other. We specify the risks and assign them to elements' costs and derive the probability distribution for the project element's cost as a by-product of the Monte Carlo simulation applied to the cost model.

Suppose we have three uncertainties with the parameters shown in Table 6.2 below. Notice that the interviewees have to discuss estimating inaccuracy independent of what they understand about other uncertainties and risks that may occur. For instance, if cost estimates are uncertain because they do not account for scope growth, it would be best to specify the risk of scope growth independently of the cost estimating inaccuracy. In this view, cost estimating inaccuracy – in this case from –5 percent to +10 percent – is due to the immaturity of the data available to make the estimate at this stage of the project.

Table 6.2   Multiple uncertainties applied to a $100 project element cost

Risk Driver	Probability	Risk factor		
		Optimistic	Most likely	Pessimistic
Labor rate may differ from assumed	100%	0.85	1.10	1.20
Construction labor productivity may differ	100%	0.90	1.05	1.15
Cost estimate is inaccurate	100%	0.95	1.00	1.10

With these three uncertainties applied to the example project element cost of $100, the probability distribution for the project element's cost is shown in Figure 6.2. Notice that the shape of the distribution and that the parameters of minimum, mean (close to most likely) and maximum that are shown in the table to the right of the histogram are derived from the three input uncertainties rather than estimated by individual SMEs doing calculations in their heads and using their judgment. We have pushed the judgment back from the impact on element costs to the more fundamental risks – judgment is still required but it is more easily applied at a fundamental level.

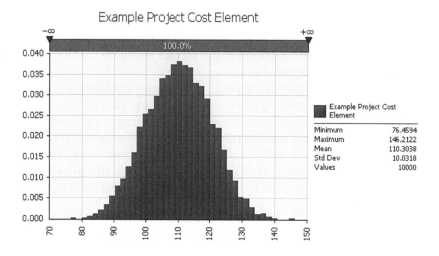

Figure 6.2 **$100 element cost probability distribution derived from three uncertainties**

Specify the Risk – Risk Events with < 100 percent Likelihood

Risks are described by their probability of occurring, and risk events have a probability less than 100 percent. If this is the case, the probability distributions for the activities affected exhibit a "spike" that represents the probability that the risk will not occur and a triangle specified that includes the rest of the probability. The following example in Table 6.3 shows a risk event, Cost of Long Lead Equipment is Unpredictable:

Table 6.3 **A risk event with 60 percent probability of occurring**

Risk Driver	Probability	Risk factor		
		Optimistic	Most likely	Pessimistic
Cost of long lead equipment is unpredictable	60%	0.85	1.10	1.20

If this risk is applied to our example element with a cost estimate of $100, we derive the cost probability distribution shown in Figure 6.3. Notice that with a 60 percent probability of occurring, there are 40 percent of the iterations on which the risk does not occur and its factor is set to 1.0. On those iterations, chosen by the computer at random, the cost of this project element is multiplied by 1.0 and the cost is the same $100 as estimated. In the other 60 percent of the iterations the cost is multiplied by a number chosen at random from a triangular distribution of .85 – 1.10 – 1.20. Notice that the triangle contains the value of 1.0 so in some cases even when the risk occurs the cost is as estimated, which is $100. This fact leads the spike in Figure 6.3 to be greater than simply 40 percent of the iterations in which the risk does not occur at all.

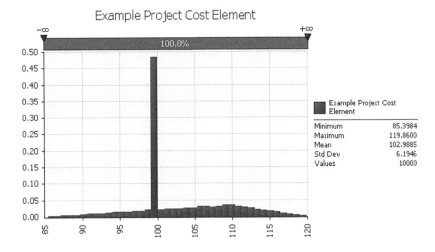

Figure 6.3 Activity with risk of 60 percent probability of occurring the spike contains more than 40 percent of the probability

Element Cost With Two Risks that are < 100 percent Likely Assigned

A project cost estimate may have more than one risk assigned to it. Let us consider three risks that may be applied to our example project element cost as shown in Table 6.4.

Table 6.4 Assigning three risk events with probability < 100 percent

Risk Driver	Probability	Risk factor		
		Optimistic	Most likely	Pessimistic
Joint venture may be out of alignment	30%	1.00	1.05	1.10
Cost of long lead equipment is unpredictable	60%	0.85	1.10	1.20
Quality key staff availability is not known	50%	0.90	1.05	1.15

In this case, the mechanics are:

- The impact multiplicative risk factors for each risk are selected at random for an iteration. Say, for the Joint Venture being out of alignment, which means the JV partners do not have the same objectives or decision-making cultures, the computer chooses 1.08 for an iteration. Note that it is assumed in the Risk Driver method that fundamental Risk Drivers are not correlated.

- For any iteration, the computer flips a coin with the probability of coming up heads listed in the probability column for the corresponding risk. If the coin comes up tails, a risk factor of 1.0 is substituted for the randomly generated risk factor originally chosen for that risk.
- For each iteration, the risk multiplicative factors for each assigned risk are multiplied together and the product multiplies the cost of the project. Repeating this operation thousands of times leads to the result shown below in Figure 6.4.

Notice that the probability distribution has a spike because each element is less than 100 percent certain to apply to this project. Based on experience in project risk interviews conducted in many industries (commercial and government) and in several countries over 20 years, the evidence is that it is very unlikely that the traditional 3-point estimate of cost uncertainty would have this shape. This is true even though, if questioned directly, the interviewees understand that each risk event may or may not occur.

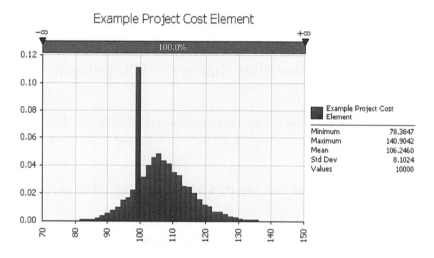

Figure 6.4   A cost element that has three Risk Drivers with <100 percent probability assigned

Assigning Risks and Uncertainties Together to One Project Element Cost

If all six of the risks that have been presented previously in Tables 6.2 and 6.4 were assigned to the example $100 project element cost, the spike tends to melt away. Figure 6.5 overleaf shows the result of applying the three risk events and three uncertainties to the example element cost. If so many risks were identified as influencing one project element's cost it is doubtful that interviewees would specify a 3-point estimate that approximates this probability distribution. In the Risk Driver method we model this distribution from the Risk Driver fundamentals.

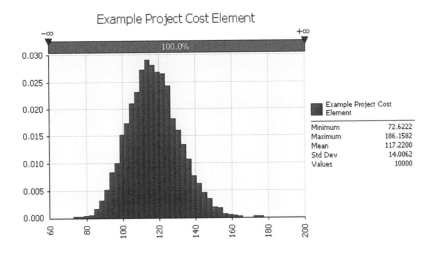

Figure 6.5   Cost element with six risks assigned

Modelling Correlation using Risk Drivers

In Chapter 5 we discussed the important subject of correlation between project element costs. In that chapter we indicated that correlation was important because as element costs vary, if they vary together there is a larger chance for very high and very low total project costs than if the elements' costs vary independently of each other. In project management we experience many examples of elements' costs varying together since they are affected by some of the same risks.

The discussion in Chapter 5 also indicated that specifying correlation coefficients that calibrate the degree of correlation between elements' costs is difficult. It is even possible that judgmentally generated correlation coefficients could be internally inconsistent when viewed as a system in a correlation matrix. There are ways in simulation software to "fix" an inconsistent correlation matrix, but those fixes do not necessarily make the correlation coefficients realistic.

A better way to specify correlation between project element costs is to model how that correlation arises. The Risk Driver approach provides a clear and transparent modelling solution to project element cost correlation. The Risk Driver method models how correlation arises and avoids the need to estimate the correlation coefficients.

Let us take the risk event Quality of Key Staff Availability is Not Known. It is a 50 percent risk with an impact range of .90 – 1.05 – 1.15. To see how correlation is generated, we will first apply this single risk to two example element costs as shown in Figure 6.6. Notice that if the risk occurs it occurs for both elements. If the randomly selected risk factor is, say, 1.09, then it is 1.09 for both elements. It is easy to see why two element costs that are influenced by a common risk become correlated in real life and in Monte Carlo simulation.

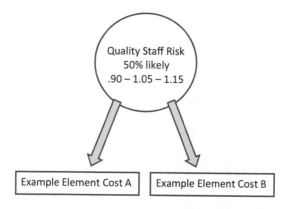

Figure 6.6   A common risk generates a 100 percent correlation between elements A and B

Correlation between Elements A and B is 100 percent, as shown in Figure 6.7.

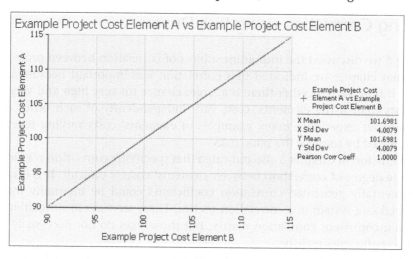

Figure 6.7   Perfect correlation between elements A and B with one common risk assigned

It is likely during project risk analysis that the same two project element costs would be affected by several risks and the chance that they would all be common is relative unlikely. If risks that are not common to the two activities affect them, the correlation coefficient will be less than 100 percent but we are not expert in specifying the correlation coefficient nor are we expert in making the calculations in our heads that would allow us to apply directly a specific correlation coefficient. This is the most common way correlation arises and the situation where interviewing for correlation coefficients will typically be the least likely to identify the correct correlation coefficient. How do interviewees calibrate the correlation between element costs when there are some risks that are common and some risks that are not common to the two activities under consideration?

The Risk Driver approach relieves the interviewees of having to answer any questions about correlation coefficients by modelling the way correlation occurs. Consider the correlation between cost elements A and B that is shown in Figure 6.8.

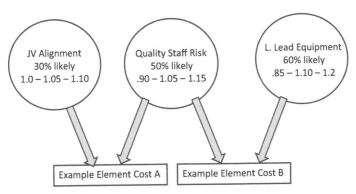

Figure 6.8   Correlation with risks that are common and not common to element costs

The correlation between example element cost A and example element cost B has been reduced to 45 percent by the addition of the two "confounding" or non-common risks, joint venture may be out of alignment, and cost of long lead equipment is uncertain.[6] This is shown in Figure 6.9. One question is: "Which interviewee would have guessed that the correlation is now 45 percent?" Another question is: "Why put the interviewees through the exercise of trying to estimate correlation coefficients when we can just model them?" Finally, this method of calculating rather than using judgment to estimate correlation coefficients will produce a correlation coefficient matrix that is always positive semi-definite, passing the Eigenvalue Test for internal system consistency, a serious benefit.

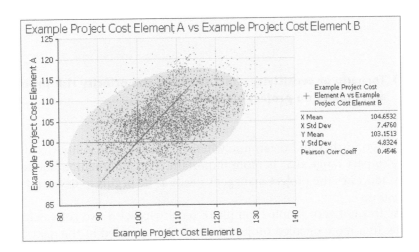

Figure 6.9   Correlation derived from risks that are both common and not common to cost elements A and B

---

6   The correlation coefficient of 45 percent is found by running the simulation of these two project elements 10,000 times, exporting the cost A – cost B pairs to Excel and running Excel's correlation function on the data.

Sensitivity Analysis using Risk Drivers

When users want to know the source of total project cost risk they have traditionally been limited to looking at the Tornado Charts showing the sensitivity of total project cost to project element line items. This is not the type of information that can lead directly to risk mitigation.

Using the Risk Driver method, the sensitivity analysis can be conducted on the Risk Drivers themselves and calculated at some relevant percentile, such as P-80.[7] That means we can tell the project manager or other stakeholders which risks drive overall cost risk at the P-80 and by how much. This is a major advantage of the Risk Driver method since the traditional method can only show sensitivity or criticality by project element cost, not by risk.

To test this approach, look again at Figure 6.8. It shows that project element cost B is driven by two risks, the quality staff risk and the long lead equipment risk. Using the tornado diagram that focuses on the risks we can tell which of these risks is more important in driving that element's cost. It seems that the cost of long lead equipment risk is more important than that of the quality of staff availability risk. The tornado or sensitivity of the cost of project element B to the two risks that affect it is shown in Figure 6.10 as follows.

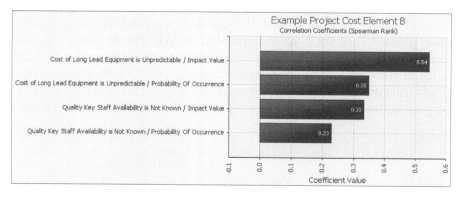

Figure 6.10 Tornado or sensitivity chart showing the priority risk probability and impact on project element cost B

In fact we can go further and determine whether it is the probability that the risk will occur or the impact range that is more important. This information about individual risks directly addresses the project manager's needs as he begins to develop targeted risk mitigation actions.

Of course this is a very simple example of sensitivity with two risks assigned to one cost estimate. In a more detailed project, such as the one used in the next section, the impact of a risk will depend not only on its probability of occurring and its impact range

---

7   The cost risk sensitivity tornado diagrams are based on correlation concepts that are themselves defined relative to the means of the input and output distributions. The risks that are important at the P-80 level may not be those that are important in describing differences from the distributions' means.

if it does occur, but also on the project element costs that it affects. The Tornado Chart of project risks affecting the total project cost will take account of all of those factors, so it is very complete.

Even with the Tornado Chart of project risks we may want to know how much cost contingency reserve money is being required to be held against each risk. Since we look at the 80th percentile in this book, let us try to sort out which of these two risks contributes most to the risk of this $100 project cost element at the P-80. To do that, we can:

- Simulate the element cost with both risks to determine the "all in" contingency between $100 and the P-80 value.
- Take out the risks one at a time (with replacement), by making their probability zero percent, and see how much contingency is needed to the P-80 with the other risk only.
- Sort the net impacts of the two risks by the dollar impact they cause by being assigned to project element cost A.

The three simulation results are shown below in Figure 6.11. (The vertical elements of the S-curves represent the spike at $100 because the risks are not 100 percent likely to occur.)

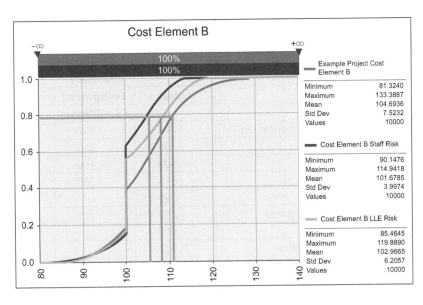

Figure 6.11 Project element B with two risks and with each risk separately

Compared to the estimated cost of Project element B of $100, the results at the P-80 show that:

- The P-80 value for both risks is $111.1.
- The P-80 value for the LLE risk only is $109.0 (set the Staff Risk probability to zero).
- The P-80 value for the Staff risk only is $105.1(set the LLE Risk probability to zero).

Now the project manager sees that if he were to be able to completely eliminate the LLE risk the contingency reserve would decline from $111.1 to $105.0, so the marginal impact of that risk is about $6, higher than the $2 impact ($111.1 minus $109.0) of eliminating the staff availability risk. The implication is that risk mitigation should start to work on the LLE cost uncertainty risk first. Of course that is what the tornado diagram implied, but here we have dollars attached and focus on the impact to the P-80 cost.

Apply the Risk Driver Method to a Refinery Construction Project Cost Risk Analysis Cost Model

The cost model used for this example is simple. It has several project element line items and some have both labor and material components. The estimate is shown below in Table 6.5.

- The total cost as estimated without contingency is $6,535 million.
- The estimator has added $980 million or 15 percent to the estimate as a contingency reserve for a total estimate of $7,515.
- In this section we will be dealing with the $6,535 estimate without contingency and build up the contingency with the Monte Carlo simulation of risks.

Table 6.5   Summary refinery cost estimate for case study

	Cost element	Labor	Baseline Equipment	Total
			($ millions)	
	Long lead equipment (LLE)	15	330	345
	Equipment	200	850	1,050
	Materials	400	1,400	1,800
Total direct field costs		615	2,580	3,195
	Supervision	260		260
	Time-related overhead	250		250
Total indirect field costs		510		510
	Direct/indirect labor	1,125		
	Construction management	500		500
	Material-related	180	400	580
	Home office engineering staff	540		540
	Overhead and fees		560	560
Total contractor related		2,345	3,540	5,885
	Project management team	350		350
	Materials		300	300
Total owner-related		350	300	650
Total base estimate				6,535
	Estimator contingency @ 15%			980
Total base estimate incl. contingency				7,515

Identifying the Risks

In this simplified example the Risk Register risks have been culled and consolidated to eight strategic risks. For a real project there would be more risks, but realistically a list of 30–45 important or strategic risks should cover the main concerns for the project, even for a multi-billion dollar project. There are numerous detailed technical risks that do not make it onto this list but which still should be handled by the project team.

Table 6.6   Example of risks selected and summarized from the Risk Register

Risk Driver
Joint venture may be out of alignment
Cost of long lead equipment is unpredictable
Quality key staff availability is not known
Single EPC contracting strategy may affect bids
Design changes may differ from expected
Construction labor productivity differs from expected
Labor rate differs from assumed
Cost estimate is inaccurate

Notice that these risks are specified at a strategic level. That is by design. These are the risks the project manager and the organization's management are concerned with every day. Technical risks are often left to the project team, although some technology-rich projects such as those of the National Aeronautics and Space Administration (NASA) may have very important technical risks. The risks of this simple case study of a refinery design and construction project cover the areas of:

- Decision-making – joint venture partners may be out of alignment, leading to difficulty making decisions.
- Procurement of long lead equipment (LLE) such as heat exchangers and heavy-walled vessels – the cost may be uncertain at this time.
- Availability of quality key staff on the project management team may be in short supply, leading to pressure on the team, overtime hours, inability to coordinate among the contractors.
- Contracting strategy of putting the entire $6–7 billion out to a single EPC contractor as a lump-sum-turnkey (LSTK) contract may limit the number of bidders, reduce competition and drive up the bid price.
- Design changes caused by the owner may occur even though "this project will be different – there will be no changes." Changes lead to delays and extra scope that must be paid for to achieve the objectives.

- Construction – Construction labor productivity has been assumed based on surveys and experience, but actual productivity may be different – either higher or lower – from plan on this project at this time with the labor and supervision available.
- Construction labor rate may be different than that assumed, based on the number of other projects going ahead at the same time, leading to higher or lower daily rates.
- Cost estimates are always inaccurate. Estimators know or have practice guidelines for representing the degree of accuracy at each stage in the contract. As more design is completed and more information comes in from potential suppliers and bidders the estimate is expected to become more accurate. Throughout the project until financial completion the uncertainty in cost is usually thought to be more likely to overrun the estimate than underrun it.

Assessing the Probability and Impact Factor for the Risks

These risks have been the subject of interviews with the project team, others in the organization that are not involved directly in the project, and the project manager. Sometimes the contractor may be interviewed if the contract has been awarded, although contractors have a different position vis a vis the contract and the owner so their risk information is usually deemed to be not entirely reliable. As mentioned above we interview about the probability that the risk will occur on this project, and about the impact range in multiplicative factors if it does occur. We also interview about the project element costs that each risk will affect if it occurs.

Now, let us suppose that we have interviewed specialists in the project's planning, execution and risk, and have collected the information shown in Table 6.7 below:

Table 6.7 Risks probability and impact derived from the risk interviews

Risk Driver	Probability	Risk Factor		
		Optimistic	Most likely	Pessimistic
Joint venture may be out of alignment	30%	1.00	1.05	1.10
Cost of long lead equipment is unpredictable	60%	0.85	1.10	1.20
Quality key staff availability is not known	50%	0.90	1.05	1.15
Contracting Strategy may affect EPC's bids	60%	1.00	1.10	1.30
Design changes may differ from expected	50%	0.95	1.10	1.30
Construction labor productivity differs from expected	100%	0.85	1.10	1.20
Labor rate differs from assumed	100%	0.90	1.05	1.15
Cost estimate is inaccurate	100%	0.95	1.00	1.10

These parameters are distilled from many interviews. In practice we have conducted as few as 8 interviews (probably not enough) to as many as 50+ interviews (probably too many). On the one hand, in interviews some subject matter experts (SMEs) may not have opinions about each risk. On the other hand, we may get the opinions of several SMEs on the same risk. The risk analyst is faced with the task of distilling the information down to the data inserted in this table. There are two common problems found by experienced risk-analyst interviewers:

- The assessment of the probability of occurring is often too low. Individual respondents may have difficulty expressing sufficient probability on the risks, particularly if the SMEs are inexperienced in risk analysis or the risk is particularly severe. Also, the interviewees are reluctant to specify too high a probability for fear of jeopardizing the project.
- The range of impacts is often too narrow. This is often a problem if the SMEs are inexperienced with risk analysis exercises on this or similar projects. Interviewees naturally wish to avoid discussing the extreme values (in statistical terms, we want the "outliers") that can be attached to a risk. Of course, the interviewees do not want to show too much high-side or overrun impact, again for fear of jeopardizing the project.

These common biases have to be recognized and can be addressed by the risk analyst before using the data to drive the simulation.

Assigning the Risks to the Activities

Once the data are assembled, the risks have to be assigned to the project element costs that they will affect if they occur. In the interviews the SMEs are asked which project element costs are affected by the risks. There are often risks that are assigned to more than one element cost and costs with more than one risk assigned. In this simple example we have made the assignments shown in Table 6.8.

Table 6.8   Table of Risk Drivers and their assignments to project element costs

Cost element	Risks							
	JVAlign	LLE	Staff	Contract	Changes	Const labor	Labor rate	Cost est.
Long lead equipment (LLE)		X		X	X			X
Equipment				X	X			X
Materials					X			X
Total direct field costs								

Table 6.8 *Concluded*

Cost element	Risks							
	JVAlign	LLE	Staff	Contract	Changes	Const labor	Labor rate	Cost est.
Time-related overhead								
Total indirect field costs								
Direct/ indirect labor				X		X	X	X
Construction management			X	X			X	X
Material related				X		X	X	X
Home office engineering staff	X		X		X			X
Overhead and fees								
Total contractor related								
Project management team	X		X					X
Materials					X			X

Each risk is assigned to at least one activity and some construction activities are affected by supervision and logistics. This is just a simple example of assigning risks to project element costs.

Iteration using Risk Drivers[8]

The simulation is run with both the uncertainties (if any) and the specific Risk Drivers. The steps for each iteration are:

1. For each Risk Driver an impact factor is selected at random from the distribution in Table 6.7, shown previously, developed by the analyst from the interviews.
2. For an iteration the Risk Driver is selected either to exist or not based on the probability derived from the interview, also shown in Table 6.7. If it exists it will take on the value (or risk factor) selected in step 1. If it does not exist it is assigned the value of 1.0.

---

8   Appendix B describes the spreadsheet's structure and logic to accomplish these steps

3. The value of the Risk Driver selected in step 2 multiplies the project element cost in the cost estimate shown in Table 6.5 according to the assignments shown in Figure 6.8.
4. If more than one Risk Driver is assigned to an activity, the selected values or factors (from step 2) are multiplied together and the project element cost is multiplied by the resultant impact product of factors. The result of step 4 is the cost of that project element cost for that iteration.
5. The total project cost is calculated for each iteration by summing down the column of costs derived in step 4.
6. Histograms of possible total project costs are developed from the thousands of iterations since each iteration can produce a different value and we do not know which one will be this project.

The results of the simulation with all of the Risk Drivers active and assigned as indicated in the tables above are shown in Figure 6.12 below.

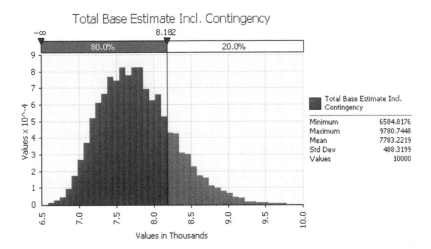

Figure 6.12 Total project cost risk results with all risks considered

The results can be shown in a cumulative distribution as in Figure 6.13. The 80th percentile is highlighted only because the project manager and other stakeholders have chosen it as their desired degree of certainty given the current plan and the identified and quantified risks.

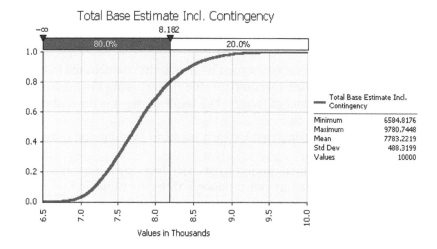

Figure 6.13 Cumulative distribution of total cost including contingency

The results focused on the cumulative distribution can also be shown in a table format that provides other percentiles for the project to look at. The table of percentiles and total cost is listed in Table 6.9, along with a column for the implied contingency reserve and the percentage contingency reserve based on the estimate of $6,535 million.

Table 6.9   Cumulative distribution of total cost and contingency from the cumulative distribution

Simulation results		Contingency reserve	
Percentile	**Total cost $ Millions**	**$ Millions**	**Percent**
10%	7,189	654	10%
20%	7,352	817	13%
30%	7,486	951	15%
40%	7,615	1,080	17%
50%	7,742	1,207	18%
60%	7,862	1,327	20%
70%	8,014	1,479	23%
80%	8,182	1,647	25%
90%	8,445	1,910	29%

Notice that we were given (in this made-up case study) a contingency reserve of 15 percent by the engineering firm that provided the original estimate. The results in Table 6.9 indicate a contingency of 15 percent will only cover about 30 percent of the known and quantified risks.

A common finding is that the contingency estimated by the engineering firm is about right at the P-50 but that is subject to analysis. In the usual case, the owners want to provide more that a 50–50 chance of success to provide for the known and quantified risks. They know that there are other risks yet to be revealed and that those risks are more likely to be threats than opportunities. In the hypothetical case study the better bet is to provide about $1,647 million in contingency reserve, or 25 percent over the base estimate of $6,535 million for this grass-roots refinery project.

Which Risks are Most Important? Explaining the Contingency

DETERMINING RISKS' CONTRIBUTIONS TO THE CONTINGENCY RESERVE

If the project manager or client does not want to add a $1,647 million contingency to achieve an 80 percent likelihood of success, the next step will be to mitigate the important risks. The question is: Which risks should be the focus of our attention? The quantitative risk analysis will help the project manager prioritize the risks for effective mitigation.

Traditional cost risk analysis, which starts with the 3-point estimate on the project element costs, uses a risk criticality or correlation – sensitivity Tornado Chart analysis to identify the activities that are most likely to be important in determining the variability in the project cost at completion. As a guide to risk mitigation this tells which project element costs are most in need of attention but not which individual risks. The traditional tornado diagram that results from using the 3-point estimate approach does not focus on the risks themselves. It is important to distinguish important risks from important project elements because:

- It is obvious that effective risk mitigation focuses on project risks and uncertainties, not on project element costs. Because the Risk Driver approach to project risk analysis also focuses on risks from the Risk Register, it is uniquely aligned with the needs of a developing risk mitigation program.
- Project element risks are not equivalent to project risks or uncertainties.
- A project element may be risky because of several different risks that affect it, so the 3-point estimate that is traditionally applied to the element's cost cannot be uniquely traced to a specific risk. Since several risks are involved in determining the project element's uncertain cost range, the mitigation steps if the traditional 3-point estimate method has been used cannot be pointed to a specific risk event or uncertainty.
- Perhaps more important than several risks affecting a single element cost, a risk may have an impact on several element costs. Looking at element costs one at a time will miss the totality of many of the risks' impacts on total project cost since it does not include the impact on more than one element's cost at a time. The Risk Driver approach deals with risks in their entirety, including their impact on all element costs that they affect. Hence the assessment of the importance of the risk or uncertainty will be inclusive with Risk Drivers.
- The Risk Driver approach can assess the impact of each risk on the total project cost estimate at any percentile that the project manager designates as the target level of certainty. In the typical tornado diagram, the basis is correlation between the risk or the element cost and the total project cost. The concept of correlation is centered on

the means of the variables, not some other percentile. Below we will show how to assess the impact at the P-80, a value that the project manager in our case study has specified as being important to the success of the project.

With the Risk Drivers we can get a total impact of the risk on the schedule. The steps are:

- Subtracting the risks one at a time from the overall project risk analysis. This is done by setting the risk or uncertainty probability to zero and re-running the simulation.
- Once a risk has been neutralized by setting its probability to zero, determine the improvement to the cost including contingency at the desired level of certainty, say the P-80 by subtracting the P-80 result without the risk from the P-80 result with all risks included.
- Each risk and uncertainty will be taken out, the simulation re-run and the P-80 impact calculated from the P-80 value with all the risks. In this way we will have "explained" the cost contingency in terms of the dollars explained by each risk in the analysis. The risks can then be re-ordered in a table that shows the risks with the highest impact at the top.

The priority of a risk will be influenced by the combination of contributions of the following characteristics:

- its probability of occurring on this project
- the range of impacts, in percentage terms, that the risk will have on project element costs if it occurs
- the number and size of the element costs to which it is assigned.

For the simple project we have used as an illustration of this technique, most cost estimates have only one or a couple of risks assigned. In a more complex project many risks will be assigned to multiple project elements so taking a risk out of the system by setting its probability to zero neutralizes its effect on several project elements all at once. Comparing the simulation results with and without the risk included reveals the impact of the risk on all elements it affects.

Selecting the Risks to Analyze, in Priority Order

Identifying the individual risks that are most important in driving the cost risk and calibrating the impact of each on the contingency to help identify the high-priority risks is the subject of this section.

The Tornado Chart or sensitivity of the overall project cost to the individual risks with all risks included is shown in Figure 6.14. Notice that a risk may enter with both its probability and its impact value, since each has its own impact on the final outcome. The Tornado Chart indicates that the contracting strategy, the possibility of design changes and basic cost estimation inaccuracy seem to be the top three individual risks.

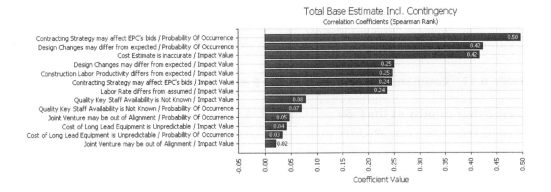

Figure 6.14 Risk Driver sensitivity (Tornado Chart) showing priority risks

The sensitivity chart in Figure 6.14 is centered on the means of the risks and the mean of the total project cost including contingency. If the project stakeholders want to focus on the P-80 they want to know which risks affect that percentile cost, and the important risks may not be those that are highest in the Tornado Chart. Let us see, in Table 6.10, which risks are important at the P-80 level by taking out risks one at a time (by setting the probability to zero) as described above and see which has the greatest impact on the P-80 value.

Table 6.10   Impact of each risk at the P-80

Risk Driver	Impact on P-80 of risks taken out one at a time
Contracting strategy may affect EPC's bids	371
Design changes may differ from expected	278
Labor rate differs from assumed	252
Cost estimate is inaccurate	150
Construction labor productivity differs from expected	97
Quality key staff availability is not known	27
Cost of long lead equipment is unpredictable	20
Joint venture may be out of alignment	9
Total	1,204

Notice that taking each risk out one at a time accounts for only $1,204 million of the $1,647 million contingency needed to achieve the P-80. The difference, $443 million, represents the interaction between risk factors when they are multiplied together, the "cross product" of risk factors. In simpler terms, when a risk is added to the mix, it does not only multiply the baseline cost estimate of the elements it affects, but it also multiplies the other risks that are likely to occur on those elements that it affects.

The risk at the P-80 has a slightly different priority listing than that of the tornado diagram, as shown in Table 6.11 below.

Table 6.11 Compare risk priorities at the P-80 and the mean

Risk Driver priority at the P-80	Risk Driver priority from the Tornado
Contracting strategy may affect EPC's bids	Contracting strategy may affect EPC's bids
Design changes may differ from expected	Design changes may differ from expected
Labor rate differs from assumed	Cost estimate is inaccurate
Cost estimate is inaccurate	Construction labor productivity differs from expected
Construction labor productivity differs from expected	Labor rate differs from assumed
Quality key staff availability is not known	Quality key staff availability is not known
Cost of long lead equipment is unpredictable	Cost of long lead equipment is unpredictable
Joint venture may be out of alignment	Joint venture may be out of alignment

Selecting Risk Mitigation Actions

MITIGATING THE "CONTRACTING STRATEGY MAY AFFECT EPC'S BIDS" RISK

Both the Tornado diagram and the results of the simulation at the P-80 indicate that the risk Contracting Strategy may affect EPC's Bids is the highest-priority risk. What was meant by that risk was that the owner of the refinery has decided to award one single, large contract on a lump-sum-turnkey (LSTK) basis with the successful bidder responsible for the entire project management role. The risk is that in today's contracting environment the contract may be too large for all but a very few EPC contractors to bid on, and that those potential bidders are unwilling to bid LSTK since they are aware of the same risks that we have seen driving our analytical results. In fact, if a potential EPC contractor were to bid a 25 percent contingency reserve the owner might pull the invitation to bid (ITB) back, re-think the entire contracting strategy and break it up into smaller more digestible pieces, playing the project management role between several EPC contractors.

According to the risk interviews and historical precedence, this risk is judged to be 60 percent likely. If it occurs it cannot help the project cost to be lower, so the optimistic risk factor is 100 percent. The most likely factor is 110 percent and the pessimistic or high risk factor is 130 percent. The implication is that if the risk occurs there is a serious chance of an "abusive" bid, a bid that the owners cannot accept. This risk has a serious implication for the project, both for the cost and for the schedule. What should the project manager and owner do to mitigate this risk?

Seeing the results of the cost risk analysis the owner and project manager may get together and change their contracting strategy. If they see the results of the analysis soon enough they might have a chance to split the packages into smaller ones that would attract several bidders each without any time penalty. If the ITB packages have not been issued yet they could be revised for the new strategy. It would perhaps cost more because the owner has to take more project management and coordination responsibility, but say it costs an additional $100 million. Would that be worth it? What would adopting this risk mitigation strategy do to the risk parameters mentioned above?

Suppose that the owner thinks about the benefits of altering the strategy and thinks that the probability of a risk would be reduced to 10 percent and the impact range would be reduced to 100 – 105 – 115 as shown in Table 6.12.

Table 6.12   Effect of risk mitigation on contracting strategy risk parameters

Probability	Risk factor		
	Optimistic	Most likely	Pessimistic
Risk before mitigation			
60%	1.00	1.10	1.30
Risk after mitigation			
10%	1.00	1.05	1.15

Would that reduce the risk enough to reduce the total cost at the P-80 after the additional $100 million cost of the mitigation? Let us re-run the simulation using these new parameters for the contracting strategy risk.

Table 6.13 shows the cumulative distribution before and after mitigating the contracting strategy risk. It shows that the people developing the new contracting strategy believe that the lower probability and narrower impact range will save $345 million at the P-80. Compared with a cost of $100 million it seems like a winning strategy.

Table 6.13   Risk results before and after mitigation of contracting strategy risk

Percentile	Total cost $ millions	
	Before mitigation	After mitigation
10%	7,189	7,064
20%	7,352	7,190
30%	7,486	7,295
40%	7,615	7,387
50%	7,742	7,483
60%	7,862	7,583
70%	8,014	7,697
80%	8,182	7,837
90%	8,445	8,056

The results are also shown in Figure 6.15 that compares the cumulative distributions of the total project cost before and after mitigation of the Contracting Strategy risk.

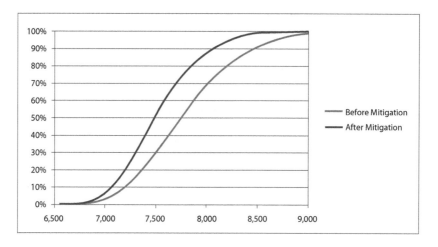

Figure 6.15 Cumulative distribution of before and after mitigating the contracting strategy risk

If the project management team is correct that breaking up the ITB into smaller pieces at a cost of $100 million to the owner will reduce the probability and impact ranges as specified, the recommendation should be to go ahead since the benefit at the P-80 is $345 million, more than paying for the extra project coordination necessitated because of supervising several prime contractors. We have just mitigated the most important risk to cost.

Chapter Summary

This chapter introduces a new approach to project cost risk analysis, the Risk Driver approach. It is contrasted to the traditional cost risk analysis that:

- Focuses on the impact of risks on project element costs.
- Does not link directly to the Risk Register prioritized list of risks.
- Makes no explicit recognition of the probability of risks' occurring.
- Requires estimation of correlation coefficients by using expert judgment.
- Cannot identify those risks that determine the uncertainty in the result because it focuses on the impact of risks on project costs rather than the risks that drive them.

The new approach, the Risk Driver approach:

- Focuses on the risks themselves, usually derived from the Risk Register that uses qualitative risk analysis methods to prioritize individual risks. The link between qualitative and quantitative analysis is made explicit.

- Characterizes the risks by both their probability of occurring and their impact on duration if they do occur, fitting well with the traditional definitions of risk events.
- Can represent uncertainties that have a 100 percent probability of occurring but an uncertain impact.
- Assigns the risks to all project element costs that they affect. Project elements can be affected by multiple risks, and risks can affect multiple project element costs.
- Activities affected by multiple risks have the risks' percentage factors multiplied, if they occur, in each iteration.
- Models correlation as it happens in the real world, eliminating the need to estimate correlation coefficients and the possibility of inconsistent correlation matrices (see Chapter 5).
- Prioritizes the risks rather than the activities and paths.
- "Explains" the generation of a needed cost contingency reserves at a percentile reflecting management's desire for cost certainty by sorting the risks in priority order. Using this list management can judge importance of risks in determining the need for the contingency.
- Management can also use the prioritized list of risks that results from the quantitative risk analysis (Monte Carlo simulation) to create an effective risk mitigation program. The risks that are highest on the priority list should be considered first for mitigation.

The Risk Driver approach promises to be a direct and useful approach to conducting schedule risk analyses.

References

Hulett, D., K. Hornbacher and W. Whitehead. (2008). "Project Cost Risk Analysis: The Risk Driver Approach Prioritizing Project Risks and Evaluating Risk Responses." Palisade Users Conference, New York City, Palisade Corporation

Hulett, D. (2009a). *Practical Schedule Risk Analysis*. Farnham, England, Gower Publishing.

Hulett, D. (2009b). "Project Cost Risk Analysis: The Risk Driver Approach Calculating Overall Project Cost Risk, Prioritizing Project Risks and Evaluating Risk Responses." Crystal Ball Users Conference, Denver, CO, Oracle.

PMI (2008). *A Guide to the Project Management Body of Knowledge*. 4th Edition. Newtown Square, PA, Project Management Institute.

Appendix B
Formulae behind the Risk Drivers Calculations Using @RISK for Excel

Table 1 Risk Factors

1	0

Risk #	Risk Driver	Probability of Occurrence			Risk Factor				
		Probability			Optimistic	Most Likely	Pessimistic	Impact Value	Factor
JVALIGN	Joint Venture may be out of Alignment	0.3	=1-C6	=RiskDiscrete(C$1:D$1,C6:D6)	1	1.05	1.1	=RiskTriang(F6,G6,H6)	=IF(E6=0,1,I6)
LLE	Suppliers of Long Lead Equipment may be busy	0.6	=1-C7	=RiskDiscrete(C$1:D$1,C7:D7)	0.85	1.05	1.15	=RiskTriang(F7,G7,H7)	=IF(E7=0,1,I7)
STAFF	Quality Key Staff availability is not known	0.5	=1-C8	=RiskDiscrete(C$1:D$1,C8:D8)	0.9	1	1.1	=RiskTriang(F8,G8,H8)	=IF(E8=0,1,I8)
CONTR	Contracting Strategy may affect EPC's bids	0.3	=1-C9	=RiskDiscrete(C$1:D$1,C9:D9)	1	1.1	1.3	=RiskTriang(F9,G9,H9)	=IF(E9=0,1,I9)
CHANGE	Design Changes may differ from expected	0.5	=1-C10	=RiskDiscrete(C$1:D$1,C10:D10)	0.95	1.1	1.3	=RiskTriang(F10,G10,H10)	=IF(E10=0,1,I10)
CONLAB	Construction Labor Productivity may differ	1	=1-C11	=RiskDiscrete(C$1:D$1,C11:D11)	0.9	1.1	1.2	=RiskTriang(F11,G11,H11)	=IF(E11=0,1,I11)
LABRATE	Labor Rate may differ from assumed	1	=1-C12	=RiskDiscrete(C$1:D$1,C12:D12)	0.9	1.05	1.2	=RiskTriang(F12,G12,H12)	=IF(E12=0,1,I12)

Table 2   Cost Model

Cost Element	Labor	Equipment	Total	Factors Assigned	Risked Cost	JVALIGN	LLE	STAFF	CONTR	CHANGE	CONLAB	LABRATE
	Baseline											
	($ millions)					=Risks!J6	=Risks!J7	=Risks!J8	=Risks!J9	=Risks!J10	=Risks!J11	=Risks!J12
Long Lead Equipment (LLE)	15	330	=SUM(C6:D6)	=J6*M6*L6	=D6*G6		=J$5		=L$5	=M$5		
Equipment	200	850	=SUM(C7:D7)	=L7*M7	=D7*G7				=L$5	=M$5		
Materials	400	1400	=SUM(C8:D8)	=M8	=D8*G8					=M$5		
Total Direct Field Costs	=SUM(C6:C8)	=SUM(D6:D8)	=SUM(E6:E8)									
Supervision	260	0	=SUM(C10:D10)									
Time-Related Overhead	250	0	=SUM(C11:D11)									
Total Indirect Field Costs	=SUM(C10:C11)	=SUM(D10:D11)	=SUM(E10:E11)									
Direct / Indirect Labor	=C9+C12			=L13*N13*O13	=C13*G13				=L$5		=N$5	=O$5
Construction Management	500		=SUM(C14:D14)	=O14*L14*K14	=C14*G14			=K$5	=L$5			=O$5
Material Related	180	400	=SUM(C15:D15)	=L15*N15*O15	=D15*G15				=L$5		=N$5	=O$5
Home Office Engineering Staff	540		=C16	=K16*M16*I16	=E16*G16	=I$5		=K$5		=M$5		
Overhead & Fees	560	560	560		=E17							
Total Contractor Related	=SUM(C13:C17)	=SUM(D9:D17)	=C18+D18		=SUM(H6:H17)							
Project Management Team	350	0	=SUM(C19:D19)	=I19*K19	=E19*G19	=I$5		=K$5				
Materials	0	300	=SUM(C20:D20)	=M20	=E20*G20					=M$5		
Total Owner-Related	=SUM(C19:C20)	=SUM(D19:D20)	=SUM(E19:E20)		=E21							
Total Base Estimate			=E18+E21		=SUM(H19:H21)							
Estimator Contingency @ 15%			=E22*0.15									
Total Base Estimate Including Contingency			=SUM(E22:E23)		=RiskOutput()+H18+H22							

7 Preparing for Integrated Cost and Schedule Risk Analysis

Introduction

This chapter and subsequent chapters define the buildup approach to integrated analysis of cost and schedule risk, the best way to estimate the appropriate level of cost contingency reserves required on projects. The main contribution of this approach is to include the impact of schedule risk on cost risk and hence on the need for cost contingency reserves. Additional benefits include the prioritizing of the risks to cost, some of which are risks to schedule, to assist in understanding the best ways to mitigate cost risk. Risk mitigation may be conducted in an efficient way using the prioritized risks.

We start with the project schedule. In an earlier book (Hulett 2009) the requirements of a successful schedule risk analysis are described in detail. Here they will be summarized for the reader as they impact the integrated cost-schedule risk analysis.

The methods presented in this chapter are based on integrating the cost estimate with the project schedule by resource-loading and costing the schedule's activities. The simulation of the cost-loaded schedule, using Monte Carlo techniques, then calculates multiple (thousands) of possible results for both time and cost simultaneously. During this simulation the cost of the time-dependent resources is partially determined by the uncertainty in activity durations, permitting the impacts of schedule risk on cost risk to be calculated automatically.

For this method the project needs to have a complete critical path method (CPM) schedule and a comparable cost estimate. A summary or intermediate level schedule (for example, 300–1,000 activities) is preferred because:

- it is easier to evaluate and debug a summary schedule than it is a detailed schedule of many thousands of activities in preparation for simulation, and
- a risk analysis is a strategic analysis, in contrast to a daily project plan, so a summary schedule works well to highlight the strategic project elements.

An important component of the integration of project cost and schedule is assessing the candidate schedule against critical path method (CPM) scheduling best practices. Another key element involves inserting the resources into the project schedule again at a summary level of detail. These two aspects of getting ready for integrated cost-schedule risk analysis are the subject of this chapter.

Context of the Analysis

In previous chapters we have analyzed cost risk by itself, without referring to schedule risk. However, that approach is partial and incomplete. Because schedule drives cost in creating the basis of estimate for the project cost, so schedule risk drives cost risk to a large extent. Capturing this influence of schedule risk on cost risk gives us a better estimate of cost risk and also a better understanding of the factors that influence cost risk since some of the most important cost risk drivers are in fact caused by schedule risk.

Trying to estimate cost without explicit reference to the project schedule is an awkward analysis that is usually incomplete and/or inaccurate. Estimating the risk to both schedule and cost simultaneously, in the same Monte Carlo simulation, is the correct way to capture the effect of schedule risk on cost risk when the project is mature enough to have both a schedule and a cost estimate.[1]

This build-up method has been applied to cost and schedule risk in many industries and in commercial as well as governmental projects, so it is powerful yet generic. We have found in applications of integrated cost-schedule risk analysis that some of the most important cost risks are actually risks to time that may extend the use of resources to more workdays with their added cost. This integrated approach shows that addressing the effect of schedule risk on cost risk directly using a complete cost-schedule model helps us to estimate this effect more accurately than by other methods. The model is a resource-loaded project schedule.

The reality is that many schedule slippages happen during the team's trying to perform the scope of work (SOW). How can this affect cost?

- If the activity that is using the resources takes longer than the original cost estimate assumed, that activity will cost more than originally estimated based on the going-in assumptions because some resources are paid more the longer they work.
- If other activities take longer than originally assumed, parallel activities often called "level of effort" or LOE activities have no opportunity to demobilize the resources so as not to pay them during the delay. In fact, it is sometimes true that as tasks take longer the management will want to add resources to keep from slipping further.

In this analysis the interaction between schedule risk and cost risk is modelled explicitly to develop several useful outputs:

- a histogram and cumulative distribution describing the probability of the current plan to finish on or before given dates
- combining the cumulative distribution with the owner's desire for certainty in the estimate produces an estimate of the schedule contingency reserve
- the histogram and cumulative distribution for cost which also produce the estimate of required cost contingency reserve
- the priority risks leading to the need for these reserves of time and budget.

---

1   Earlier in the project life cycle the cost and schedule and their risk analysis are conducted parametrically. This book does not cover parametric analysis of cost and schedule.

A later chapter describes how these results lead to efficient mitigation actions to mitigate both time and cost risk.

Simulating a resource-loaded project schedule produces the cost risk implication of all known and quantified risks to the project, whether they be risks directly to cost or risks affecting cost indirectly through their impact on schedule. The main benefits of this approach are to improve, over the cost-risk only approach described in prior chapters:

- the accuracy of the cost risk estimate including the necessary contingency reserve
- the identification and prioritization of the sources of cost risk including risks to the schedule
- to focus the risk mitigation measures where they are most likely to produce results, making people aware of the full implication of those mitigation measures. One specific result is an estimate of the implications for the necessary holding of cost contingency reserves of mitigating schedule risk.

The risk analysis is correct only for the current plan, which is not surprising since the schedule and cost estimates are current as of the time the analysis is conducted. Project managers have the option of re-planning and re-scheduling in the face of new facts such as an uncertain event (for example, a risk) that may occur to jeopardize the project objectives. This analysis does not include the conditional planning, which is available to all project managers. Rather it is an attempt to analyze these risks in advance of their occurring so the project manager can mitigate risks, a much better strategy than recovering once the risks have occurred. A new plan will emerge and we can perform a risk analysis of that plan after the risk mitigations have been developed.

Hence, the results of this analysis:

- Hold only for the current plan. That is understandable since we only have today's project plan (schedule and cost estimate) to analyze.
- are analytical results for the current plan and are intended to provide a tool for Improving the plan rather than a report card showing how late and over-budget the current plan is. In other words, we hope that the analysis will not become a forecast. The whole purpose of the risk analysis is to help the project manager to anticipate and respond appropriately to the high-priority risks. In doing so, the project plan can be improved. The results of the risk analysis are best viewed as inputs to project management rather than as forecasts of how the project will be completed.

It is common for the results of the risk analysis to be close to the results of the project once it is complete. Experienced risk analysts have many times found that the risk analysis report findings were ignored, or the project management argued with the results and disbelieved them, which goes hand in hand with a reluctance to change the project plan. In this case the analytical results become forecasts since the risks are not mitigated.

Getting Ready: The CPM Schedule

The platform for the integrated cost-schedule risk analysis is a resource-loaded and costed CPM schedule. That means that in addition to putting the resources on their respective activities the resources have to have costs attached. The best way to do this is to specify that the cost of a resource is $1 and then the number of resource units amount to the total cost for that activity, since the recommendation is to use summary resources (for example, construction labor) which will be applied to several (construction) activities. The resources are often specified at a summary level and are not meant for other resource analyses such as overloading leading to resource leveling, or to detailed resource planning.

For an integrated cost-schedule risk analysis (and for a simple schedule risk analysis) a summary schedule that is integrated is often used. This integrated summary schedule includes representation of all the work, has activities properly linked with logic and includes enough detail to highlight the main project milestones that may be used. Experience shows that schedules of 300–1,000 future activities (not including completed activities) can be used in a risk analysis, even of projects as large as $10 billion.[2] This means that we often do not need to deal with the detailed schedule supplied by the contractor.

Often the project has a detailed schedule provided by the contractor. These schedules often have activities numbering in the tens of thousands. One problem with schedules of this size is the sheer effort needed to debug them against scheduling best practices. Experience shows that most if not quite all schedules need to be debugged and improved, both for CPM best practices and to condition them for the rigors – activity durations changed randomly on purpose to develop a large number of possible projects – of Monte Carlo simulation. It is hoped that the project scheduler will cooperate by developing the summary schedule, but this is not always the case.

The scheduler will often not want to create a separate summary schedule for the purpose of a risk analysis because of the extra work involved, the need to make sure that the summary schedule is consistent with the detailed schedule and the need to keep them both synchronized as time passes and changes are made to the detailed schedule. This concern can be appreciated, and often the risk analyst has either to develop a summary schedule or work with larger, detailed schedules. One alternative, for the risk analyst to build a separate schedule, may raise a credibility problem if the project management disavows the new schedule because it is not their own. If building a summary schedule will be used to support the risk analysis, working closely with the project scheduler will be key to gaining acceptance for the new simpler model.

The first task in the risk analysis of cost and schedule is to debug the schedule. The schedule needs to follow CPM scheduling recommended practices because it needs to calculate the milestone dates and critical paths correctly automatically during Monte Carlo simulation, according to CPM principles. It is not feasible to make corrections by hand since activities' durations change for each iteration during the simulation.

The scheduling principles that are particularly important to the success of a Monte Carlo simulation include (USGAO 2009):

- All work needed to complete the project must be represented in the schedule. It is not uncommon for people to try to compute schedule risk analyses focusing only on the CPM critical paths, perhaps including near-critical paths. The problem

---

2   Some risk analysts recommend conducting schedule risk with schedules as small as 25–30 activities, although it is difficult to count on such a small schedule being able to take all of the strategic risks of the project and the key logical dependencies.

with that approach is that since we do not know how long the activity durations will be – the basic rationale for conducting a schedule risk analysis is that activity durations are probabilistic – we do not know which path is risk-critical and therefore most likely to delay the project. It is common for the ultimate critical path to differ from that identified earlier in the project using CPM techniques, just as it is common to experience the critical path's changing during a project. It is also common to omit activities representing the work of fabrication and delivery of equipment (for example, compressors) or material (for example, steel) that are procured from and built by suppliers. Since the fabrication and delivery are done by others, some schedulers omit them or place only a promised date milestone into the schedule, assuming that (1) the items will materialize as promised, or (2) if they are late the contractor can pass on the blame to the supplier. The cost-schedule risk analysis needs to establish the entire project risk without regard to which party is responsible for a project delay. The prioritization of the risks that is another result of quantitative risk analysis will establish where the key risks originate. Instead of representing the final delivery of procured material and equipment with a milestone tied in time with a constraint, we should represent the procurement process with work-type activities from Invitation to Bid (ITB) or Request for Proposal (RFP) to the submissions of bid proposals by contractors or suppliers, to award of the work, and then to the fabrication and final delivery of the equipment. Each of these steps is uncertain and it is best to identify and quantify the risks to each step so we know the source of our problems getting procured equipment or material on time and the extent of the possible problem. This is a good approach, even though we cannot detail the work underlying the supplier's fabrication of the equipment because we have no details of suppliers' processes.

• The schedule should not contain any open ended activities, called "danglers." This means that each activity needs a predecessor to its start date and a successor from its finish date. (PMI 2007) A picture of this requirement is shown in Figure 7.1 below.

Figure 7.1   CPM logical relations required for best quality scheduling

This logic requirement is important because we are using a method that could be called "dynamic scheduling," (Uyttewaal 2005), making sure that the project schedule provides the correct dates and critical paths if durations change, as they will during a project or a simulation of the project.

   This definition of open ends is more complete than the most common injunction, that "each activity needs a successor." That commonly understood rule is necessary but it is not sufficient. "Each activity needs a successor from its finish date" would be a good start. Add to that, "Each activity needs a predecessor to its start date" for the complete cure for dangling activities.

In other words, there is nothing wrong with a start-to-start successor, but if the activity does not have a finish-to-start or a finish-to-finish successor as well its duration can increase until it bumps up against the finish milestone without affecting any successor activity. This phenomenon is probably not accurate for most activities, and an activity would need justification if it does not have an F-F or F-S successor. Similarly, an activity can have a finish-to-finish predecessor, but if that is its only predecessor it will simply start earlier if its duration is greater than scheduled in some iteration. However, when the project gets to that point it may be too late to start the activity earlier just because its duration is longer than originally scheduled.

Activity logic must be fixed before the simulation is conducted. There is no minimal amount of logic incompleteness that is all right, since until the logic is complete we do not have confidence in the dates or critical paths of the schedule.

- The schedule should not rely on date constraints but rather the dates should be outputs of the schedule that are determined by the logic and duration of the schedule. Date constraints are often used to start activities or keep their finish dates from being later than some promise date. The proper use of date constraints is quite limited, to such things as availability of funding in a new fiscal year or the end of the monsoon season's affecting offshore oil and gas platform heavy lifts. Most of the use of date constraints would be better accomplished by predecessor logic and durations. Relying on date constraints makes the network into a calendar, not a schedule. Constraints are usually restrictions placed on the computer file to make the schedule behave as someone wants it to do. However, placing constraints on a computer file somewhere does not constrain the project as it is executing. The essence of a project schedule is that the dates are an output of project scheduling, not an input.[3] Usually if date constraints are used the project management has an idea of the dates that are acceptable to the customer or are included in the contract and wants a schedule document that supports those dates. A better approach is to plan a realistic project and see whether the required dates are supported. If they are not, re-plan the project, perhaps including more resources or less scope, until the dates are supported or known to be unsupported, after which a discussion with the customer is required. Some schedulers use start-not-earlier-than (SNET) constraints to build some contingency into the schedule. These SNET constraints are not effective since we do not know how much contingency will be needed at the end of the project and, when we get to that point in the project we do not know what dates would be appropriate. They also alert the manager of the successor activity to start on a date that may be later than necessary and hence the project will lose an opportunity to advance the project schedule. There may be some appropriate SNET constraints that represent actual calendar-related factors such as weather or budget fiscal years. Generally it is a bad practice to rely on SNET dates in the schedule but if the project plans to delay starting activities according to these constraints that behaviour should be modeled in the simulation. In general, activities should be started with predecessors and logic and start dates determined by the schedule. SNET constraints will delay the starting

---

3   The PMI definition of a "schedule" as a set of completion dates is wrong. The schedule is the set of input data and rules that produce important dates and critical paths, along with other information, as outputs, not inputs. See PMI (2008), *A Guide to the Project Management Body of Knowledge*, Newtown Square, PA, Project Management Institute.

of some activities, which is counterintuitive since most projects want to finish as soon as possible (ASAP). These SNET constraints dates will surely be observed by the scheduling software during a Monte Carlo simulation, and the results will reflect the planning inefficiency represented by the constraints. Some backward pass constraints such as finish-not-later-than (FNLT) will be ignored during Monte Carlo simulation. They are not effective in keeping the project from being delayed but will cause negative float, which can be helpful during schedule development. Mandatory constraints (must-finish-on or must-start-on, for instance) will not be ignored by the simulation software. These so called "hard constraints" will be observed during simulation and may cause the schedule risk analysis to underestimate the risk to the schedule, and hence to the cost of the project. They must be taken off, allowing the schedule to determine those dates. In general, a good CPM schedule does not rely on constraints but on logic and durations to drive dates. The principle is that the dates are outputs of the schedule, not inputs. This is what we need for CPM scheduling and for simulation. Quantitative risk analysis of cost and schedule does not require any more rigorous logic than a good CPM schedule.

- Lags are to be avoided. Lags are definite amounts of time that will always delay the successor by a fixed number of days. Lags do not represent work but rather mandatory durations that cannot change. There are few instances of appropriate use of lags, such as "watching concrete cure." This activity takes time (given the environmental conditions) but no resources (well, maybe a watchman or an inspector) and cannot be longer or shorter. A common use of this lag is when the framework of the house cannot be installed until the concrete foundations have cured. Some schedulers put lags in to represent the time a regulatory agency takes reviewing an application, or how long it takes to install a piece of equipment after delivery but before commissioning that equipment. In general, it is better if these lags are replaced with activities even if that increases the number of activities in the schedule, since the work is of uncertain duration and activities can be risked. Most activities represented by lags are not risk free. Leads (negative lags) are to be avoided in general in project scheduling.

- The schedule should be recently statused. In statusing a schedule the activities that have completed are discovered by the scheduler and given "actual" finish dates. Activities that are started but not complete are given "actual" start dates and their remaining duration is estimated anew, perhaps changing their total duration from that originally estimated because of new information. In other words, the schedule is brought up to date periodically (weekly or monthly is common) by the scheduler using information provided by activity managers. Finding actual dates in the future or activity completions in the past with no actual dates would be a good indication of a lack of statusing of the schedule and might indicate the presence of some risk that has occurred but not been incorporated in the schedule. In statusing a schedule there will be instances of activities starting before their predecessors finish. This is common and is called "progress override" (progress in the field overrides the schedule logic). The scheduler should review these instances of "broken logic" and resolve them by changing the schedule logic if necessary before the status is complete.

- Are the durations realistic, created without bias and attainable given the scope, resources and other factors that are realistic to assume about the project? Duration estimating is an art and it is also unfortunately a political process. Often management or the customer has a "required" date for completion of the project, and one way the scheduler can comply with his instructions is to shave the durations to force-fit the size-11 foot into a size-9 shoe.[4] Even if there is not political pressure on the scheduler to shorten (not usually to lengthen) the schedule, is the information available to estimate the durations? Are some participants forced to guess rather than estimate based on data or bids? A common issue is when long level of effort (LOE) activities are represented as normal activities with a long duration. LOE activities should be represented by hammocks (Primavera is now calling these "Level of Effort" activities) that expand or contract their durations according to the durations of the detailed activities they support. There are several reasons to examine the activity durations.
- The schedule should have resources loaded. This is important for resource planning including to see whether resources are overloaded in any work period. Resource planning can be done in physical units such as hours of specific skill sets. For integrated cost-schedule risk analysis the resources need to be costed, that is they need to have unit rates (cost per hour or per day for resources with time-dependent costs) or total costs (for resources with time-independent costs) applied to them. Loading and costing resources will permit the entire budget to be included in the schedule. This will be discussed in the next section.
- The levels of total float ("slack" in Microsoft Project) should be reasonable. Examining the levels of total float is another way to examine the completeness of the schedule logic, since large float values occur mostly when activities do not have proper successors. Of course some activities can accurately exhibit large total float values in the project plan, but experience shows that these large float values are often spurious. We find that the project manager or team leads do not believe the float values when made aware of total float in the hundreds or even thousands of days. It is a comment on the managers' general disinterest in total float as a signal of project tightness that the risk analyst needs to point out that the project seems to have a lot more flexibility than the managers really believe. Total float values have to be reasonable, since artificially long float values will invalidate the project schedule risk analysis by causing underestimation of schedule risk.

A schedule risk analysis does not invalidate the CPM schedule; it builds upon it with added information to generate added results. The results indicate when the project is likely to finish without the project team's taking additional risk mitigation steps. For this purpose the CPM schedule needs to obey best scheduling practices such as those in this list.

In this chapter and the one following, a simple schedule of a 28-month construction project is shown in Figure 7.2.

---

4   It would be naïve to assume that all project participants (team leads, schedulers) are given the permission to make objective, realistic and most-likely duration estimates, or that the scheduler has all the knowledge to do so available to him.

ID	Description	Remaining Duration	Start	Finish	Total Cost	Resource Loading	2011	2012	2013	20
1	Total Project	850	01-Jan-11	29-Apr-13	$624,220					
1.1	Initiation	1	01-Jan-11	01-Jan-11	$0					
0010	Project Start	0	'01-Jan-11		$0		01-Jan-11			
1.2	Planning	290	01-Jan-11	17-Oct-11	$53,470					
0015	Approval Process	90	01-Jan-11	31-Mar-11	$2,070	MGT[Normal];PMT[Normal]				
0017	Project Sanction	0		31-Mar-11	$0		1-Mar-11			
0018	Environmental	180	01-Apr-11	27-Sep-11	$5,400	ENV[Normal];PMT[Normal]				
0020	Design	200	01-Apr-11	17-Oct-11	$46,000	ENG[Normal];PMT[Normal]				
1.3	Execution	560	18-Oct-11	29-Apr-13	$570,750					
0030	Procurement of Equipment	360	18-Oct-11	11-Oct-12	$210,800	PROC[Spread];PMT[Normal]				
0040	Construction	460	18-Oct-11	19-Jan-13	$335,800	CONS[Normal];PMT[Normal]				
0045	Install Equipment	90	12-Oct-12	09-Jan-13	$7,650	CONS[Normal];PMT[Normal]				
0050	Commissioning	100	20-Jan-13	29-Apr-13	$16,500	COMM[Normal];PMT[Normal]				
1.4	Completing	0	30-Apr-13	29-Apr-13	$0					
0060	Project Turnover	0		29-Apr-13	$0				29-Apr-13	

Figure 7.2 Example construction project schedule[5]

Notice that general resources (for example, PMT for Project Management Team and (CONS for Construction) are loaded in the schedule and the budget is $624,220 million. The resources and their costs are introduced in the next section.

Getting Ready: The Cost Estimate

The cost estimate is a basic input to the integrated cost and schedule risk analysis. The cost estimate is generally built up using engineering estimates, reference to analogous projects, application of expert judgment, and information provided by suppliers and subcontractors as well as obtained from market surveys (such as wages of construction workers).

- Often a below-the-line cost contingency is added by the engineering contractor to the raw costs without contingency. It is a simple matter to ignore the contingency below the line, promising to build it up again as the result of the integrated cost-schedule risk analysis.
- A more difficult situation to deal with is when the individual project elements' costs have padding designed to provide for risk embedded in them. In this case the individual cost estimates are not just based on engineering estimates, time and material, or quantity and unit rate calculations. They often have specifically inserted amounts of padding that intend to provide for risk of each activity. This padding for risk must be taken off the costs before loading them into the schedule.

Some estimators are uncomfortable about stripping the contingency amounts from the estimate, but the Monte Carlo simulation will re-estimate the contingency reserve that is appropriate for (1) the risks to the specific project, and (2) the desired level of certainty of the project management and other stakeholders.

---

5   This figure and several others shown below are screen shots from Primavera Risk Analysis, formerly Pertmaster Risk Expert, now owned by Oracle.

Padding each individual cost element cannot be justified and is a dangerous practice. Think of a risk as an uncertain event that will affect the cost of the project element only if it occurs. What happens if an individual project element's cost is padded for risk?

- On the one hand, in some cases the risk will not occur at all and any padding will just be budget wasted, that is not needed, but probably spent by the project team unwilling to give any money back to be used on other activities.
- On the other hand, nobody can justify adding padding to provide for all the risks that could possibly occur, so some smaller amount of padding might be added. However, if the risks do occur, the padding will be insufficient for the recovery that is necessary.
- In each case, where the risk occurs or does not occur, the padding added to an individual cost element is incorrect: in the first case it is too large and in the second it is too small.
- The conclusion is that provision for cost risk is correctly made at the total project level and that the project manager has the span of control and perspective needed to allocate the contingency where and when it is needed.

The best way to look at project cost elements, and schedule durations, since it is a parallel argument, is to keep the cost elements and schedule durations as pure, non-biased and realistic as possible. Contingency reserves will be computed at the total project level. The integrated cost-schedule risk analysis is consistent with this approach. To avoid double-counting of risk, the cost elements themselves must be free of padding, leaving the risk analysis to calculate a risk contingency reserve of cost to add to the entire estimate.

In this chapter we will use a simple project as an example. It is a construction project, pictured in Figure 7.2 above, estimated to cost $624 million over a 28-month period. The cost estimate is shown in Table 7.1.

Table 7.1   Example project cost by activity

Activity	Cost estimate ($ millions)
Approval process	$ 2.1
Environmental	$ 5.4
Design	$ 46.0
Procurement	$ 210.8
Install equipment	$ 7.7
Construction	$ 335.8
Integration and test	$ 16.5
Total estimated cost	$ 624.2

Loading Resources into the CPM Schedule

Loading resources into the CPM schedule for the purpose of integrated cost-schedule risk analysis can be accomplished using summary resources; it does not require a list of resources at a detailed level. We usually can represent enough detail with 8 to 10 summary resources, even for large (multi-billion dollar) projects. Summary resources might include:

- front-end (FEED) design
- detailed engineering
- direct construction labor
- procured equipment
- procured material
- project management team
- installation of equipment
- commissioning of equipment

These summary resources are not sufficient to perform resource planning and leveling functions. Their purpose is to get the entire budget into the project schedule. Simple categories of resources that can be given budgeted values and placed on the activities they work on are needed.

The resources need to be identified by type, either labor or materials. Resources used on the simple construction project are shown in Table 7.2 below.

Table 7.2   Resource for example construction project

ID	Description	Type	Default loading
COMM	Commissioning	Labor	Normal
CONS	Construction	Labor	Normal
ENG	Engineers	Labor	Normal
ENV	Environmental	Labor	Normal
MGT	Management	Labor	Normal
PMT	Project Management Team	Labor	Normal
PROC	Procurement	Materials	Spread

In addition, the resources need to be tagged as labor-type or material-type resources:

- "Labor type" resources are those that will cost more if they work longer. These time-dependent resources include contract labor, engineering labor, the project management team, and equipment that is billed by the day or the hour such as cranes, earth movers, drill rigs, installation barges and the like. These resources have the characteristics that they will cost more (1) if they are employed longer such as when activity durations are lengthened, and (2) if more units of the resource are applied per work period. Both the length of the activities and the units per day ("burn rate") are risky and are handled in integrated cost and schedule risk analysis.

- "Material-type" resources include those that have uncertain costs but do not necessarily cost more if their activity takes longer. The main examples of these resources are manufactured equipment and bulk raw materials. Equipment may take longer to arrive at the project, since the suppliers may be busy or otherwise not able to stick to agreed fabrication and delivery schedules, but that may not necessarily make the equipment or raw materials cost more. Or, the equipment may arrive on time but its delivered cost may be uncertain, particularly if the contract has not been signed, because of competition, fluctuation of market cost of materials or demand pressure in the supplier's shop. Their costs may be uncertain but not because of time.

The purpose of resource loading the schedule for integrated risk analysis is to allocate the entire contingency-free budget to schedule activities. This approach will provide two attributes needed for the integration of cost and schedule risk:

- The entire budget is represented, so any change in the duration of activities supported by resources that cost more if the duration is longer (labor-type resources) will capture the cost effect of schedule uncertainty.
- Placing resources on individual activities will place the costs correctly in time, permitting the computation of probabilistic cash flow by month or other periodicity as desired. The more the activities can be placed on individual activities correctly the more accurate the probabilistic cash flow will be.

An alternative method of applying resources to the schedule is to develop hammocks that span the activities that get the resources.

- A hammock is a good approach to take when applying level-of-effort (LOE) resources such as the project management team. That team will be active from the beginning of the project to turnover and a hammock (or LOE activity as it is named in some scheduling software) is the appropriate way to handle that type of resource usage.
- Hammocking a set of detailed work activities is sometimes necessary when the detail for resources is at a higher level than the detail for scheduling. Putting resources on hammocks in this instance will put those resources on just one activity representing several activities so the timing of the resource will be evenly allocated across time. Evenly distributing costs of a phase across its entire duration may be correct for the project management team. However, for other resources, placing them on specific activities shows concentrations of resources as those activities tend to stack up in some work periods as they will in the real schedule.

The software that handles integrated cost-schedule risk analysis spreads out the costs evenly along the entire duration of the resource-loaded activity.[6] Putting the total construction labor resource on a hammock that covers the entire construction period will not result in a cost curve that represents real construction cost curves. It is better to put the construction resources on individual construction activities.

---

6   There are some software utilities that could cause a cost curve with a shape other than uniform, but these are really in beta test at this time.

Integrating Inconsistent Cost Estimates and Schedules

One problem that must be addressed in applying resources or costs to the schedule is that the cost estimate and schedule have evolved separately to some extent during the progress of the project. When the baseline was established the cost estimate and the schedule were probably consistent in several ways:

- They both start with the WBS structure and descriptive titles.
- The basis of estimate (BOE) for costs assumes durations that are in the baseline schedule.

However, as the project progresses the cost estimate and schedule documents become specific to them and become more dissimilar from each other in structure, nomenclature and level of detail as the project progresses. Schedulers will insert various activities into the schedule as the team leads indicate that more detail is needed to represent their plans. If the scheduler and cost estimator – indeed the entire project controls organization – is not careful the schedule will depart from its original WBS focus.

In most instances the schedule is statused each week or each month, and changes are made to the schedule as a result. Since a key part of the BOE, the activity durations, may have changed, it is fair to ask whether the cost estimate is changed accordingly. In most instances, the cost estimate is not changed as a result of changes to the schedule. Why not?

Often the schedulers and cost estimators do not talk to each other on a daily basis. Some companies specifically separate their cost personnel from their schedule personnel organizationally because they are believed to do very different things. Often the cost estimators make estimates using quite different methods, for example, parametrics used in aerospace projects, and many cost estimators do not rely on or much care about schedules.[7] In some cases, after a few months the schedule and cost estimates are so different, including using different descriptive titles, that on first impression they may be describing different projects.

So these two basic documents that should have so much in common may be inconsistent with each other. This inconsistency is discovered when costs are integrated into the schedule, and it is often, surprisingly, the risk analyst who discovers it first.

When costs are applied to the schedule, daily rates of resources will be implied by dividing the cost by the number of days of activity duration. For instance, if $100,000 is applied to a 10-day activity it implies that $10,000 per day of the resource is used each workday. The problem in many practical instances is that the costs in the cost estimate and the durations in the schedule are inconsistent at any point of time. This inconsistency is revealed in inaccurate or unbelievable daily rates of resource expenditure when costs are entered into the schedule.

For instance, suppose at a given Friday status review the new estimate of duration is 13 days rather than 10 days. Then suppose the three-day slip cannot be recovered and the project manager reluctantly agrees that 13 days is realistic. Does this mean that the

---

7   There are even some people, mostly in aerospace, who are trying to implement parametric methods on schedules. This may be because the parametric approach is all they know and they are unfamiliar with the profession of scheduling. This development calls for integrating the two staffs and forcing them to talk regularly.

cost estimate (current, not baseline) should be changed to $130,000 at $10,000 per day? Arguably yes, unless the extra days of duration are caused by a lower resource allocation than originally planned. However, cost estimators are not in the room and are not generally kept informed about changes in the schedule, nor are they asked about the impact of schedule changes on the cost estimate.

Inconsistency between cost and schedule is not a minor consideration. An actual project case, applying the estimated amount to the cost of drilling offshore wells implied that the same drill rig and crew was going to cost more on a per-day basis on one well than on another, even though it was the same drill rig with the same crew and hence the same daily rate. In another case, the cost of a heavy-lift barge was computed (dollars divided by days) to be only about one-third of the known daily rental (working or idle) of the barge. In these cases the cost estimate was ultimately changed, because there was no reason to change the activity durations.

The cost estimator and scheduler need to address these inconsistencies in daily rates that are discovered when the cost estimate is inserted into the schedule. Usually the cost estimator is delighted to have finally put the entire budget into the schedule and does not check the daily "burn rates." This is unfortunate for the simulation of cost risk.

During simulation the daily rates will be used to compute the cost impact of schedule delays for labor-type resources. This is exactly the purpose of integrated cost-schedule risk analysis and represents the essential connection between cost and schedule, the reason cost and schedule actual data are seen to be correlated. The risk analyst, working with the scheduler and the cost estimator, may find that durations may be wrong or costs may be wrong or both. It is a failure of project controls organizations if the risk analyst, because he is the first to integrate the budget into the schedule, is the first person to find out that cost and schedule are not consistent.

Placing the resources on the example schedule, shown above in Figure 7.2, details the cost by activity and resource, shown in Table 7.3 below. The activity total costs are made up of resources applied to the activities with daily rates and total duration or by lump sum for procured items.

Table 7.3   Cost for example construction project showing resources

Cost estimate by resource and activity ($ thousands)								
Activity	PMT	MGT	ENV	ENG	PROC	CONS	COMM	Total
Approval	720	1350						2,070
Environmental	900		4500					5,400
Design	6,000			40,000				46,000
Procurement	10,800				200,000			210,800
Install equipment	2,250					5,400		7,650
Construction	13,800					322,000		335,800
Commissioning	1,500						15,000	16,500
Total	35,970	1,350	4,500	40,000	200,000	327,400	15,000	624,220

Risk Data Inputs[8]

First principles require that the risk of the project cost and schedule be driven by identified and quantified risks.[9] The risks are quantified by their probability of occurring and their impact on the project if they do occur. (Impact is often specified as a range of possible impacts.) The risks are then assigned to the activities and resources they affect. During the Monte Carlo simulation, on any iteration, a risk will occur or not depending on its probability and, if it does occur, the affected durations and time-dependent costs will be increased or decreased according to the impact (chosen from the impact range) for that iteration.

Risks to project schedule and cost are generally classified in two different types:

- Risk events. These are events that may or may not happen, but if they do happen they will have a positive or negative impact on the cost or schedule or both.
- Uncertainties. These include ambiguities such as estimating error and uncertainties such as the level of labor productivity or the price of steel. These uncertainties are 100 percent likely to occur but their impact on the project cost or schedule is uncertain.

Risk events and uncertainties are characterized by their probability of occurring and their impact on the project if they do occur. Each can have a positive or negative impact on the project, but whether they do has a lot to do with the statement of the risk.

- "It may be difficult to find qualified, experienced engineers." This risk event has a probability and an impact if it happens, but the way it is stated the impact is likely to imply a higher cost (a threat rather than an opportunity).
- "Labor productivity may not be what we assumed." This ambiguity has a 100 percent probability of occurring, since it is generally impossible to estimate labor productivity precisely. However, productivity may be better than assumed or it may be worse, so this is a combined opportunity and threat.
- "The cost estimates are inaccurate because we do not have contractor bids yet." This is an uncertainty, again with 100 percent likelihood since it is impossible to estimate project element costs with precision until final accounting after the project turnover. Cost estimates based on immature data are often expressed as plus and minus estimates, such as "plus 20 percent, minus 10 percent."

Collection of risk data is based on the results of the processes of the risk identification and risk prioritization (PMI 2008) (APM 2004).

- Generally, risk identification is conducted in risk workshops and/or interviews. Devices such as the Risk Breakdown Structure may be used to help participants think of risk that may be outside of their specific assigned area but which they know about and might affect the project.

---

8   This topic is covered in more detail in Chapter 4.

9   In this approach the risks from the Risk Register drive the simulation. In more traditional approaches the activity durations and component costs are given a 3-point estimate of potential impact. These 3-point estimates, introduced in Chapter 2, result from the workings of, potentially, several risks, the influences of which are difficult to disentangle. We are using the Risk Driver approach that is introduced in Chapter 6.

- Risk assessment, sometimes called qualitative risk analysis, is the process of prioritizing identified risks for the project in question. Usually the risks are prioritized according to a combination of their probability of occurring in the project and the impact on project objectives if they do occur. Best practice is to prioritize risks according to their impact on the different objectives rather than their impact on the entire project.
- The result of risk prioritization is to group the identified risks into high risk, moderate risk and low risk for time, cost, scope and quality. These results constitute the beginning of the Risk Register.
- The Risk Register risks that are judged to be high and moderate for time and cost are used in the risk data collection phase for the quantitative risk analysis of cost and schedule.
- During risk data collection new risks may emerge as well, and the risk interviewer should be alert to and encourage interviewees (or risk workshop participants) to identify and quantify the probability and impact of new risks.

To provide the data to support the Monte Carlo simulation the risk analyst needs to interview subject matter experts about the probability that the risk will occur on this project and, if it occurs, the impact of that risk on the schedule and cost. The impact of any risk is often specified as a range determined by the optimistic (low), most likely (most probable) and pessimistic (high) impacts on the activities to which it is assigned. The range is specified as a multiplicative factor so it can be applied to both longer and shorter activities. The analyst will also try to identify those activities and costs that are affected by the risk so risks can be assigned accurately to the cost-loaded schedule.

The input risk data are usually collected in risk workshops or interviews. In workshops the people may be influenced by strong personalities or people in higher positions in the organization. Alternatively, in individual interview sessions, usually protected by promises of confidentiality, people can discuss their concerns and make estimates without feeling the influence of others. However, the process of interviewing individuals for risk data usually takes longer than conducting a risk workshop. The trade-off is that the quality of data gathered during risk interviews is generally more reliable than that from workshops.

Interviews are conducted with a wide diversity of interviewees, representing all disciplines on the project team. Others interviewed may include management and people with knowledge of the project who are not assigned to the project – these people often have different perspectives than those of project team members and the project manager and are less likely to be biased in favor of underreporting risk. Contractors may be interviewed, but their position on the other side of the contract often causes some caution in crediting their information.

Summary-level risks are required for a strategic analysis of project cost and schedule risks. Often even very large, multi-billion dollar multi-year, projects can be risk analyzed with 20–40 strategic risks. If the risks are stated at a summary level the probability and 3-point estimates of impact are fairly easy to collect, even from people who do not know anything about statistics. However, with multiple interviews there is a variety of data that needs to be summarized and turned into the risk data that will be used in the simulation. The risk analyst should be willing to use good judgment in distilling the best risk information from the different inputs to produce the specific data to be used for each risk.

Summary

This chapter covers the main tasks in getting ready to do an integrated cost and schedule risk analysis. With a good CPM schedule we can define summary resources to enable us to put into the schedule the total contingency-free cost estimate that is consistent with that schedule. If the cost and schedule are not consistent the cost can be adjusted to match the schedule so we have good quality realistic daily rates of expenditure. With the risk data and a consistent resource loaded schedule we are ready to perform integrated cost-schedule risk analysis.

The purpose of integrating the risk analysis of project schedules and cost estimates is to introduce the risk of the schedule into the cost risk. This is because if some activities take more time they will cost more money given the type of time-dependent resources they employ. This integration improves our estimate of cost risk and our understanding of the main causes of that risk to the total cost of the project.

It is not surprising that we need a project schedule to perform integrated cost and schedule risk analysis. We have introduced the critical path method (CPM) schedule in brief, since it is the subject of other books and covered more fully in (Hulett 2009). We discussed several best-practice criteria for project scheduling because having a schedule with realistic durations and total float values, with tight and complete logic that does not rely on constraints and lags and that has been statused recently is needed if the results of Monte Carlo simulation are to be correct. Unfortunately, experience shows that the integrity of the project schedule cannot be assumed. A simple CPM construction project schedule of 28 months was introduced and will be used in subsequent chapters to illustrate the methods.

We also discussed the project cost estimate that is used. We require that the costs be stated without contingency, either below the line or embedded in the estimates. The purpose of the simulation is to re-estimate the contingency that is applicable to the project under study, with its own cost and schedule risks and taking into account the project owners' desire for certainty in cost projections. A cost estimate of $624 million was introduced and applied to the simple schedule using very summary resources. The resources were applied to each of the work-type schedule activities, although one resource was specified to be a material-type resource with a cost that is independent of its activity's duration.

We have found by experience that costs and schedules are not always consistent with each other. In specific, the basis of estimate (BOE) showed the schedule assumptions that were made when the cost estimate was conducted, but those assumptions change as the project planning and execution proceed. In specific, activity durations may change as frequently as weekly, and cost estimators generally do not keep their estimates up to date with those changes in the schedule. Often the project risk analyst is the first person to discover that cost has not kept up with schedule changes since the baseline was established, because the risk analysis of cost and schedule may be the first attempt to put the project's budget into the schedule. In specific, the risk analyst may be more interested in the daily rates implied when the cost and duration of activities are placed side-by-side, since the costs of time-dependent resources depend on the daily rates of expenditure. The cost and schedule must be made consistent since inconsistency causes implied daily rates of expenditure to be unrealistic. It is these daily rates of expenditure that will be used to transmit the schedule risk to the cost estimate during simulation, effectively implementing the integration of cost and schedule risk analysis.

References

APM (2004). *Project Risk Analysis and Management Guide (PRAM Guide)*. Buckinghamshire, UK, Association for Project Management Publishing Limited.

Hulett, D. (2009). *Practical Schedule Risk Analysis*. Farnham, England, Gower Publishing.

PMI (2007). *Practice Standard for Project Scheduling*. Newtown Square, PA, Project Management Institute.

PMI (2008). *A Guide to the Project Management Body of Knowledge*. Newtown Square, PA, Project Management Institute.

USGAO (2009). GAO Cost Estimating and Assessment Guide.

Uyttewaal, E. (2005). *Dynamic Scheduling with Microsoft Office Project 2003*. Boca Raton, FL, J. Ross Publishing.

8 Essentials of Integrated Cost and Schedule Risk Analysis

Introduction

The integration of cost and schedule risk analysis allows us to model the interaction between cost and schedule risk on a project. It has been observed by people looking at historical data that cost and schedule results for projects are correlated. The longer project schedules occur with higher cost. Of course long projects cost more, at least because they generally have more scope to accomplish in the extra time required. The questions are:

- If the duration of a specific project is longer than planned because of risks, is the cost of the project always higher, and in what relationship to time?
- What is the nature of the relationship between cost and schedule results – is it close (for example, one-for-one) or is it loose (not related at all)?
- Why would cost and schedule grow together on a specific project that is affected by risks to the schedule? What is the mechanism that links cost and schedule?

We have indicated that when activities' durations grow their costs grow if they use time-dependent resources such as labor or rented equipment or facilities. We can model that relationship in the resource-loaded project schedule (see Chapter 7) and simulate both cost and schedule simultaneously. We can calculate the correlation coefficient between cost and schedule from the results produced by the simulation to estimate the degree of correlation. And we can identify the risks that cause the results including the correlation between cost and schedule.

Other results are available as well. We can calculate the Joint Confidence Level (JCL), favored by NASA that indicates the combinations (there are many, but we want to concentrate on a highly likely combination) of cost and schedule that has some desired probability of meeting both objectives.[1] Also, because the resources are assigned to the activities and the activities occur in time we can calculate the risk-adjusted project cash flow, putting the project expenditures on the right month.

This chapter will explain and show the fundamental results so the reader can understand what is happening when cost and schedule are simulated. Hopefully the

---

1   According to NASA Policy Directive (NPD) 1000.5A, Policy for NASA Acquisition (Revalidated March 17, 2010), Programs are to be baselined or re-baselined and budgeted at a confidence level at which there is a 70 percent (or the level approved by the decision authority of the responsible Agency-level management council) chance of project cost and schedule success.

reader will gain a good understanding about what is happening during simulation and during the conduct of a real project. The next chapter applies this method to a simple project and derives results such as the JCL and risk-adjusted cash flow including the implied performance measures of internal rate of return and net present value.

Simulation using Risks as Drivers

The method used in this and subsequent chapters to describe risks and their parameters and to assign the risks to activities and resources is called the Risk Driver Method. The Risk Driver method focuses on the risks themselves so it is a more fundamental analysis than the more traditional 3-point estimate placed directly on activity durations or costs. In fact, one complaint about quantitative risk analysis has been that it deals with impacts rather than with the risks that cause them, meaning that the risk information used as a basis for simulation is the impact of risks on activity durations. That criticism is correct. The Risk Driver method was created to focus on the risks.

This is not to say that 3-point estimates or Risk Register (existence risks) cannot be used in addition to the Risk Driver approach. The basic ways these three methods can be used together recognize their different characteristics:

- Risk Drivers allow the user to identify and calibrate the risks that affect the durations of activities that are included in the schedule. Risk Drivers result from risk events that make the current plan activities take longer.
- Risk Register or existence risks result from risk events that cause new activities to occur. This means that a risk event has occurred that results in a discontinuous result, some activity that was not in the schedule to begin with now appears with its own probability and duration and/or cost.
- Three-point estimates can be used to represent an uncertainty with 100 percent likelihood of occurring, such as duration or cost estimating error. It is possible that this estimating error would be applied to the entire schedule, or differentially to large segments of the schedule. The estimating error specification, usually expressed in percentages below or above the estimates of durations or costs, must be devoid of any effect of specific risks, since those risks would be either Risk Drivers or Risk Register/existence risks.

With the Risk Driver method the risks can be specified with both of their fundamental parameters (probability and impact), whereas the traditional "3-point on durations" approach, which also affects the durations and costs of activities already in the schedule, focuses on just the impact and requires mental gymnastics to incorporate risk events that may not occur.

Using Risk Drivers a risk can be modelled to affect two or more activities, so those activities' durations become correlated. Using the traditional 3-point estimate applied to activity durations, the correlation between two activity durations or costs can only be achieved by specifying the correlation coefficient between activities' durations. We no longer have to estimate the strength of correlation between activities since that correlation is produced by modelling the effect of individual risks on activities during the simulation.

Prioritizing risks is possible with the Risk Driver approach and it captures the entire effect of the risks on all activities that the risk affects. With the more traditional 3-point estimate approach the activity durations are the units of measure of risk so:

- we cannot capture the effect of any particular risk on an activity, unless there is only one risk that affects that activity, and
- any sensitivity of overall project risk to individual activity uncertainty will miss the true impact of most risks because it does not capture the risks' impact on more than one activity at a time.

Risk Drivers uses the risks from the Risk Register as risk factors that can apply to:

- the duration of an activity in the schedule or several (many) such activities
- the burn rate per work period (day) of labor-type (duration dependent) resources
- to the total cost of material-type (duration independent) resources. [2,3]

To summarize, the risks operate on the cost and schedule as follows:

- A risk has a probability of occurring on the project. If that probability is 100 percent then the risk occurs in each iteration. If the probability is less than 100 percent it will occur in that smaller percentage of iterations, chosen at random by the computer program during the simulation.
- The risks' impacts are specified by 3-point estimate of a multiplicative factor that will be applied to the activities to which the risk is assigned. The impacts are multiplicative, so a schedule risk, for instance, will multiply the duration of the activity that it is assigned to, and it can be applied multiplicatively to long or short activities. The 3-point estimate is converted to a triangular distribution. For any iteration the software selects a multiplicative factor at random from the distribution specified for that risk by the analyst and uses that factor for that iteration, if the risk occurs in that iteration, to multiply the durations of all activities it affects. If the risk does not occur the Risk Factors program sets the impact value to 1.0 which is a neutral value when multiplied into the activity durations or costs.
- The cost risk factor is applied differently depending on whether the resource is labor-type or equipment-type.
  - For a labor-type time-dependent resource, the cost risk factor varies the daily burn rate, representing more or fewer resources applied per day. If the burn rate varies the cost of that activity could differ even if the activity's duration estimate were perfectly accurate. Of course for these resources, their total cost is also affected by the uncertainty in the duration.

---

2   The examples in this chapter and the next use the Risk Factors Module of Primavera Risk Analysis (previously Pertmaster). Primavera Risk Analysis will read projects from Primavera P3 and P6, Microsoft Project and Open Plan Professional. If the project is scheduled in Microsoft Project the @RISK for Project tool can be configured to derive most of these results.

3   Basic cost impacts of project schedule risks can be calculated with risks specified as 3-point estimates on durations in Risk+ from Deltek, which is a Microsoft Project add-in.

– For material- and equipment-type time-independent resources the cost risk factor varies the total cost since for these resources the cost may be uncertain but it is not affected by time.

The way these risks work in the model can be shown below. Suppose there is a $600,000 home construction project with a 13-month schedule, shown in Figure 8.1, that consists of:

- a 100-day decision process activity with no resources chargeable to the project
- 300-day construction activity with 1,000 units per day of construction resources for a cost of $300,000
- 200-day procurement activity with a total equipment and material cost of $300,000

ID	Description	Remaining Duration	Start	Finish	Remaining Cost	2011	2012
0010	Project Start	0	*01/01/11		$0	ⓘ 01/01/11	
0020	Decision Process	100	01/01/11	04/10/11	$0		
0030	Construction	300	04/11/11	02/04/12	$300,000		
0040	Procurement	200	04/11/11	10/27/11	$300,000		
0050	Project finish	0		02/04/12	$0		▶ 02/04/12

Figure 8.1   Schedule to illustrate basic integration of cost and schedule risk[4]

We will build up the characteristics of integrated cost and schedule risk analysis one step at a time.

One Schedule Risk on Time-Dependent Resource

The first principle we want to introduce is the direct relationship between schedule risk and cost risk. In the first instance let us introduce only one risk, Labor Productivity may be Uncertain, and assign it to the duration of the construction activity. Assume this is an uncertainty with 100 percent likelihood of occurring as shown in Table 8.1.

Table 8.1   One risk on the construction activity duration

Risk ID	Risk	Probability	Duration impact ranges		
			Minimum	Most likely	Maximum
1	Labor productivity may be uncertain	100%	95%	105%	120%

---

4   This figure and other figures in this chapter are derived using Primavera Risk Analysis. The author has no financial interest in this software product or Oracle that owns it.

Notice that the most likely duration of any activity affected by Risk 1 is specified as being 5 percent above the duration in the schedule. This is quite common, that when people look at the assumptions they believe the assumed value not to be the most likely value.

Since construction is conducted with a time-dependent resource, construction labor that is paid more if it works longer, cost is increased proportionately with time.[5] The histogram and cumulative distribution of the cost of the project from the Monte Carlo simulation with only this schedule risk is derived from simulating the resource-loaded schedule and is shown in Figure 8.2 shown below.

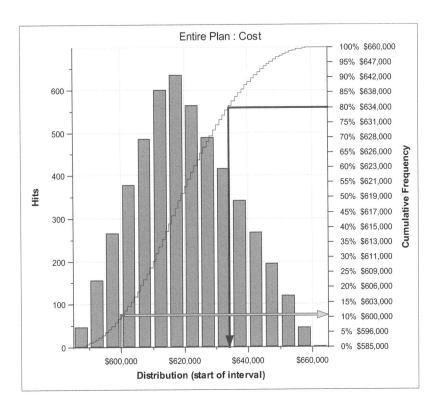

Figure 8.2 Cost risk caused by duration risk on construction activity

Notice that we did not assign any risk directly to the cost of the construction activity but only to its duration. The only way cost is affected is through the effect of schedule risk on the time-dependent resource construction labor.

The results show that there is an 11 percent probability that the budget of $600,000 will be sufficient for this project. Adopting the P-80 value for the desired level of certainty the cost is $634,000 for a $34,000 or 6 percent cost contingency reserve.

---

5   Time and cost may not be proportional depending on when the risk occurs, whether the activity is a highly mobilized state or not. However, since we do not know when during the construction period this risk will occur it is acceptable to assume proportionality.

What is the relationship between cost and schedule when there is just one risk applied to an activity with a resource which has a cost dependent on time? That relationship is direct and uncomplicated. It is shown in a scatter diagram that plots the finish dates and cost pairs of numbers for each iteration. In other words, there are 5,000 possible finish dates and total costs that are consistent with each other since each pair is the result of an iteration and schedule drives cost. The cost-schedule results are shown in Figure 8.3 below.

Since, in this case, cost is entirely determined by time, the "scatter diagram" is a straight line at a 45 degree angle.

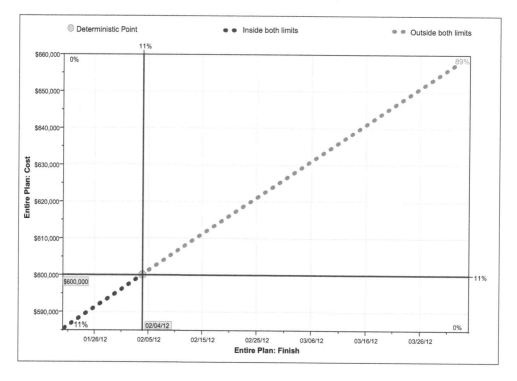

Figure 8.3 Scatter of completion dates (X-axis) and corresponding cost values (Y-axis) (cross-hairs are set to the deterministic values)

Notice that in Figure 8.3 the cross-hairs are set at the deterministic values for this project, to finish February 4, 2012 and to cost $600,000. Most of the probability, 89 percent of the time-cost pairs are in the upper-right-hand quadrant, is for overruns of both cost and schedule. This corresponds to the probability of overrunning cost in Figure 8.2 of 11 percent. Cost and schedule results are correlated 100 percent because the only cost risk comes from the time dependent resources' reaction to a single schedule risk that is 100 percent likely.

Add Uncertainty of the Burn Rate for Construction Labor

Suppose there is some uncertainty about how many construction resources are needed (or their wage rate) compared to the base assumption. That uncertainty can be added to the duration risk as shown in Table 8.2 below in the three columns labeled "Cost Impact Ranges." Notice that the uncertainty in the burn rate is symmetrical in this case – equally likely to be below as it is to be above the estimate of $1,000 per day. It does not have to be symmetrical depending on the risk data collected compared to the daily cost ($1,000).

Table 8.2   Adding burn-rate risk to duration risk, construction labor

Risk ID	Risk	Probability	Duration impact ranges			Cost impact ranges		
			Minimum	Most likely	Maximum	Minimum	Most likely	Maximum
1	Labor productivity may be uncertain	100%	95%	105%	120%	90%	100%	110%

The cumulative distribution including uncertainty in the burn rate, shown in Figure 8.4, shows more risk at the tails of the cumulative distribution since burn-rate risk has been added on top of the impact of construction duration on construction labor risk.

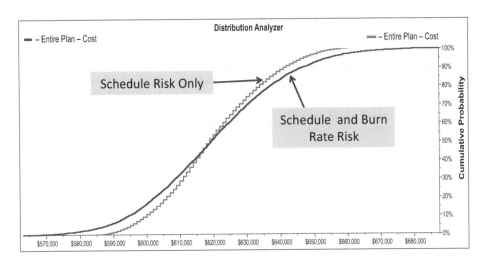

Figure 8.4   Impact of adding burn-rate risk to duration risk for construction labor

Notice that the addition of a symmetrical uncertainty on the burn rate per day ($1,000) of this home construction project does not increase the risk to cost at the P-50, but it has the result of spreading the tails and increasing the overall uncertainty in what the house will cost once constructed.

The scatter diagram from this simulation, shown in Figure 8.5, now looks more like a scatter since the burn-rate risk adds risk to cost that is not entirely schedule-related.

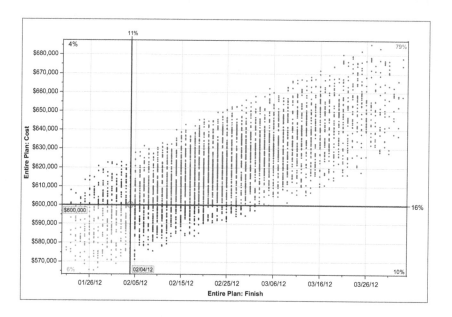

Figure 8.5   Impact of adding burn-rate risk to duration risk for construction labor (cross-hairs set at the deterministic values of time and cost)

These two values – cost and schedule – are correlated 76 percent. This is found by exporting the cost and schedule data to Microsoft Excel and performing the Correlation function on the two columns of numbers. The reason they are not correlated 100 percent as they were in Figure 8.3 is that there is some cost risk, the risk of the uncertain burn rate, which is independent of time.

Add Risk to the Procurement Resource

Finally, let us look at the risks on the Procurement activity. Procurement resources are assumed to be uncertain but not dependent on time, they are "material" resources in Primavera Risk Analysis. Let us specify a procurement risk, suppliers may be busy. This risk, we assume, may cause the suppliers to raise (not to lower) their prices but we assume it does not affect the duration of the procurement activity (this assumption is not material to the cost results but might affect the completion date). The two risks that now affect the home construction project are shown below in Table 8.3.

Table 8.3   Adding procurement risk to duration risk on construction labor

Risk ID	Risk	Probability	Duration impact ranges			Cost impact ranges		
			Minimum	Most likely	Maximum	Minimum	Most likely	Maximum
1	Labor productivity may be uncertain	100%	95%	105%	120%	90%	100%	110%
2	Suppliers may be busy	100%	100%	100%	100%	90%	110%	130%

Assigning the risk "Suppliers may be Busy" to the $300 million procurement activity increases the cost risk of the project and spreads the scatter diagram because procurement cost risk is not driven by (or correlated with) schedule uncertainty. This is shown in Figure 8.6.

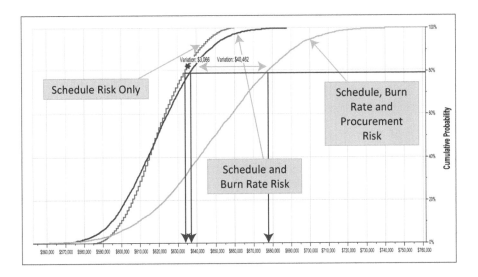

Figure 8.6   Adding procurement cost risk

Notice that adding burn rate risk added only $3,066 to the cost of the house at the P-80 but adding uncertain procurement risks (buying kitchen appliances, heating and air conditioning units, bathroom fixtures, and so on.) adds $40,462 at the P-80 confidence level. These results are shown in Table 8.4.

Table 8.4   Effect on cost of adding schedule risk, burn rate risk and procurement risk

Scenario	Budget	P-80	Cost added at P-80
Deterministic cost	600		
Cost with schedule risk		634	34.0
Add burn rate risk		637	3.1
Add procurement risk		678	40.5

The relationship between cost and schedule is now more diffuse since there are two risks to cost, the burn rate risk on construction labor costs and the procurement risk on procurement, that are not related to schedule. The scatter in Figure 8.7 shows less concentration than that of Figure 8.5.

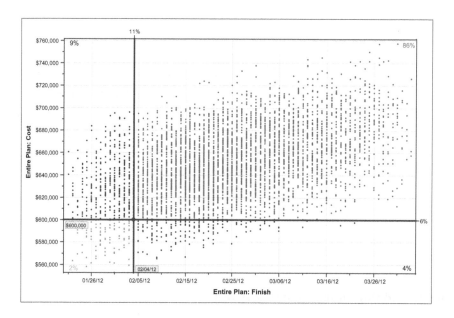

Figure 8.7   Adding procurement cost risk increases scatter (cross-hairs set to the deterministic values)

The correlation between cost and schedule now is only 47 percent. The reduction in correlation coefficient from 76 percent to 47 percent is because the risk to the equipment cost is independent of time.

Decomposing the Risk Results by Cause

These results taken together demonstrate that schedule risk can affect cost risk, and that we can also model cost risk that is independent of schedule risk. One other comparison can be made, that with cost-type risks only, with schedule-type risks only and with both cost- and schedule-type risks. This comparison, shown below in Table 8.5, illustrates the benefit of including both types of risk in gaining both (1) an accurate estimate of cost risk, and (2) a fundamental understanding of the sources of cost risk.

Table 8.5   Comparing results of scenarios with schedule risks only, cost risks only and with both schedule and cost risks

Cost and risk		P-5	Mean	P-80	P-95	Spread P-5 – P-95
Deterministic Cost	600					
Just Schedule Risk		596	820	634	647	51
Just Cost Risk		584	630	654	675	91
Both cost and Schedule Risk		598	650	678	701	103

In this comparison the cost risks (uncertain burn rate and uncertain equipment cost) contributes $54,000 to the cost of the home at the P-80 while schedule risk contributes $34,000 at the P-80. In some other analyses the results are reversed and the effect of schedule uncertainty on the cost contingency reserve exceeds the effect of cost-type risks. When both types of risk are included the contingency reserve is $78,000. The sum of the two is $88,000, more than the total risk at the P-80 level since there is some cancelling out (the schedule-driven cost is high on iterations when the burn rate or procurement cost may be low or moderate.

Also, with both types of risk the spread from the P-5 to the P-95 values, indicating the degree of certainty we have in the cost estimate is $103,000 with both cost and schedule risks considered. These results clearly indicate the benefit of including both cost and schedule risks in the analysis.

In Figure 8.8 the two more-vertical S-curves on the left are those with just schedule risk or just cost risk. The curve to the right includes both cost and schedule influences on project cost risk, illustrating once again, as Table 8.4 showed, the importance of including both schedule and cost risks to get the most accurate estimate of cost risk. Since schedule risk is important in developing estimates of cost risk and cost contingency, the integration of cost and schedule risk analysis is a requirement for best-practice cost risk analysis.

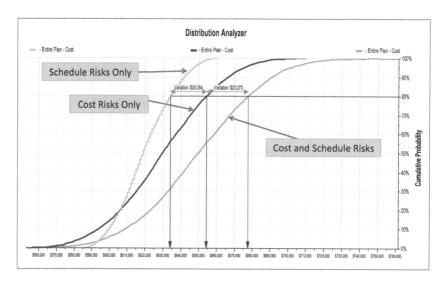

Figure 8.8   Cumulative distribution showing the effect of analyzing both cost and schedule risks to project cost risk

Getting Ready: Other Risk Data

CORRELATION

The degree of correlation between the activity durations has long been viewed as being important for project cost risk analysis. Chapter 5 discussed correlation between cost elements and correlation in schedule risk analysis as discussed in (Hulett 2009) Correlation between project elements costs arises if one risk affects two (or more) activities. We create or model cost correlation so that every iteration in a simulation has values that are internally consistent. In other words, each iteration is a possible combination of durations and costs. For instance if the steel price goes up it would be expected that the cost of structural steel, steel pipe and cables and equipment such as large rotating compression equipment that have steel content would all go up, together. It is the "together" aspect that is the correlation. If during a Monte Carlo simulation the cost of structural steel is chosen on the high side of its distribution, one would think that steel pipe and equipment with steel content would also have costs on the high sides of their distributions. If in some iteration structural steel costs is high and steel pipe costs are low, that iteration would not be internally consistent.

Correlation is observed between costs in a cost estimate and between activity durations in a schedule. Because several or many activities powered by time-dependent labor-type resources may be longer or shorter together the potential for correlation to affect project cost is serious and should not be overlooked.

Using risks to drive the simulation as discussed in Chapter 6 solves this correlation problem. It models the way correlation occurs by assigning risks to activities that also drive the cost risk. When the risk occurs it occurs for all activities it affects and they become correlated as desired.

PROBABILISTIC BRANCHING

Probabilistic branching in project schedule risk is another type of risk data. (Hulett 2009) Some risks may cause activities to occur only if the risk occurs and it would be surprising if those activities were in the original schedule. An event such as the failure of a test or commissioning activity, if it occurs, may require new activities such as finding the root cause of the failure, determining the recovery plan, executing the recovery plan and retesting the article. These activities will all take time and increase project schedule and cost if they occur. The problem is that recovery activities are not typically included in the baseline project schedule so they have to be added with the probability that they will occur. They can be inserted in the schedule as probabilistic branches with time and cost implications if they occur. Another way to handle probabilistic activities (but not branches of logic-linked activities) is to use the Risk Register function.

PROBABILISTIC CALENDARS

Probabilistic calendars may be required for simulating a project schedule and its cost implications. For instance, some activities contained in offshore oil and gas projects in south-east Asia often run into the problem if a heavy lift of a module on a platform is scheduled during the monsoon season, typically November–February. Heavy lifting activities to place the jackets on the sea floor, or to place the modules on top of the jackets cannot be done if the waves are too large or their periodicity is not acceptable. The cost of losing a module or jacket in rolling seas during monsoon season is prohibitive, so these activities are delayed or are advanced, if possible, to avoid the monsoon season.

If a heavy lift occurs during November–February the project typically will delay the lift, including the arrival of the heavy-lift barge that costs serious money on a daily basis, until March. Of course the cost of the barge will be delayed as well. The probabilistic calendar specifies the percentage of non-work days in any time period, typically but not always months. The monsoon calendar would be assigned to the installation of the jacket and the lifts of the modules, so that any iteration that puts these activities in the four months of monsoon will be delayed.

Using Hammocks in Scheduling to Analyze Costs

For some cost-schedule risk analyses it is convenient and proper to put the resources on a hammock. Commonly the level of effort (LOE) support labor-type time dependent resources can be put on a hammock. The characteristic of a hammock (in Primavera P6 it is actually called a "level of effort" activity) is that it takes its duration from the activities it supports. Its predecessor is an activity that starts the group of activities that are supported using a start-to-start (S-S) relationship. The successor of the hammock is the end of the last activity that the resource supports using a finish-to-finish (F-F) relationship.

A common use of the hammock activity is to represent the level-of-effort work of the project management team. We can use the home construction project to illustrate this point. Installing the hammock on the entire schedule from the beginning of the decision process to the end of construction, we have the schedule shown in Figure 8.9.

ID	Description	Remaining Duration	Start	Finish	Remaining Cost	2011	2012
0010	Project Start	0	*01/01/11		$0	01/01/11	
0015	PMT Hammock	400	01/01/11	02/04/12	$80,000		
0020	Decision Process	100	01/01/11	04/10/11	$0		
0030	Construction	300	04/11/11	02/04/12	$300,000		
0040	Procurement	200	04/11/11	10/27/11	$300,000		
0050	Project finish	0		02/04/12	$0		02/04/12

Figure 8.9   Schedule with project management team hammock at $80,000

Notice that we have allocated $80,000 to the project management team (PMT), and the cost of the project is now $680,000. Notice also that the duration of the PMT Hammock was not specified in advance but rather takes its 400 day duration from the total project duration.

If the construction takes 400 days instead of 300 days the PMT Hammock will extend to cover the new project duration and the PMT cost will increase to $100,000 while Construction costs increase to $400,000 and the total project costs $800,000. This possible scenario, which might be an iteration in the Monte Carlo simulation, is shown in Figure 8.10:

ID	Description	Remaining Duration	Start	Finish	Remaining Cost	2011	2012
0010	Project Start	0	*01/01/11		$0	01/01/11	
0015	PMT Hammock	500	01/01/11	05/14/12	$100,000		
0020	Decision Process	100	01/01/11	04/10/11	$0		
0030	Construction	400	04/11/11	05/14/12	$400,000		
0040	Procurement	200	04/11/11	10/27/11	$300,000		
0050	Project finish	0		05/14/12	$0		05/14/12
TOTALS					$800,000		

Figure 8.10 Construction duration increase is also in the duration and cost of the PMT Hammock

The scatter diagram produced by simulating this schedule is shown in Figure 8.11.

Because the cost of the PMT is completely determined by the duration of the overall home construction schedule the scatter looks tighter than the previous one in Figure 8.7. The correlation of time and cost for this scenario is 61 percent, higher than the 47 percent of the earlier Figure because the added PMT resource is completely determined by schedule risk.

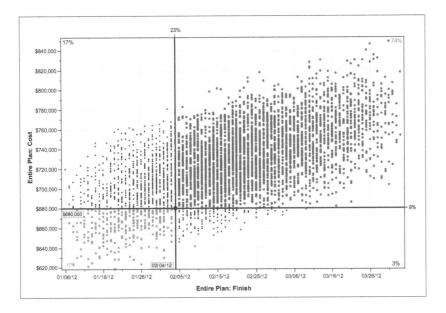

Figure 8.11 Scatter diagram when the PMT Hammock is introduced

Joint Confidence Level

The Joint Confidence Level (JCL) can be calculated from the scatter diagram, for instance the one in Figure 8.11 above. The JCL is the term given by NASA to the points where there is a 70 percent probability that the cost and time values will both be met.[6] This is found by freezing the percentage in the south-west quadrant to 70 percent. There are many cost-time points where the probability of meeting both is 70 percent. In Figure 8.12 we have chosen one combination of cost and time with a 70 percent joint likelihood that looks like it is in the densest part of the scatter diagram. There are many other such points that would satisfy the JCL criterion of 70 percent, and those are indicated by the iso-joint-probability curve shown on the scatter diagram.

In this case the date of completion is March 8, 2012 (the plan says February 4, 2012) and the cost is $756,781 (the plan says the cost is $680,000 including the PMT). If we adopted these cost and schedule goals we estimate that there is a 70 percent probability that the home construction project will come in on or below both of those two values. Notice the bold line running through this pair of numbers, called the JCL iso-probability curve. Any value on this curve (in this figure it is approximated) will produce a joint cost and schedule success probability of 70 percent.

---

6   "Programs are to be baselined or rebaselined and budgeted at a confidence level of 70 percent or the level approved by the decision authority of the responsible Agency-level management council. For a 70 percent confidence level, this is the point on the joint cost and schedule probability distribution where there is a 70 percent probability that the project will be completed at or lower than the estimated amount and at or before the projected schedule. The basis for a confidence level less than 70 percent is to be formally documented" (NASA, 2010).

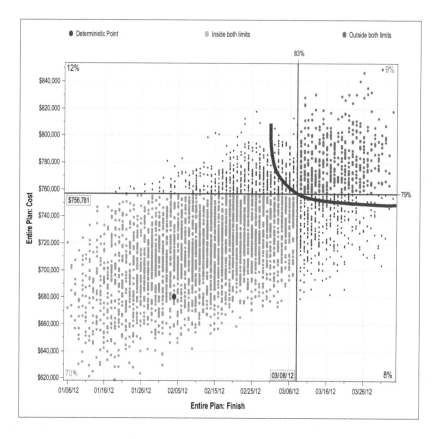

Figure 8.12 The same scatter diagram with a JCL-70 percent probability of success

The project cannot actually choose any particular point on the JCL curve as a budget and a finish date. Rather, the iso-probability or JCL curve is a probabilistic curve with most of the probability concentrated in the center where the time-cost scatter is most concentrated. Think of a 3-dimensional chart where the high point would be about where the cross-hairs are and the height of the curve is reduced as you travel out toward the ends of the curve. Given the current plan and the quantified risks, the project will probably end up at a point along the iso-probability or JCL curve where the cloud of cost-time pairs is densest.

If the project wanted to try to ensure an earlier date it would first have to change the plan by mitigating the schedule risks and then review the risks on this new plan. Finally we re-run the simulation and find the new cost-time pairs where 70 percent of the results are in the south-west quadrant. We might find that the 70-percent curve shifts to the left but also to the top since the risk mitigation steps probably add to the cost.

Summary

In this chapter we have introduced the concept of integrated cost and schedule risk analysis. This approach to cost risk recognizes that schedule slips can add to project cost since the labor and rented equipment will charge more if they work more. This is true to a large extent even if there is a fixed-price contract with a contractor since delays are often compensable and the contractor will make claims for more money claiming that there were compensable events that caused the delay. Often some large portion of the claim will be paid.

Another concept that was introduced was the application of the Risk Driver approach to schedule risk. Similar to the use of Risk Drivers to costs, introduced in Chapter 6, Risk Drivers can be used for schedule risk using the Risk Factors module in Primavera Risk Analysis (formerly Pertmaster Risk Expert). We used a simple 3-activity home construction schedule and applied two resources, construction labor and equipment, on it to illustrate some fundamental concepts of integrated cost and schedule risk analysis.

In applying Risk Drivers to schedule we are also applying it to cost for those resources that are identified as time-dependent (for example, labor-type). The resource-loaded schedule (see Chapter 7) is simulated with schedule risks affecting their time-dependent resources so cost results are correlated with schedule results 100 percent.

We then introduced the uncertainty in the burn rate of time-dependent resources. The number of people or their compensation per hour may be uncertain. Even if they work the same hours as in the baseline and the basis of estimate, the total cost may be different than estimated because the burn rate is not certain. In this chapter we have called the uncertainty in the burn rate a "cost risk" to distinguish it from the cost implications of schedule risk. When uncertainty in the burn rate is introduced there can easily be more risk at the P-80 or some other risk tolerance threshold. The correlation between cost and time in the Monte Carlo simulation is clearly not 100 percent any more – in our example it dropped to 76 percent – because the uncertainty in burn rate is independent of time, even when added to a resource with a cost that is time dependent.

The cost of materials or equipment is also uncertain. In the integrated cost and schedule risk analysis we can put risk on the total equipment cost and that cost will vary but not because of schedule uncertainty. Doing this further loosens the linkage between cost and time, and in our example the correlation coefficient was reduced to 47 percent.

The concept of hammocks is introduced for the purpose of installing the cost of the level of effort (LOE) resource, exemplified by the Project Management Team. (While this may be a stretch for a home building project, management does have to be paid.) Hammocks are also used when the level of detail at which cost is specified is not as fine as the detail in the schedule. Since the PMT works until the project is completed, a hammock activity that takes its duration from that of the overall schedule is an appropriate place to put the PMT resource. In this case we are introducing another time dependent resource and the correlation increased from 47 percent to 61 percent.

Finally the concept of the Joint Confidence Level (JCL), used by the United States' National Aeronautics and Space Administration (NASA) was introduced. The JCL is set at 70 percent by agency policy, a level of certainty that is comfortable to the project sponsors for meeting both cost and schedule targets. Turning this around, if a 70 percent target for both cost and schedule is desired, then 70 percent of the cost–time pairs resulting from the Monte Carlo simulation will be in the lower-left quadrant. There are many combinations of time and cost that will achieve any particular percentage.

Using the home construction project we picked a point that produced a 70 percent success level and that, to the naked eye appeared to be in the densest part of the scatter diagram. This would be more likely to occur than some point on the iso-probability JCL curve that occurs in a less dense part of the scatter cloud. If the project manager wants to budget time and cost to the 70th percentile of success, the point chosen should be one of the most likely points on the JCL curve, recognizing that other points on the curve may occur since they are generated from the project plan and its risks.

Integrating cost and schedule risk provide a more accurate estimate of cost risks and also an idea about which risks are important. In our home construction example the schedule risk contributed significantly to the overall cost risk at the P-80 level. We will also identify high-priority specific schedule and/or cost risks that affect project cost. Working directly with resource-loaded schedules we have more confidence in our cost risk analysis than if schedule were ignored or approximated using spreadsheet models. Hence, the best approach to cost risk uses the project schedule as its platform. To conduct this complete cost and schedule risk analysis requires the knowledge of project scheduling.

References

Hulett, D. (2009). *Practical Schedule Risk Analysis*. Farnham, England, Gower Publishing.
NASA (2010). NPD 1000.5A, Policy for NASA Acquisition (Revalidated March 17, 2010), US National Aeronautics and Space Administration.

9 Integrated Cost and Schedule Risk Analysis: Method and Case Study Basic Results

Introduction

In Chapter 8 we illustrated the fundamental principles and results of integrated cost and schedule risk analysis. These principles used a very simple home construction project with few resources and few risks.

In this chapter we will show how to implement integrated cost and schedule on a somewhat more complicated schedule. In this chapter we continue to focus on the fundamental risks to drive the Monte Carlo simulation by using the Risk Driver method first introduced in Chapter 6 applied to cost risk but applied now to schedule and cost risk using the schedule as the model, as shown briefly in Chapter 8. This chapter shows what happens when risks are assigned to more than one activity and when some activities have several risks assigned to them. We have some uncertainties with 100 percent probability and some risk events with less than 100 percent probability in the list of risks.

The result of doing the risk analysis this way is that we are able to:

* estimate the risk to the overall project schedule
* estimate the cost risk of the project, taking into account the impact of schedule risk on cost risk directly and clearly
* prioritize the risks, which is essential for efficient risk mitigation.

Prioritizing the risks using the Monte Carlo simulation model enables us to identify the important risks. For instance, many of the risks to cost are actually risks to schedule, operating on activities with resources that have costs that depend on the activities' durations.

Conducting risk mitigation is important because we do not want to give the project a report card but rather a tool to improve performance.

* If the project manager believes that the risk analysis is like grading his homework he will be unenthusiastic about the exercise and will not be willing or cooperative when his team leads are bothered by workshops, meetings and interviews. In fact some of these project managers will argue with the results or discard them instead of deriving benefits for the project.

- However, if the project manager sees the exercise as providing information and a tool enabling management to be proactive in mitigating project risk he may become enthusiastic and even be a champion of the process.
- Sometimes, of course, project managers need to be told to do risk analysis before they can learn to embrace it. If the customer or owner wants the risk analysis done, or has a corporate policy that risk analysis is to be done, say before major decision points, then the project manager may be forced to cooperate. This sometimes works since some of these managers become believers after experiencing risk analysis.

The chapter develops the integrated cost and schedule risk analysis in a logical progression:

- Review and improve the schedule logic.
- Incorporate the project budget through assigning costed resources to activities in the schedule.
- Use the Risk Register as the basis of in-depth quantitative risk data interviews.
- Model the application of risks to the schedule durations and cost elements for a Monte Carlo simulation.
- Derive results such as the contingency reserves of time and cost as well as the prioritization of risks to time and cost.
- Lead the project team in workshops to develop a risk mitigation strategy for better project results. Analyze the mitigation strategies to determine their net impact on project time and cost risk.
- Compute the risk-adjusted cash flow and compare it to the budget for the project to determine the feasibility of the project if the budget is specified in advance.

Integrated Cost-Schedule Risk Analysis Case Study

THE SUMMARY SCHEDULE

The project that is the subject of this case study is still a simple project, but in this chapter we focus on overall schedule and cost risk. The project is another construction project, shown in Figure 9.1.

It may seem illogical to start with a schedule when the objective is to derive a cost risk assessment, but it is the best way to reflect the effect of schedule risks on cost risk and to identify separately schedule risk and cost risk impacts on cost risk for risk mitigation. Finally, if we want to know which risks are most important to determining the need for a cost contingency reserve we need to account for the schedule risks because their impact on cost risk is sometimes greater than the risks that are usually thought of as cost risks.[1]

---

1   This logically leads to cost estimators and cost risk analysts needing to be familiar with project scheduling. Experience shows that schedules need to be checked, particularly for complete logic, before they can be certified as fit for Monte Carlo simulation, and the risk analyst may be the one to check the schedules. Hence the analysis of costs starts with the project schedule and the analyst needs to be comfortable with project schedules. Some analysts may need to be retrained, which will help to make their practice of risk analysis more inclusive and accurate.

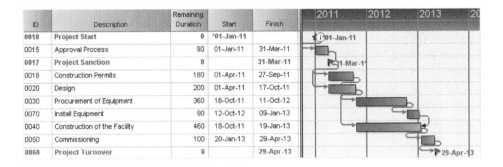

ID	Description	Remaining Duration	Start	Finish	2011	2012	2013	20
0010	Project Start	0	*01-Jan-11		★①01-Jan-11			
0015	Approval Process	90	01-Jan-11	31-Mar-11				
0017	Project Sanction	0		31-Mar-11	◆31-Mar-11			
0018	Construction Permits	180	01-Apr-11	27-Sep-11				
0020	Design	200	01-Apr-11	17-Oct-11				
0030	Procurement of Equipment	360	18-Oct-11	11-Oct-12				
0070	Install Equipment	90	12-Oct-12	09-Jan-13				
0040	Construction of the Facility	460	18-Oct-11	19-Jan-13				
0050	Commissioning	100	20-Jan-13	29-Apr-13				
0060	Project Turnover	0		29-Apr-13			◆29-Apr-13	

Figure 9.1   Simplified schedule of a 27-month construction project

Time-Dependent and Time-Independent Resources

Since the project schedule is the basis of the cost risk analysis we need to incorporate the entire contingency-free budget into the schedule. This is done using resources, which also give us the opportunity to distinguish between time-dependent and time-independent resources.

- Time dependent resources include labor, rented equipment and any resource that charges by the amount of time it is employed, such as tower cranes, drill rigs or heavy lift barges. Their costs will be affected by risks to schedule that cause them to work more days and to be paid more. The durations of the activities are key ingredients of the Basis of Estimate (BOE) that reflects the fact that the cost and schedule are, at least initially in the approved baseline, consistent with each other. When schedule risk occurs, the assumptions of the BOE are changed and the current cost estimate (not the baseline cost estimate) needs to reflect the new durations for time-dependent resources. It is common that the cost estimate does not reflect the project schedule after the project starts because the cost estimators and schedulers may not communicate with each other. They may even not be in the same department. Schedule events are often not transmitted to the cost estimators to incorporate into their current estimate.
- Time-independent resources are often procured items such as equipment and bulk materials. If the procurement process is longer than expected, the project schedule and delivery dates may change but the equipment and materials may not cost more because of the longer process. However, the cost to the project of equipment and bulk materials is usually uncertain, but just not because of the time it takes to fabricate and deliver the items after the procurement has been approved. Analysts and management are tempted to put subcontracts in this time-independent category if the subcontract is fixed price. Sometimes fixed price means fixed price and sometimes it is just the basis for claims that will be settled later, usually increasing the price paid to the subcontractor. In general we need to be skeptical and not rely on the certainty of fixed prices when we analyze cost risk.

The resources need not be detailed to be used in an integrated cost and schedule risk analysis. Indeed, identifying the resources at a summary level may be preferable for the risk analysis. It becomes more difficult to price detailed resources and place them on the activities. Experience shows that you can analyze multi-billion dollar projects with 8 to 12 summary resources. These summary resources cannot be used for resource planning or resource leveling because they are too general for that. But keeping the resources at the summary level makes the loading of the project budget feasible and accurate both in the overall total cost sense and the time phasing of the budget to individual activities. These are both crucial to the success of the integrated cost and schedule risk analysis. The example case study uses the resources shown below in Figure 9.2.

ID	Description	Type	Default Loading	Cost
COMM	Commissioning	Labor	Normal	$1
CONS	Construction	Labor	Normal	$1
ENG	Engineers	Labor	Normal	$1
ENV	Environmental	Labor	Normal	$1
MGT	Management	Labor	Normal	$1
PMT	Project Management Te...	Labor	Normal	$1
PROC	Procurement	Materials	Spread	$1

Figure 9.2   Summary resources used to place the project budget in the schedule[2]

Notice that the procurement resource is designated as "Materials" whereas all the others are "Labor." This means that the Monte Carlo simulation using the Primavera Risk Analysis Risk Factors Module will treat the effect of risks on procurement differently depending on its type. Any risk that is assigned to an activity with procurement resources will vary the activity as follows:

- Schedule risk on procurement activities may delay the fabrication and delivery of procured equipment, and hence any installation or commissioning successor activities, but will not change the cost.
- A cost risk assigned to that activity will affect the cost of the procured equipment even if the schedule is not risky, that is, independent of its schedule risk.

The other resources are designated as "Labor" resources. The cost of those resources can be affected using the Risk Driver approach (implemented in Pertmaster's Risk Factors Module)[3] in two ways:

- Any schedule risk that is assigned to an activity with labor resources will affect the activity's cost proportionately to the impact on the activity's duration, since the average burn rate per day will be extended (or reduced in the case of opportunities) by the number of days the risk adds (or subtracts). The proportionality assumption

---

2   The images in this chapter come from Primavera Risk Analysis (formerly Pertmaster), an Oracle product.

3   Some other simulation software can be configured to do the same processes. @RISK from Palisade can replicate some of these functions if configured correctly.

can be interpreted as reflecting agnosticism concerning when during the activity the risk occurs. The risk may stretch out the peak labor period, or may stretch out the mobilization or demobilization periods, but we are not sure. Hence, the default option of proportionality is appropriate. This consideration is particularly important for summary schedules in which the activities are often longer than for the detailed schedules.

- Any cost risk applied to labor resources will affect the burn rate per day. This applies to the burn rate on the scheduled duration as well as on the added (or subtracted) duration caused by schedule risks. Variation in the burn rate can reflect changes from baseline in the number of labor resources actually working on the activity or their average pay per day or both. Optimally these changes would be communicated to the cost estimators, and the risks may actually arise from discussions with the cost estimators. Varying the burn rate using a cost-type risk on time-dependent resources will cause uncertainty in those costs even when the schedule is fixed.

Notice that each resource is given a value of $1. That means that the units of the resources applied to any activity will be the total value of that resource for that activity.

Assigning the Resources to the Activities

Adding these resources to the project schedule in this chapter's case study yields a total project cost of $624,220 thousand. The cost by activity is shown in Figure 9.3 below. Notice that the milestones that represent moments in time do not take resources or cost.

ID	Description	Remaining Duration	Start	Finish	Total Cost
0010	Project Start	0	^01-Jan-11		$0
0015	Approval Process	90	01-Jan-11	31-Mar-11	$2,070
0017	Project Sanction	0		31-Mar-11	$0
0018	Construction Permits	180	01-Apr-11	27-Sep-11	$5,400
0020	Design	200	01-Apr-11	17-Oct-11	$46,000
0030	Procurement of Equipment	360	18-Oct-11	11-Oct-12	$210,800
0070	Install Equipment	90	12-Oct-12	09-Jan-13	$7,650
0040	Construction of the Facility	460	18-Oct-11	19-Jan-13	$335,800
0050	Commissioning	100	20-Jan-13	29-Apr-13	$16,500
0060	Project Turnover	0		29-Apr-13	$0

Figure 9.3   Activities with resources added to a total of $624,220 thousands

To see how these estimates are built up from resources, Figure 9.4 shows the two resources, CONS and PMT, that are assigned to the construction of the facility activity and add up to $335,800 thousand.

ID	Unit of Measure	Loading	Units/period	Remaining	Budget
CONS - Construction		Normal	700	322,000	322,000
PMT - Project Management Team		Normal	30	13,800	13,800

Figure 9.4   Resources assigned to the construction activity

Notice that the entire budget is remaining cost for this project that has no progress recorded yet because the project is still in the planning phase. Notice too that when the $322,000 thousand construction budget is assigned to construction the program automatically spreads this amount to the 460 working days of the construction activity and calculates a daily rate of $700 thousand.

The resource assignments by activity are shown in Table 9.1 below. Notice that the project management team (PMT) is spread over all activities whereas the other resources are generally assigned to one activity. If this were a real schedule of hundreds (but, hopefully, not thousands) of activities, each of these areas such as construction of the facility would be comprised of several, perhaps tens of activities. In that case the resource shown here would be spread as the estimator feels it should be over all of the construction activities, and the sum of the assigned resources would equal the budget for that particular resource.

Table 9.1   Resources applied to the schedule activities

ID	Activity	PMT	MGT	ENV	ENG	PROC	CONS	COMM	Activity total
15	Approval process	720	1,350						2,070
18	Construction permits	900		4,500					5,400
20	Design	6,000			40,000				46,000
30	Procurement of equipment	10,800				200,000			210,800
70	Install equipment	2,250					5,400		7,650
40	Construction of the facility	13,800					322,000		335,800
50	Commissioning	1,500						15,000	16,500
	Resource total	35,970	1,350	4,500	40,000	200,000	327,400	15,000	624,220

In Figure 9.5 we see the resource loading in the schedule.

ID	Description	Remaining Duration	Start	Finish	Total Cost	Resource Loading
0010	Project Start	0	*01-Jan-11		$0	
0015	Approval Process	90	01-Jan-11	31-Mar-11	$2,070	MGT[Normal];PMT[Normal]
0017	Project Sanction	0		31-Mar-11	$0	
0018	Construction Permits	180	01-Apr-11	27-Sep-11	$5,400	ENV[Normal];PMT[Normal]
0020	Design	200	01-Apr-11	17-Oct-11	$46,000	ENG[Normal];PMT[Normal]
0030	Procurement of Equipment	360	18-Oct-11	11-Oct-12	$210,800	PROC[Spread];PMT[Normal]
0070	Install Equipment	90	12-Oct-12	09-Jan-13	$7,650	CONS[Normal];PMT[Normal]
0040	Construction of the Facility	460	18-Oct-11	19-Jan-13	$335,800	CONS[Normal];PMT[Normal]
0050	Commissioning	100	20-Jan-13	29-Apr-13	$16,500	COMM[Normal];PMT[Normal]
0060	Project Turnover	0		29-Apr-13	$0	

Figure 9.5   Schedule showing resource loading

Detailed vs. Summary Schedules and Resources

Some schedulers and cost estimators who do not have experience with loading resources are concerned that resource loading will prove to be an insurmountable task. They are thinking of identifying and loading 50 to 100 resources in some detail. Of course loading many detailed resources, particularly on detailed schedules with thousands of activities, would be a daunting task. We have seen resources listed down to the named individual level for multi-hundred million dollar programs, so even this is possible.[4] Other programs have loaded detailed resources but not costed them. In this case the resources should be good for planning purposes but, without associated costs, are one step short of helping us with the cost implication of the schedule.

The main way to look at resource loading of the budget as feasible is to consider summary resources to be sufficient and to construct a summary schedule. The natural reaction of schedulers when resource loading is discussed evokes the detailed approach using both detailed schedules and detailed resources. This approach would work to do integrated cost and schedule risk analysis but it is difficult and not necessary to the generation of valuable risk analysis results. Summary schedules that include all of the work and summary resources that can place the entire project budget on the schedule is the least-aggravating way to go and should be chosen whenever possible. Executing a risk analysis with the summary schedule and cost approach is better than complaining how hard it would be to identify and load detailed schedules with detailed resources and then not doing it.

Identifying the Risks

Notice that the title of this subsection is identifying the risks, not specifying the risk. This distinction is deliberate since we are using the Risk Driver approach wherein we specify

---

4   The specific project mentioned was a program with a lot of time to do the planning and an expert scheduler-cost estimator combination in the project controls office that thought resource loading was the only way to do scheduling and cost estimating right.

the probability of occurring, impact range in multiplicative terms and the activities that they affect for individual risks, whether they are uncertainties or risk events.

We also distinguish and specify separately the schedule impacts and the cost impacts, where:

- The schedule impacts affect the duration of the activity and will affect the cost of any time-dependent resources assigned to the activity.
- The cost impacts affect the burn rate of the time-dependent resources and the total cost of the time-independent resources. Hence the effect of the cost impact depends on whether any resource assigned to the activity is time dependent or time independent.

The emphasis on using the Risk Driver approach in this chapter and indeed in much of this book (see Chapter 6) is not to imply that the traditional 3-point estimate approach has no place in integrated cost and schedule risk analysis. There are at least three main ways to specify the risk, and each has its role in a risk analysis. These are:

- Risk Drivers allow risks to affect the duration of the activities that are included in the schedule.
- The existence risks, also represented by the Risk Register method in Primavera Risk Analysis, allows the analyst to specify discontinuous activities, such as recovery after a failed test, that are not generally included in the schedule.
- Three-point estimates can be used to represent uncertainty, usually the error in estimating activity durations or project element costs. In specifying this uncertainty it is important to abstract the estimating uncertainty ranges from the additional effect of risk events, since the risk events are included in the Risk Drivers or as existence risks.

The benefits of focusing on the risks that are usually found in the Risk Register rather than on the impact of the risks on activity durations (the traditional 3-point estimate of durations) should become clear, especially in the risk mitigation section. Unfortunately the use of Risk Drivers limits the Monte Carlo software choices today, but this is not necessarily a permanent condition.

The initial list of risks is found in the Risk Register that should be available from the qualitative risk analysis. The Risk Register includes a prioritized list of risks, perhaps risks grouped as "high," "moderate," and "low" in their importance for the project. Optimally the Risk Register specifies the risks that are important for different objectives, and the ones we need to look at are those important for time and for cost. Risks to scope, quality or other objectives may have time or cost implications, and if those are important the Risk Register should indicate their cost and schedule implications.

The list of risks from the Risk Register will probably not be complete and the risk interviews tend to uncover additional risks that are added to the expanding risk list. Participating in the risk interviews or risk workshop can and will cause some to think of risks that were never on the list. This creative activity of identifying new risks is encouraged by the risk interviewer.

Specifying the Parameters of the Risks

A project risk is an uncertain event or condition that, if it occurs, has a positive or negative on at least one project objective (PMI 2008). This definition of project risk usually refers to risk events that may or may not happen with some probability. In this analysis of integrated cost and schedule risk we need to include uncertainties that are not uncertain in their probability of occurring but have uncertain impacts. The definition also refers to "risks that matter" (Hillson and Simon 2007), which are those with probabilities and impacts on cost or schedule that are sufficiently large to be material. The definition highlights the need to interview (or gather in a workshop) to collect data on both probability of occurring and impact.

We typically interview the project teams and subject matter experts (SMEs), perhaps interviewing as many as 30 to 40 different people or small groups of people with the same area of expertise. Suppose we have done this and the reports from different interviewees/workshop participants differ on the relevant probabilities and impacts for at least some of the risks. Since the participants have different personal experiences with projects they have different impressions about probability and impact. What is the risk analyst to do with these different inputs on the same risks?

We typically gather the inputs from different interview sources together for each risk and examine them. The risk interviewer and perhaps others from the project management office (PMO) have been in all of the workshops and interviews and know which interviewees were most knowledgeable about which risk. The inputs from the most knowledgeable would be given more weight, but the inputs from others should not be entirely discounted. It would be difficult to construct a set of rules to give various weights (importance) to different respondents. Ultimately the risk lead must conclude which quantitative probability and impact range parameters are going to be used for each risk.

Suppose we have finished the interviews or workshops and have concluded that the risks with their parameters are those shown in Table 9.2 below.

Table 9.2   Risk Drivers' probability and impact ranges quantified

Risk Driver	Sched. Opt.	Sched. ML	Sched. Max	Cost Opt.	Cost ML	Cost Max	Probability
Design complexity may challenge engineers	90%	100%	135%	100%	105%	110%	40%
Site conditions/site access may slow logistics	100%	110%	125%				50%
Equipment suppliers may be busy	100%	105%	115%	100%	110%	120%	60%
Capable management may not be assigned	90%	105%	110%				40%
Permitting agency may be slow	95%	110%	125%				50%
Activity duration estimates are inaccurate	90%	105%	115%				100%
Cost estimate is inaccurate				95%	100%	110%	100%
Key engineering personnel may be unavailable	85%	105%	120%	90%	100%	110%	65%

An examination of the Risk Drivers and their parameters indicates that several risks are deemed to impact schedules, and hence may impact costs of time-dependent resources, but not to have impacts in addition to these on the resources' burn rate (for time dependent resources) or total cost (for time-independent resources). These risks have blank cells under the three cost range column headings. There is one entry that has cost uncertainty implications but does not affect the schedule.

Risk Events and Uncertainties

Notice that there are two uncertainties: activity duration estimates are inaccurate and cost estimate is inaccurate. (All of the other risks represent specific risk events and have the word "may" in them, indicating that they may occur or not and their probabilities are less than 100 percent.) But the uncertainties are not risk events. They are certain to occur and their probabilities (far right-hand column in Table 9.2) are listed at 100 percent.

The schedule uncertainty and cost uncertainty can be handled (in Primavera Project Risk) by using 3-point estimates on activity durations and resources. This indicates that the traditional 3-point estimate and the Risk Driver approach can coexist if they are used properly. Since the 3-point estimate only varies the impact on activities' duration it is only appropriate to be used for uncertainties such as errors in estimating durations. There is a parallel operation to put 3-point estimates on resources which represents cost estimating error. In addition if the 3-point estimate were called upon to represent the impact on the activity's cost or duration of more than one risk we get back into murky waters. That is, developing 3-point estimates of impact representing the combined impact of more than one risk is a tricky calculation to do off-line and it is best left to the modelling process. The interviewee needs to make a number of calculations and approximations in his head to create the compound 3-point estimates. If there are two or more uncertainties on costs or on schedule durations it is best to make them Risk Drivers. Using Risk Drivers the Monte Carlo simulation process will develop during the simulation the appropriate probability distribution of cost or of schedule durations from application of multiple risks to the activity and its resources. (See Chapter 6, which illustrates this process with two risks on a single cost element.)

Assigning the Risks to Activities

Suppose we have a project with the activities shown in Figure 9.1 above and resources/ costs as shown in Figure 9.2 and distributed as in Table 9.1 above. Also, suppose we have interviewed for the probability and time/cost impacts as shown previously in Table 9.2 above. After the risks are listed and their parameters quantified they need to be assigned to the activities and their resources. For this case study the risks are assigned according to Table 9.3.

The risks, called "Risk Factors" in Primavera Risk Analysis, are indicated in the schedule for each activity in Figure 9.6.

Table 9.3   Assigning risks to activities

Risks	Approval process	Environmental	Design	Procurement	Install equipment	Construction	Commissioning
				Activities			
Design complexity may challenge engineers	X		X				
Site conditions/site access may slow logistics						X	X
Equipment suppliers may be busy				X			X
Capable management may not be assigned	X					X	X
Permitting agency may be slow		X					
Activity duration estimates are inaccurate	X		X	X	X	X	X
Cost estimate is inaccurate	X		X	X	X	X	X
Key engineering personnel may be unavailable	X	X	X		X	X	X

ID	Description	Remaining Duration	Start	Finish	RiskFactors
0010	Project Start	0	^01-Jan-11		
0015	Approval Process	90	01-Jan-11	31-Mar-11	1,4,6,7,8
0017	Project Sanction	0		31-Mar-11	
0018	Construction Permits	180	01-Apr-11	27-Sep-11	5,8
0020	Design	200	01-Apr-11	17-Oct-11	1,6,7,8
0030	Procurement of Equipment	360	18-Oct-11	11-Oct-12	3,6,7
0070	Install Equipment	90	12-Oct-12	09-Jan-13	6,7,8
0040	Construction of the Facility	460	18-Oct-11	19-Jan-13	2,4,6,7,8
0050	Commissioning	100	20-Jan-13	29-Apr-13	2,3,4,6,7,8
0060	Project Turnover	0		29-Apr-13	

Figure 9.6   Risk Drivers (called risk factors) appear in the schedule

Simulating the Resource-Loaded Schedule

The resource- and risk-loaded schedule is simulated. Each iteration will produce both schedule dates and costs that are consistent with each other. This simulation will provide the traditional schedule and cost histograms and cumulative distributions. In addition we will be able to look at time-cost scatter plots and probabilistic cash flows.

Occasionally someone will ask about the number of iterations that should be used. Without getting technical the following seems to work for simulating the resource-loaded schedule:

- For draft results for which the analyst is gaining information, testing alternative modelling strategies and making comparisons that will not make it into the final report, 1,500 iterations seems to be sufficient.
- For final report simulations more iterations are recommended, in the 3,000–5,000 iteration range. The results may not be much different from the draft runs, but the resulting distributions seem to be smoother and the customer of the analysis feels better with more iterations.

The balance of this chapter covers the results and their interpretation, as well as the use of the model to assist in the development of risk mitigation plans.

Schedule Risk Results

The schedule histogram for the case study is below in Figure 9.7. It shows that the deterministic date of 29 April 2012 is about 9 percent likely to be achieved following the current plan and without further risk mitigation actions. If we assume that the project stakeholders have agreed that their acceptable level of confidence is at the 80th percentile, it is 80 percent likely that the current project plan with all of its risks will finish on or before 22 October 2013.

Given these results, this project needs about a 5.8-month contingency reserve of time from its scheduled date to its P-80 date. At the P-80 point the project is expected to finish on that date or earlier with a probability of 80 percent, and finish later with a 20 percent probability. These results are shown in Figure 9.7 and in Table 9.4.

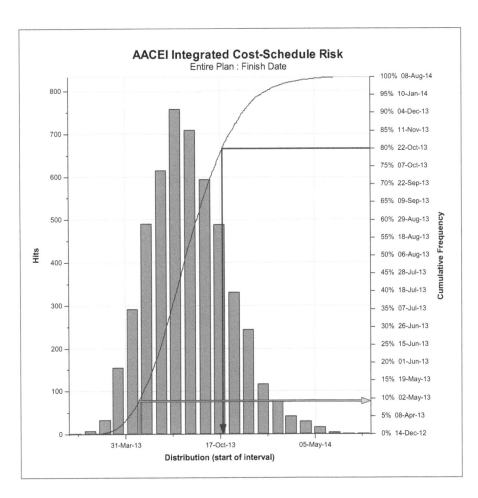

Figure 9.7   Histogram with cumulative distribution (S-curve) for the project completion date

Table 9.4   Summary schedule risk analysis results for the example construction project

						Spread
Deterministic	29 Apr 13	P-5	P-50	P-80	P-95	P95-P5
Schedule dates at percentiles		8 Apr 13	6 Aug 13	22 Oct 13	10 Jan 14	
		Months				
Difference from deterministic		−0.7	3.3	5.8	8.4	9.1

Cost Risk Results

The cost risk results, including the impact on cost of schedule risk, indicate the need for a contingency reserve of cost of about $124 million or 20 percent at the 80th percentile. At that level there is an 80 percent probability that the project will cost $748 million or less, given the risks and following the current plan. Remember that these results incorporate the impact of schedule risk on the cost of time-dependent resources. These results are shown below in Figure 9.8 and Table 9.5.

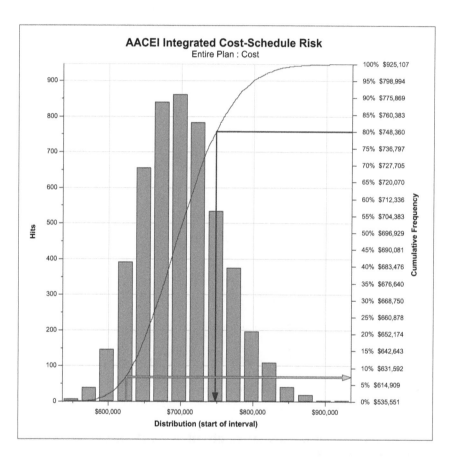

Figure 9.8   Histogram with cumulative distribution (S-curve) for the project cost

Table 9.5   Summary cost risk analysis results for the example construction project ($ millions)

						Spread
Deterministic	624	P-5	P-50	P-80	P-95	P95-P5
Cost at pecentiles		615	697	748	799	
Difference from deterministic cost $		−9	73	124	175	184
Difference from deterministic cost %		−1%	12%	20%	28%	

Source of Cost Risk: Is it from Cost or Schedule Risks?

Above we have seen standard results. However, while the cost risk results appear to be conventional, we know that the cost results are affected by the schedule risk and uncertainty as well as the cost risks and uncertainty. This additional content of the source of cost risk in the integrated analysis results occurs automatically when the resources are put into the schedule with their costs as previously shown.

One thing we can do is to see to what extent the schedule risks have affected the cost risk results. What is the contribution of the hard work we expended putting the resources into the schedule with their contingency-free costs and then simulating the resource-loaded schedule? We can find out whether cost-type risks or schedule-type risks are more important in determining the cost contingency to the P-80 point. The source of the cost contingency can be discovered by eliminating all schedule risks to compute the marginal impact of cost risks, then repeating the process by eliminating the cost risks and computing the impact of schedule risks on contingency. The results are shown below in Table 9.6.

Table 9.6   Sources of cost contingency reserve by risk type

	P-80	Marginal impact
	($ millions)	
Contingency-free cost estimate	624	
All risks	748	
Add only cost risks	673	49
Add only schedule risks	713	89
Total of two adds		138
Total contingency		124
Note: amounts do not add at P-80		

Table 9.6 shows that if only cost-type risks (burn rate risks and equipment cost risks) were added the contingency could be $49 million, whereas if only schedule risks were added (duration risk) the contingency would be $89 million. These results depend on the case study assumptions, but in many examples of integrated cost and schedule risk conducted on projects the majority of the risk to cost arises from uncertainty in the schedule rather than from cost-type risks such as uncertain equipment costs.

Notice also that the sum of the two "Adds" is $138 million, which is more than the total cost contingency reserve of ($748 − $624 = $124) $124 million. This is a case of "curves do not sum except at their means." When the mean values are considered, the sum of the two means is $75.6 million and the total contingency at the mean is $76.9 million, a very similar number.

Contribution of Cost and Schedule Risks to Overall Cost Risk

Comparing the contribution to the total contingency, Figure 9.9 shows the cumulative distributions for the curve with just the cost risks, the curve with just the schedule risks and the total risk curve with both cost and schedule risk are included. It indicates that any analysis of cost risk that does not take account of both cost-type and schedule-type influences on project risk is underestimating cost risk. This comparison shows the basis and the value of integrating cost and schedule risk.

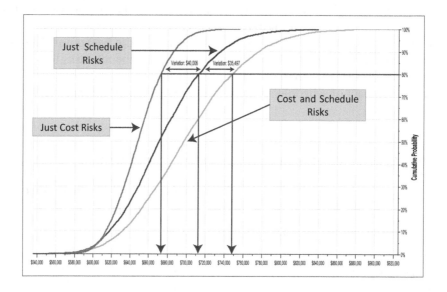

Figure 9.9 **The impact on the contingency reserve of schedule risks exceeds that of cost risks incorporating both sources of risk produces a full risk effect**

Summary

The purpose of integrating cost and schedule risk analysis is to capture the impact on cost risk of risks that are initially seen as affecting activity durations or otherwise delaying the project.[5] Historically most cost risk analyses were based on parametrics or on cost risks alone, with perhaps some nod toward the possible effects of uncertain schedules. In recent years we have seen that it is possible to integrate the two, schedule and cost risk analyses, to provide a more complete and consistent picture of project cost and schedule risk.

In the process of integrating cost and schedule risk we have captured the mechanism, direction and magnitude of influence of schedule uncertainty on cost uncertainty. The

---

5   Most risks are threats that cannot help the schedule or cost, or are mostly threats with the pessimistic results outweighing the optimistic results. This is not to rule out opportunities that can improve the schedule or cost estimate. It just recognizes reality that it is easier to delay the project, given the types of schedules we see, than to accelerate it. Experience tells us this is true (Flyvbjerg et al. 2002).

mechanism is through the impact of delays on the cost of time-dependent resources. The direction of influence is clearly from schedule to cost. The magnitude of the influence depends on both probability and impact of the schedule risk as well as the activity or activities that it affects. A few modern Monte Carlo simulation packages can model this relationship directly and accurately.

Including the impact of schedule risk on cost risk we achieve two main benefits:

- We produce a better, more accurate and complete cost risk analysis result.
- We can identify the main drivers of cost risk, many of which may be risks to schedule, which is described in Chapter 10.

In this chapter we applied the Risk Driver method to the integrated risk analysis of cost and schedule.

- Because this book emphasized cost risk analysis in the previous chapters we needed to introduce the project schedule, which will be our platform for the integrated analysis.
- We make the distinction between time-dependent and time-independent resources.
- We illustrate the process of assigning resources to the schedule activities, inserting the entire project budget in the project schedule. The resource-loaded schedule becomes our platform for cost risk analysis, and as an intermediate product the schedule risk analysis.
- A common question is whether to use detailed or summary schedules and resources. Summary schedules and resources are perfectly adequate and even preferred because:
  - a risk analysis is a strategic analysis;
  - we are interested in a best-practice schedule;
  - we are not using these resources for leveling.
- Identifying the important strategic risks is usually based on the risks prioritized using qualitative risk analysis methods and included in the Risk Register. Risk interviews often unearth additional risks, and some risks are dropped while others may be consolidated. Often even very large projects (for example, multi-billion dollar energy construction projects) can be risked with 20–40 risks.
- We have distinguished risks from uncertainties. "Risk" usually refers to risk events with probabilities of less than 100 percent, while "uncertainties" are often 100 percent likely but with impact uncertainty. Uncertainties can be handled with Risk Drivers or traditional 3-point estimates.
- Different methods of representing risk can be used together in the same risk analysis and Monte Carlo simulation:
  - Three-point estimates can represent estimating error for durations or costs.
  - Existence risks can represent a discontinuous event such as failing a qualifying test and the required recovery activities not usually in the schedule.
  - Risk Drivers that represent the uncertainty in the durations of activities that are already in the plan and schedule.

- Assigning risks to activities can lead to some risks impacting multiple activities and some activities being impacted by multiple risks, if they occur. This is how risks impact the project schedule and cost so we are modelling reality. The method has another benefit – a risk's total impact on the schedule and cost of a project can be isolated and measured even if it affects multiple activities. This characteristic will be important in developing risk mitigation actions, discussed in the next chapter.
- We have performed simulations of the schedule-based cost and schedule risk model and have achieved both schedule and cost results. Though the cost results appear to be like the other cost risk results in earlier chapters, these results have directly and clearly incorporated the influence of uncertain schedule on costs.
- We have seen that schedule risk can contribute significantly to cost risk, making the point that cost and schedule risk need to be analyzed together in an integrated way in order to estimate the complete risk to project cost.

In the next chapter results more specifically linked to the integration of cost and schedule risk are presented.

References

Flyvbjerg, B., Holm, M.S., and Buhl, Søren (2002). "Underestimating Costs in Public Works Projects, Error or Lie?" *Journal of the American Planning Association*, vol. 68, (No. 3).

Hillson, D. and Simon, P. (2007). *Practical Project Risk Management: The ATOM Methodology*. Vienna, VA, Management Concepts.

Hulett, D. (2009). *Practical Schedule Risk Analysis*. Farnham, England, Gower Publishing.

NASA PA&E (2009). Joint Confidence Level (JCL) FAQ.

PMI (2008). *A Guide to the Project Management Body of Knowledge*. Newtown Square, PA, Project Management Institute.

10 *Integrated Cost and Schedule Risk Analysis Advanced Results*

Introduction

The method of integrating cost and schedule risk analysis begins with first principles, the risks themselves, usually prioritized in the project's Risk Register. We have already introduced some schedule principles and showed how the schedule becomes the platform for the Monte Carlo simulation simultaneously not just of schedule but of cost as well. In Chapter 9 we showed that the standard histogram and cumulative distributions can be derived for both cost and schedule using this method. What is not obvious from looking at the results on cost risk is that those results integrate the impact of schedule risk on the cost of time-dependent resources and hence have an impact on cost risk from risks that are typically thought of as schedule risks. In other words, risks that can delay the project may also add to the cost contingency reserve needed.

This chapter looks at some of the more advanced results from integrated cost and schedule risk.

- The scatter diagram of finish dates and their corresponding cost and its interpretation.
- A special instance of that result is the Joint Confidence Level requirement used by the US National Aeronautics and Space Administration (NASA).
- Prioritizing the risks to schedule and to cost through the Monte Carlo simulation of the resource-loaded schedule leads to focused and effective risk mitigation. The cost of the mitigation actions and the benefits of reduced schedule to cost risk can be estimated by simulating the schedule before and after specifying the effects of the mitigation and comparing the differences in finish dates and cost, say at the 80th percentile.
- We present the concept of probabilistic cash flow wherein the risks may affect the cash outlay pattern during project execution.
- A special implication of the probabilistic cash flow is to compare the cash outflow to the planned outlay or to a limited budget, with the opportunity to calculate budget margins that are appropriate to the project risks. Oftentimes comparison of the probabilistic cash flow to the available budget leads to re-planning, usually involving stretching out activities into future fiscal years.

Integrated Cost and Schedule Risk Results

The construction project case study introduced in the last chapter is used to develop the time-cost scatter diagram shown below in Figure 10.1.

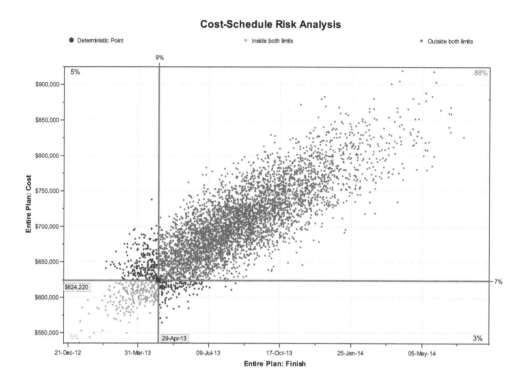

Figure 10.1 Cost and time results from the simulation with cross-hairs indicating the deterministic project plan without contingency

This scatter diagram shows finish dates along the horizontal axis and costs up the vertical axis. The scatter is made up of 3,000 points where each point represents the date and corresponding cost calculated in an internally consistent iteration of the resource-loaded summary schedule. Each point represents a possible date and the corresponding cost result that reflects the impact of the uncertain durations on the costs for our construction project. Though we cannot possibly tell which one ours will be we can make statistical statements about our project using this chart.

The scatter in Figure 10.1 is both centered and diffuse.

- The positive slope of the scatter represents an increase of about $553 thousand[1] in cost per day of delay (remember the project is estimated to cost $624,220 thousand

---

1   This calculation is made by taking the 3,000 pairs of cost and dates into Microsoft Excel and specifying a "Linest" function with a constraint. In other words, the slope does not represent the line's starting at the origin but at a positive dollar figure that fits the data.

without contingency). This positive slope indicates that the cost risks are related to the schedule risk, so the later the project finish the more it will cost.

- However, the scatter is also somewhat diffuse since, in addition to the direct cost risk implications of schedule risks there are some cost risks affecting the burn rate of labor-type resources and the total cost of procured items. Neither of these sources of project risk is related to schedule, causing a vertical dispersion for every possible completion date. The correlation of the two series, date and cost arranged in pairs corresponding to the 5,000 iterations performed, is 84 percent. This is quite high, indicating that the schedule risks are exerting a large influence on cost, which is borne out by the data in Table 9.6 of the last chapter.
- The cross-hairs shown on the diagram cross at the deterministic point of April 29, 2013 and $624.2 million. The sparse collection of points in the lower-left quadrant indicate that there is only a 5 percent chance that this project will satisfy both cost and schedule targets without contingency reserve of either project objective. There is also an 88 percent chance that this project will overrun both cost and time objectives, measured without contingency, if the current plan is followed. The cross-hairs can be re-positioned to indicate other specific joint date–cost success probabilities.

This date–cost scatter diagram indicates that the project should adopt both a cost and a schedule contingency reserve. Interestingly, while most cost estimates include a clear contingency reserve of cost most schedules do not contain a contingency reserve of time. We are seeing more schedules with contingency reserve activities at the end of the schedule just before the final milestone. Adding a schedule contingency activity at the end of the schedule is parallel in every way to the addition of a cost contingency "below the line" of a cost estimate. While we always see cost contingency reserves schedules seldom include an activity representing schedule contingency.

Joint Confidence Level used by NASA

NASA employs a concept of the joint cost and schedule confidence level[2] (NASA 2009). The Joint Confidence Level calculation provides:

- A date and cost for which the probability that the program's cost will be equal or less than the targeted cost AND its schedule will be equal or less then the targeted schedule date is 70 percent, or some other percent that is agreed with NASA management.
- A process and product that helps inform management the likelihood of a projects' programmatic success.
- A process that combines a projects' cost, schedule, and risk into a complete picture.

The joint cost and schedule confidence level is the probability that both cost and schedule will be satisfied on the project. NASA has recently adopted a requirement that their large programs, unless exempted, must establish budgets and schedules that provide a 70

---

2   The JCL policy is located in NPD 1000.5 under Section H3 with "Joint cost and schedule confidence levels are to be developed and maintained for the life cycle cost and schedule associated with the initial lifecycle baselines (for example, for space flight programs and projects baselines established at KDP-I or KDP-C)."

percent confidence level of achieving both cost and schedule. This means that 70 percent of the cost-date pairs in the scatter diagram will appear in the lower-left quadrant, as shown in Figure 10.2, which is similar to Figure 8.12 for a simpler project. The analysis to discover the appropriate time and cost contingency reserves, called the JCL analysis, is an integrated cost-schedule risk analysis as described in these chapters.

There are obviously many date-cost points that will satisfy the 70 percent criterion. Figure 10.2 shows the cross-hairs at one such point and traces generally the frontier of date-cost points through that point to others that also provide a 70 percent JCL.

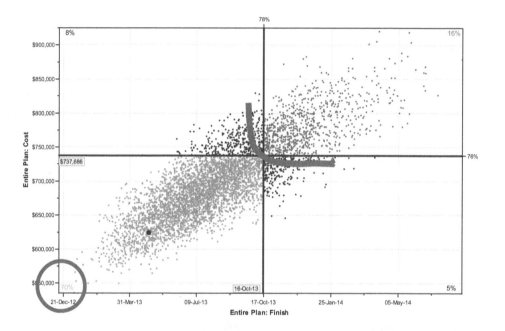

Figure 10.2 Scatter showing the 70 percent joint confidence limit (JCL) frontier

There is a temptation to look at a contour line on a chart such as the scatter plot in Figure 10.2 and say: "I want to choose an earlier date and will take on a little more cost to achieve that date. Thus, I can travel to the left and upward along the JCL contour." This is an incorrect interpretation of the JCL.

The best way to look at the scatter plot is to imagine it as a three-dimensional range of hills with the highest points ranging from lower-left to upper-right snaking through the densest part of the scatter. These high points on the 3-dimensional view of this scatter are the more likely results. It is more likely to have the cost-date combinations that are at the concentrations of date-cost points along the spine of the range of hills (peaks) than on the fringes (foothills) where the date-cost points are less concentrated. This interpretation relies on the essential truth of this display; each point is a probabilistic result, in this case each point has the probability of 1/5,000 of happening, since we performed 5,000 iterations and each point represents one of those iterations. It is more likely to end up where the concentrations of points are greatest than where those points are relatively few and far between.

There is no choice here – the results for the construction project will occur with a probability determined by the degree of concentrations of the date-cost points or iterations.

If the program manager wants to ensure a better (earlier) finish date he needs to change the plan to reduce the number of date-time pairs that are later than that date. To do this he needs to mitigate schedule risks, usually adding cost to the plan. If this happens, the cloud of scatter points resulting from the post-mitigation Monte Carlo simulation will migrate to the left and upwards and there should be fewer points (indicating lower probability of occurring) to the right of – or later than – the desired date. In other words, do the risk mitigation so the probability of the new plan has less chance of being later than the desired date and accept the cost consequences of those mitigation actions. The new JCL frontier will have shifted to the left and upward depending on how successful and costly the risk mitigations are determined to be.

Probabilistic Cash Flow

We can calculate the probabilistic cash flow because we have cost in the form of resources allocated to the activities. We have both cost and schedule risks represented in the schedule as well. The probabilistic cash flow helps organizations that want to plan their outlays by month or know the probability that they can work within annual budgets.

Figure 10.3 compares the P-80 cash flow to the plan's deterministic cash flow as shown in the risk-free schedule plan, both without contingency. The time-cost cloud or (American) "football" is the same as in Figures 10.1 and 10.2, but it is placed on a time-scale representing the entire execution period for the project and a cost scale with origins from the beginning of the project.

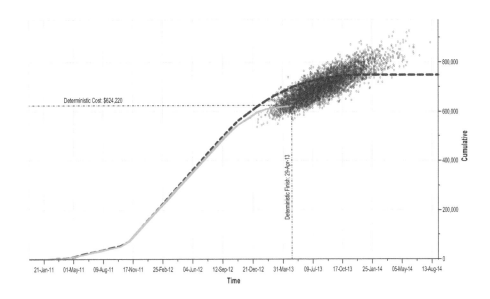

Figure 10.3 Probabilistic cash flow showing the P-80 cash flow by month compared to the plan's deterministic cash flow

Notice that the probabilistic cash flow may differ from the planned cash flow in the early months but, more dramatically, it often continues to increase for a longer time to higher costs while the planned outlays are declining toward completion and turnover. The P-80 line is higher than the planned expenditure line at the planned completion date, and then it continues rising until it hits the scatter of date-cost points. There is no specific point in that scatter that we can say will be the finish date and cost, but somewhere in the main concentration of points this project will finish. At that point this project will have exceeded both its budget and its schedule.

Adding Schedule and Cost Contingency to the Project Plan

Throughout this chapter it is assumed that the project stakeholders have chosen the 80th percentile as their acceptable threshold for cost and schedule (NASA has specified a 70th percentile for cost and schedule jointly). Taking cost and schedule individually, this threshold implies that there is an 80 percent likelihood that the cost will be $748.4 million or less (see Figure 9.8) and the project will finish on October 22, 2013 or earlier (see Figure 9.7). The chosen level may be different from the P-80, but it must be made explicitly by management.

It is recommended that these contingency reserves, needed to account for a desired margin of certainty for the risks that are accepted, be added to the project schedule and budget and that they be monitored during the project to determine if they are sufficient for the risks as the project execution progresses. Since the cost is in the schedule these two reserves can be put on the SCHEDULE-COST CONTINGENCY RESERVE activity with 176 days' duration and $124,140 thousand cost, as shown in Figure 10.4 below.

ID	Description	Remaining Duration	Start	Finish	Total Cost	2011	2012	2013	2014
0010	Project Start	0	'01-Jan-11		$0	01-Jan-11			
0015	Approval Process	90	01-Jan-11	31-Mar-11	$2,070				
0017	Project Sanction	0		31-Mar-11	$0	31-Mar-11			
0018	Construction Permits	180	01-Apr-11	27-Sep-11	$5,400				
0020	Design	200	01-Apr-11	17-Oct-11	$46,000				
0030	Procurement of Equipment	360	18-Oct-11	11-Oct-12	$210,800				
0070	Install Equipment	90	12-Oct-12	09-Jan-13	$7,650				
0040	Construction of the Facility	460	18-Oct-11	19-Jan-13	$335,800				
0050	Commissioning	100	20-Jan-13	29-Apr-13	$16,500				
0420	SCHEDULE-COST CONTINGENCY RESERVE	176	30-Apr-13	22-Oct-13	$124,140				
0060	Project Turnover	0		22-Oct-13	$0				22-Oct-13

Figure 10.4 Schedule-cost contingency activity is added

Will We Stay Within Our Budget?

Perhaps more important than the overall program cost result is whether the program will overrun its budget in the next fiscal year. Usually the program plan is arranged so that there is not much margin between projected expenses and the available budget. However, this plan does not account sufficiently for cost and schedule risk.

Often, when the risk is taken into account there is some likelihood that the current plan will overrun the budget, and may overrun by enough to require re-planning, scope-cutting or plan-stretching.

The probabilistic cash flow may be different from the planned cash flow during most of the planned execution period. This does not mean that the probabilistic cash flow or the planned cash flow agree with any imposed budget, nor does it mean that there is sufficient margin to buffer the cost against project risk. And, what would happen if the owner or Congress cut the funding below what was expected when the plans were made? Even if the plan had sufficient margin to accommodate the risks with the original budget, reducing the budget will usually eliminate more than the margin – it often cuts into the meat of the project and leads to re-planning of the project.

A simple case study will be used to illustrate how the probabilistic cash flow can be compared both to the planned outflow and to an imposed budget. In this example we will use the P-70 level of confidence that was relevant to the NASA audience of the referenced presentation (Hulett and Neatrour 2010). After assessing the plan and the P-70 probabilistic cash flow the project management and owner/customer may get together and:

- re-plan the project to stretch out the expenditures, meeting the reduced budget on an annual basis with the same scope but extending the period of performance
- increase the budget to coincide with, or provide a margin over, the probabilistic outlay
- reduce the scope, or
- a combination of the strategies.

Of course there is a fourth strategy, not likely to succeed – that is, to insist that the project meet its budget and schedule in the face of evidence to the contrary.

Using the simple schedule shown below in Figure 10.5 and the resources shown in Figure 10.6 we compute the probabilistic cash flow shown in Figure 10.7.

ID	Description	Remaining Duration	Start	Finish
000001	Project Start	0	'01 Jan 11	
000002	Hardware	425	01 Jan 11	29 Feb 12
000003	Design Hardware	75	01 Jan 11	16 Mar 11
000004	Build Hardware	275	17 Mar 11	16 Dec 11
000005	Test Hardware	75	17 Dec 11	29 Feb 12
000006	Software	415	01 Jan 11	19 Feb 12
000007	Design Software	65	01 Jan 11	06 Mar 11
000008	Code Software	300	07 Mar 11	31 Dec 11
000009	Test Software	50	01 Jan 12	19 Feb 12
000010	Integrate and Test	150	01 Mar 12	28 Jul 12
000011	Integrate HW and SW	100	01 Mar 12	08 Jun 12
000012	Test System	50	09 Jun 12	28 Jul 12
000013	Project Finish	0		28 Jul 12

Figure 10.5 Simple hardware- software-integration and test project

ID	Description	Remaining Cost	Resource Loading
000001	Project Start	$0	
000002	**Hardware**	**$19,020,000**	
000003	Design Hardware	$1,920,000	HW DESIGNERS[Normal]
000004	Build Hardware	$15,400,000	HW BUILDERS[Normal]
000005	Test Hardware	$1,700,000	HW TESTERS[Normal];TEST HARDWARD[Spread]
000006	**Software**	**$10,816,000**	
000007	Design Software	$1,456,000	SW DESIGNERS[Normal]
000008	Code Software	$7,560,000	SW CODERS[Normal]
000009	Test Software	$1,800,000	SW TESTERS[Normal];SOFTWARE TEST LAB[Spread]
000010	**Integrate and Test**	**$4,400,000**	
000011	Integrate HW and SW	$3,200,000	INTEGRATORS[Normal]
000012	Test System	$1,200,000	SYSTEM TESTERS[Normal]
000013	Project Finish	$0	
TOTALS		**$34,236,000**	

Figure 10.6 Resources loaded and costs by activity

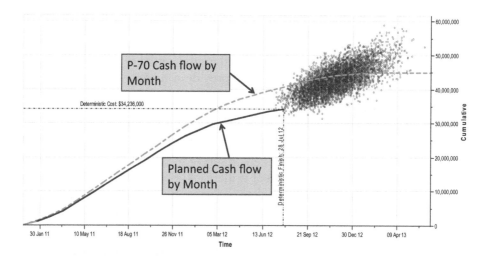

Figure 10.7 Cumulative probabilistic cash flow compared to the planned cash flow

The resources are loaded and produce the costs shown in Figure 10.6.

The simulation leads to the probabilistic cash flow with the P-70 cash flow compared to the planned cash flow shown in Figure 10.7 below. (Notice that, unlike the P-80 values shown in Figure 10.3 above, the values in Figure 10.7 show a probabilistic P-70 cumulative outlay indicating that some organizations prefer a degree of confidence different from the P-80.) The P-70 estimate for this plan exceeds the planned outlays at almost every point on the graph. This is not an uncommon result that depends on the risks assigned, their probability, impact and assignment to activities. The correlation between the finish dates and costs is 69 percent.

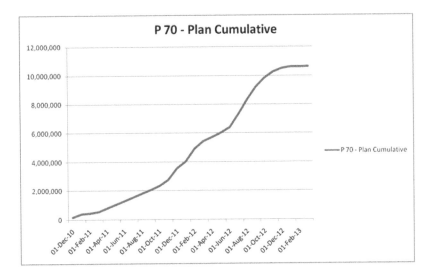

Figure 10.8 Difference between the probabilistic cash flow at P-70 and the planned cash flow

Comparing the probabilistic cash flow at the P-70 value with the planned cash flow for each month yields the curve plotted in Figure 10.8.

Suppose that the project is faced with a budget that is allocated at a fixed rate during the execution of the project. Suppose also that the budget has been set so that a 10 percent margin over the risk-free estimate without contingency for the total project. This is shown in Figure 10.9 below.

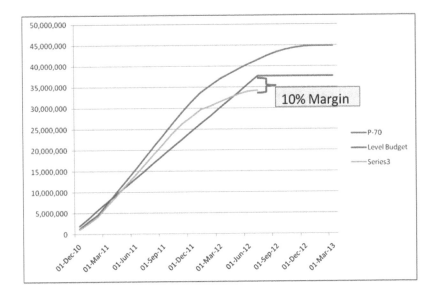

Figure 10.9 Compare the level budget including a 10 percent margin to the plan and to the P-70 probabilistic cash flow

Notice that even the planned cash flow exceeds the planned level monthly release of funds. However, the overall finish-of-project cumulative availability of funds seems to be sufficient before risk is taken into account. The overspending that is actually planned is not too large and does not occur during too many months. At least it looks that way before risk is considered.

The P-70 risked cash flow presents a different and more disturbing picture. The over-budget spending is significantly greater than even the funds provided by the 10 percent margin. These two different pictures of the cash flow prospects of the project – one without considering risk and the other considering both cost and schedule risk – compared to the level budget available to the project are shown in Figure 10.10.

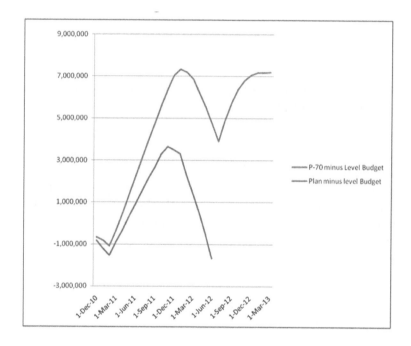

Figure 10.10   Risked cash flow at P-70 exceeds the level budget by much more and for more months than the planned cash flow

Figure 10.10 shows that the project needs to re-plan in each fiscal year because the risks place the cash flow significantly above the level budget for most months of the project's execution. This result should lead to the project manager's re-planning with the team leads so that the cash flow including risk is more in line with, actually conforms to, the funds that will be made available.

This result occurred without reducing the program budget, but many programs face reduced budgets after they have established their plan. Even if the margins were acceptable before the budget reduction, they may experience the problems shown here after action by Congress or management to limit their budget.

Of course this analysis can be applied if the budget is not level, conforming the budget line in Figure 10.8 to whatever the projected budget is in total and in monthly increments.

Prioritized Risks to Cost and Risk Mitigation

Often the risk results for schedule and for cost imply cost and schedule results that are not acceptable to the project manager and the owner/stakeholders. The PM and other stakeholders do not want to give up their dates and budget, since they have promised to others that they will finish on a date and at a cost. About these promises:

- On the one hand, the cost they have promised to others would include contingency since estimating a cost contingency is mandatory, so the cost risk result from the simulation may not be extremely off from plan.
- On the other hand, often the scheduled completion date they have promised does not include a time contingency, since time contingency is rare, so the entire risk analysis result may come as a rude surprise.

There is a misimpression about the risk analysis results. They are not foregone conclusions. Rather, the risk analysis shows what may happen if the project stays with its current plan in the presence of the risks that have been identified, quantified and applied to the resource-loaded schedule. These results are frequently an unpleasant surprise to the organization, but the project manager and project team do not have to accept those results as what will happen, only what might happen unless they mitigate the risks.

The risk analysis results do not need to become a *fait accompli* for the project. Instead, the risk analysis model and data along with the analysis using Monte Carlo and Risk Drivers can become a tool for improvement of the project plan. In order to improve the project's prospects through risk mitigation the risk analysis needs to provide the project management team with prioritized risks to serve as a guide.

Prioritizing Risks to Cost

The analyst can prioritize the risks for the project manager who will want to mitigate the highest-priority risks first. Taking a P-70 threshold for acceptable cost risk this is done by:

- taking each risk out of the project one at a time
- running the Monte Carlo simulation
- computing the impact on cost at the P-70 risk threshold
- replacing the risk before taking out the next risk for analysis
- for each risk, comparing the P-70 simulation result to the results at the P-70 with all-risks-in results, replacing the risk and repeating the process one risk at a time.

Table 10.1 below shows the risks that were applied to the resource-loaded schedule shown in Figures 10.5 and 10.6 in this section. Notice once again that these are just examples of typical risks and are intended to stand in for the real risks to the project that would be discovered during the risk workshop called to develop the Risk Register or during the risk interviews.

Table 10.1 Typical Risk Drivers applied to the resource-loaded schedule

	Schedule risk impacts			Cost risk impacts			Probability
	Minimum	Most likely	Maximum	Minimum	Most likely	Maximum	
Design risk	90%	105%	120%	90%	110%	130%	60%
HW build risk	85%	110%	125%	85%	105%	115%	50%
Software coding risk	95%	115%	135%	90%	105%	120%	90%
HW test risk	90%	105%	115%	90%	105%	120%	80%
SW test risk	90%	115%	135%	90%	100%	115%	80%
Integration risk	85%	100%	140%	90%	105%	120%	80%
System test risk	85%	110%	145%	90%	110%	125%	90%
Schedule duration estimating error	95%	105%	130%				100%
Cost estimating error				90%	105%	119%	100%

These risks are assigned to the schedule as shown in the column labeled "Risk Factors" in Figure 10.11 below.

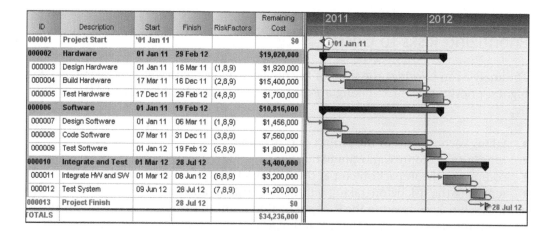

Figure 10.11 Schedule showing the assignment of risks to the activities

Using the procedure described above, taking each risk out by replacing its probability with a value of zero (0.0) and re-running the simulation, the marginal impact of each of the risks is calculated and shown in Table 10.2 below.

Table 10.2   Highest priority risks to project cost at the P-70 level of confidence

Risk ID	Risks	Contribution to the P-70 contingency
		($ thousands)
8	Schedule estimating error	4,350
9	Cost estimating error	2,549
3	Software coding risk	1,928
2	Hardware building risk	1,080
6	Integration risk	607
1	Design risk	577
7	System testing risk	445
4	Hardware testing risk	284
5	Software testing risk	271

Of all the risks to cost the most important is risk No. 8, Schedule Estimating Error, which is actually an uncertainty representing schedule estimating uncertainty. This implies that $4.35 million of the cost contingency reserve is being held as a provision against schedule risk. Since a schedule estimating error is most important it might be good to discover the main schedule risks.

Prioritizing Risks to Schedule

Finding the most important schedule risks is somewhat more difficult than finding the most important cost risks. The extra difficulty comes from the fact that schedules have predecessor-successor logic. For costs, if a cost risk is mitigated the project cost is reduced. However, if one risk is very important but on a schedule path that is not the most risk-critical, no amount of risk mitigation on that risk will shorten the schedule. That is because a different path is parallel and risk-critical.[3]

The most critical schedule risk will be on the risk-critical path, because mitigating it will actually reduce the possible schedule overrun, at least until reducing its duration causes a different path to be risk-critical. Finding the risk that will cause the greatest improvement in the project schedule can be a tedious procedure since there is no foolproof method (such as the risk tornado diagram) to determine which is the most

---

3   "Risk critical" means that, with risks considered, that path will usually be longer than parallel paths and it will generally determine the schedule's finish date.

important risk. The procedure needed to find the most important risk requires examining the marginal impact of several candidate risks one at a time and selecting the one that, when it is deleted from the risk list, makes the biggest impact on the results, say at the P-70 level.

Once the most important risk on the risk-critical path is mitigated it may uncover an important risk on a different path that was not risk-critical in the presence of the most critical schedule risk. Then, when the second risk is mitigated, an important risk on a different path, or on the mitigated risk-critical path, may be the next most important risk. The steps to prioritizing the schedule risks are:

- Identify the risk that will cause the greatest improvement in the project completion date when it is taken out of the risk list. One way to do this might be to look at the risk factors tornado diagram in Primavera Risk Analysis (this is the software that we are using here). However, the tornado diagram is not an infallible guide to identify the most important risk.
- The steps are:
  - Take each of the most likely candidate risks out one at a time by changing their probability to zero and re-running the Monte Carlo simulation.
  - When one risk is neutralized and the simulation is re-run, write down the P-70 (or a different certainty level, whatever level is chosen by the project).
  - Replace the first risk's original probability level and select another likely candidate to test for its importance. Set that risk's probability to zero, run the simulation again and record the P-70 date.
  - The risk that when it is neutralized results in the earliest date can reasonably be identified as the most important schedule risk.
- Once that risk is excluded, leave its probability at zero. Then check the risk factor's tornado again to identify the next most likely candidates. You may have to zero-out several risks one at a time to assure yourself that you have identified the next most important risk.
- Repeat the process of taking risks out and leaving them out in order of most impact to the finish date at the target certainty level. Ultimately there will be enough risks removed that the P-70 schedule date equals the schedule date without risk, or is very close to it.

We have followed that procedure on the simple schedule used in this section. The prioritized risks are shown in Table 10.3.

Table 10.3 Risks to project schedule prioritized for their impact at the P-70 level of confidence[4]

Risk ID	Risks removed in order of impact on the P-70 date	P-70 Date	Days saved at the P-70
	All risks in – no mitigation	21 – Dec – 12	
8	Schedule estimating error	6 – Oct – 12	76
3	Software coding risk	3 – Sep – 12	33
2	Hardware building risk	20 – Aug – 12	14
6	Integration risk	12 – Aug – 12	8
7	System testing risk	4 – Aug – 12	8
1	Design risk	1 – Aug – 12	3
4	Hardware testing risk	28 – Jul – 12	4
	Schedule date – no risks	28 – Jul – 12	

Notice that the most important schedule risk is schedule estimating error, which accounts for 76 calendar days to the P-70 level. The schedule estimating error uncertainty has a probability of 100 percent and a range of multiplicative factors of 95 percent – 105 percent – 130 percent and is applied to each activity in the schedule. This is also the main risk to cost, as shown in Table 10.2, because of the time-dependent resources that are affected by the uncertain durations in the schedule. A picture of the way the P-70 improves as we take these risks out in turn is shown in Figure 10.12.

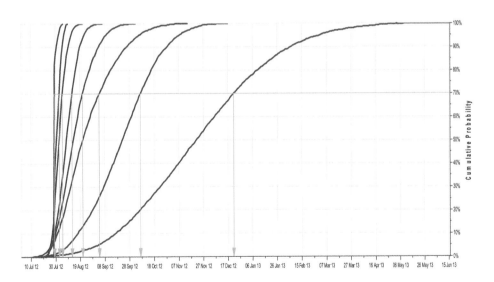

Figure 10.12 Comparison of distributions as risks are removed in priority order

---

4   Notice that removing Risk 4, hardware testing risk, subtracts 4 days while removing Risk 1, design risk, subtracts only 3 days. An inversion of the days' saved values often happens. Risk 4 saves less than 3 days unless Risk 1 has already been removed. However, after removing Risk 1, Risk 4 will save 4 days.

Prioritizing the risks by computing their marginal impact from simulation of the resource-loaded schedule is much more accurate and useful than the prioritizing that goes on through the qualitative development of the Risk Register. This improvement is accomplished by:

- quantifying the risks' parameters
- assigning them to the schedule's resource-loaded activities
- assessing their impact on cost and schedule by simulating the schedule model, and
- comparing the risks at the P-70 (or whatever level of certainty the customer desires).

Quantifying the risks and analyzing their impact using modern Monte Carlo techniques adds to our understanding, provides a measure of credibility for the results and is more understandable by management.

Mitigating Project Risks

If the project manager wants to control project costs the first thing to work on is the risk that shows the highest marginal impact, Risk 8, schedule estimating error. What mitigation action could be taken on this risk? It might be possible to increase the maturity of the data on which the schedule estimates are made. For instance, after letting the contract an early delivery is the contractor's schedule that provides information valuable to schedule estimating. We can also gather delivery proposals from prospective suppliers and put long lead procurement items under contract. This type of information always improves the accuracy of the schedule and should be used as well in improving the accuracy of the cost estimates. Another suggestion is to add planners/schedulers who can improve these estimates. There may be other ways to improve the estimate of schedule durations, such as improving the estimating methodology, with those newly hired planners/schedulers, by linking more closely the resources, productivity and duration estimates.

Suppose each of these actions were to be pursued. What do those risk mitigations cost? Suppose it is $4 million. Would it be worth doing? The answer to that question depends on the improvement in the parameters of the risk. Table 10.4 shows the current parameters of the schedule estimating error risk along with the assessment of the improvement in those parameters that $4 million of mitigation actions could bring.

There is one consideration with this particular risk, which is actually a 100 percent likely uncertainty (estimating error exists, almost by definition, but with uncertain impact). Until project turnover there will always be schedule uncertainty so the uncertainty's likelihood will be always 100 percent. Hence, the improvement in the project cost and date at the P-70 can only come from a narrowing of the impact ranges. Suppose that with the application of $4 million we believe that we can improve the quality of the estimate from its current range of 95 percent-105 percent-130 percent to a narrower range of 95 percent-100 percent-110 percent, making it a better class ("definitive") of schedule estimate. The results for this particular schedule are shown below in Table 10.4.

Table 10.4   Effect of mitigating the schedule estimating error uncertainty

Risk	Description	Minimum	Most likely	Maximum	Likelihood	Schedule P-70	Cost P-70
	Before mitigation						(millions)
8	Schedule estimating error	95%	105%	130%	100%	21 – Dec – 12	45,010
	After mitigation						
8	Schedule estimating error	95%	100%	110%	100%	19 – Oct – 12	42,383

Notice that the reduction of the Scheduling Estimating Error uncertainty improves the schedule by 2 months. In doing so, it reduces the contingency that would be needed by over $2.6 million because some of the contingency reserve of cost is intended to provide for schedule risk. Notice that the improvement of $2.6 million from partially mitigating this risk is less than the $4.4 million, which is shown in Table 10.2, for taking that risk out completely. The estimate of $2.6 million saved is more realistic, since it is not practical to imagine fully mitigating any risk.

The typical risk mitigation exercise starts after the risks are prioritized. It includes the project manager and key team leaders as well as the risk analyst. There may be some off-line analyses, illustrated by an experience where the drilling program was completely revised to save time. At the end there will be a number of risk mitigation steps that have been analyzed using the risked resource-loaded schedule. The result of the analysis of risk mitigation shows clearly:

- what the cost and date results would be if the current plan is followed, with the risks as are known at the time
- which risk mitigation steps are being recommended (some the project manager can accomplish on his own but some may require involvement of corporate management) and what they might cost
- the cost and date results that would result if these risk mitigation steps are taken.

In this way the initial risk analysis results are seen correctly as intermediate steps between where we are with the risks as they stand today and where we are going. It also provides the mechanism to move from pre-mitigation results to post-mitigation results. Management can relate to this analysis and appreciates its clarity and quantification.

Summary of Integrating Cost and Schedule Risk Analysis

The last chapter and this one illustrate that integrating cost and schedule risk into one analysis based on the project schedule loaded with resources from the cost estimate:

- provides a more accurate cost estimates than if the schedule risk were ignored or incorporated indirectly

- illustrates the important contribution of schedule risks to cost risk and the need for cost contingency reserves when the durations of activities using labor-type or time-dependent resources are risky.

Many activities such as detailed engineering, construction, software development, drilling and installation offshore, fabrication of equipment, and commissioning the final product for use are mainly conducted by people and rented equipment that need to be paid even if their work takes longer than scheduled. Level-of-effort resources, such as the project management team, are extreme examples of time-dependent resources, since they clearly work longer if the project duration exceeds its planned duration.

The integrated cost-schedule risk analysis is based on:

- A best-practice CPM schedule with logic complete enough so that it will provide the correct dates and critical paths when the durations vary during simulation. A linked, end-to-end integrated summary schedule with complete logic and that represents all of the work is recommended. A detailed schedule is acceptable but it causes more difficulty in debugging and in allocating resources to activities.
- A contingency-free estimate of project costs expressed as resources that are allocated to the schedule's activities. Below-the-line contingency and padding/contingency embedded in the line item estimates are to be eliminated before the analysis, since the cost contingency that we need to add to most-likely cost estimates will be one of the results of the analysis. Summary-level resources are recommended that include the entire project budget.
- Placing resources and the costs into the schedule, resolving inconsistencies between the cost estimate and the schedule. The inconsistencies are often revealed by the implied but improbable daily rates of expenditure.
- Good-quality risk data that are usually collected in risk workshops or interviews involving the project team, management and others knowledgeable in the risk of the project. The risks from the Risk Register are used as the basis of the risk data as an expression of the basic principle that risks and uncertainties cause overall project cost and schedule risk. The Risk Driver method is used for this analysis. Parameters for these risks include their probability of occurring, the impact range expressed as multiplicative factors if they do occur, and the schedule activities and resources they impact.
- The Risk Drivers method models how risks affect the activities that are in the schedule. It can be combined with the Risk Register/risk existence/probabilistic branching that will add activities not in the schedule with some probability and impact. Finally, 3-point estimates can also be used on durations and resources to represent uncertainties like the 100 percent likely estimating error for duration or cost.
- A Monte Carlo simulation software program that can simulate schedule risk, burn-rate risk and time-independent resource risk. During the simulation the time-dependent or labor-type resources will cost more if the schedule is longer and if the burn rate is uncertain. Also, equipment and materials may cost more or less but these variations are not generally thought to be because of schedule uncertainty.

The results include the standard histograms and cumulative distributions of possible cost and time results for the project. However, by simulating both cost and time simultaneously we can collect the cost-date pairs of results and hence show the scatter diagram ("football chart") that indicates the joint probability of finishing on time and on budget. This scatter is either diffuse if there are many time-independent risks such as risk on equipment and material procurement and on daily burn rates, or they can be tight if most of the cost risks are caused by variation of duration on activities with time-dependent resources. A particular use of the scatter diagram is made by the US NASA, which instructs programs to calculate the Joint Confidence Level and to schedule and budget, so the probability of achieving both time and cost is 70 percent.

It is recommended that the contingency reserves of cost and of time, calculated at a level that represents an acceptable degree of certainty and uncertainty for the project stakeholders, be added to the project cost estimate and to the project schedule for strategic planning purposes. Adding contingency amounts to the cost estimate is a standard procedure, but adding a contingency to the schedule is not as common and is often resisted. One way to add contingency would be to add a schedule-cost contingency activity to the end of the schedule where it belongs, and give it the duration and cost that are calculated by the analysis.

We showed that this analysis can produce results needed to assess whether the project will overrun its budget. This analysis uses the probabilistic cash flow and overlays the project budget on it. We have used a linear budget for simplicity, and the project cost on a monthly basis may have an expected spending curve that follows the hills and valleys of resource mobilization and equipment or material procurement costs. If the risked or probabilistic cash flow exceeds the budget in any month or cumulatively the project team may need to re-plan, probably shifting activities into the next fiscal year, reducing scope or asking for more money.

Finally, if the cost and schedule estimates including contingency reserves derived from the Monte Carlo analysis are not acceptable to the project stakeholders, the project team should conduct risk mitigation workshops and studies, decide which risk mitigation actions to take, and re-run the Monte Carlo simulation to determine the possible improvement to the project's objectives. The list of priority cost and schedule risks will assist in making this risk mitigation exercise more efficient.

The result of the risk mitigation exercise is to create a better project plan. It also shows management that the entire exercise was not just for the purpose of giving a report card to the project. Rather it provides the project with a valuable tool for further optimizing and managing the project. This is the main objective of the integrated cost and schedule risk analysis.

References

Hulett, D. and Neatrour, J. (2010). "Will We Overrun Our Budget?" presented to the NASA Cost Symposium, Kansas City, MO.

NASA (2009). Joint Confidence Level (JCL) FAQ, NASA HQ-PA&E (URL: http://www.nasa.gov/pdf/394931main_JCL_FAQ_10_12_09.pdf).

11 *Summary of Integrated Cost and Schedule Risk Analysis*

Introduction

The most important concept introduced in this book is the integration of cost and schedule risk. There is no substitute for the direct application of schedule risk to cost risk, and there is no excuse for not realizing that many risks to cost arise from those risks that cause schedule uncertainty. Compared to traditional approaches to analysis of cost risk, we get a more accurate estimate of cost risk and of the risks that cause it by starting with the resource-loaded project schedule.

The second important concept contained herein is the Risk Driver method of conducting risk analysis.[1] Using the Risk Register's high-priority risks as the drivers of project cost and schedule risk represents getting back to basic principles, namely by driving overall cost and schedule risk by the risks that cause the uncertainty in schedule activities and cost estimates. It is a significant improvement over the more traditional use of the 3-point estimate on durations and costs which focuses on the impact of the risks on duration and cost.

Key success factors for performing effective cost-schedule risk analysis include close cooperation and communication between the cost estimators and the schedulers on a project. Often the estimating and scheduling functions are performed by people who do not know much about each other's function. When things happen on the scheduling side, as they do regularly during schedule updates, the cost estimators are not often involved or even informed. Cross-training and integration of these functions organizationally is important for the success of the integrated cost-schedule risk analysis exercise.

The appropriate applicability of integrated cost-schedule risk analysis to projects is specific to the organization. While quantitative risk analysis is not difficult, it must be undertaken with a healthy regard for the expertise, time and resources that are needed. This analysis properly done will provide important information at key decision points for projects that are large or risky, that expose the stakeholders to damage to their organization, and of course when required by the contract between performer and owner.

---

1   The Risk Driver concept is discussed in Hulett, D. *Practical Schedule Risk Analysis* (2009 Gower) in Chapter 6.

Integration of Cost and Schedule Risk Analysis

"Time is money," said the businessman. If this is so, then "time risk is money risk" and it is unwise to ignore the impact of uncertainty about how long activities will take on the cost of the project. The objective of holding cost contingency reserves is to provide for the uncertainty of how much money will be needed to complete the scope of work. An increase in the duration of some activity, say because of low labor productivity, will cause that activity to cost more than was originally expected if the resources are paid by the hour, day or some other work period.[2]

The project schedule is the correct platform for the integrated analysis of cost and schedule risk. For an effective analysis the analyst might consider constructing a summary schedule of 300–1,000 activities rather than using the larger detailed project schedule. A summary schedule is useful in part because it is feasible to debug a summary schedule whereas the problems with a detailed schedule with many thousands of activities are too daunting to be resolved for a risk analysis. Also, a risk analysis is a strategic analysis rather than a daily assignment and progress-reporting analysis. A summary schedule that is integrated by proper scheduling logic and includes all the activities at a summary level of detail is a viable instrument. It is important for the accuracy and credibility of the analysis that a summary schedule be reviewed by the project scheduler and others of the project teams to ensure that it is a fair summary representation of the project.

The schedule needs to be resource-loaded to allow the effects of schedule fluctuations to be transmitted to the cost. The resource loading allocates the entire budget (expressed as most likely costs without additional padding for risk) to the appropriate schedule activities in the schedule. This can be accomplished by the use of summary resources unless we want to level resources, perhaps because of our uncertainty in their adequacy, in this schedule. Usually 8 to 10 summary resources (for example, at the general level of "commissioning," "detailed engineering," "construction," "procurement," and so on) can be used to allocate the entire budget to the activities. If the cost estimate is available at a more-summary level than the schedule activities, hammocks, level-of-effort or summary tasks can be used to take the resource assignments. Resources need to be distinguished by time-dependent (those resources that will cost more if the activity takes longer) and time-independent (those resources that may be uncertain but not because of uncertain time) for the Monte Carlo simulation of both cost and time simultaneously to record all of the influences on cost risk correctly.

A cost contingency must be estimated and identified whenever the cost estimate is presented to management. Since the costs are assigned to the activities without any padding to account for risk, the Monte Carlo simulation will estimate the risk and allow the selection of the proper contingency reserve of both time and cost.

This contingency reserve provided for time and cost can be represented as a cost-loaded activity at the end of the project schedule, adding the appropriate cost and duration to the plan. It is not appropriate to spread the cost or time contingency reserves to the project's activities because the amount of contingency will not be correct for any activity.

---

2   Even if the contract specifies a "fixed price" contract, there will be circumstances leading to schedule delays that may be "compensable" so the contractor will get more than originally budgeted.

- If the risks do not occur or have less than the anticipated effect the cost and time contingency allocated will be too large, but the activity managers may use it anyway.
- If the risks occur or have more effect than anticipated the contingency of time and cost will be too small and management will need to allocate more than was spread.

The best way to understand the contingency reserve is that it is the net effect of all of the risks that may or may not occur on the project, and only at the end of the project or below the line can we accumulate and account for all of the risks in one place.

Part of that cost contingency will be held against the very real possibility that activities may take longer than planned in the baseline schedule and, hence, in the cost basis of estimate (BOE). If those activities require, or are supported by resources that cost more if they are employed longer, the "time-dependent" resources, schedule uncertainty will lead to cost contingency. Experience shows that a significant amount of cost risk, sometimes the majority of cost risk, occurs as the result of schedule risk.

There are clearly many factors other than schedule uncertainty, such as the market price of bulk materials or the cost of manufactured equipment that will affect cost, and these factors also contribute to the need to hold reserves. Finally, even if the project holds to its schedule, the cost of time-dependent resources may be uncertain due to factors that make their burn rate – cost per unit of working time – uncertain. The uncertainties that cause the burn rate to be uncertain are classified as cost-type risks that affect cost directly rather than indirectly through their impact on schedule because they affect cost even if the schedule is not uncertain. Once the resources are assigned to schedule activities the cost-loaded schedule is simulated using the Monte Carlo technique. Normal work activities' durations will change during the simulation ans will durations of level of effort (LOE) activities, which are assigned resources such as the project management team that are time-dependent. Monte Carlo simulation is best practice for cost and schedule risk analysis.

During simulation the software will collect data on both cost and schedule including cost-and-finish date pairs representing the thousands of possible projects (represented by individual iterations in the simulation). Standard histograms and cumulative distributions for schedule risk and for cost risk are produced. Some of the simulation programs will produce scatter diagrams of finish date and cost pairs to show the likelihood of completing both on time and on budget, and to show the correlation between time and cost. Some of the programs will also calculate and show the probabilistic cash flow so the project can see whether it is complying with its budget as the project progresses. If the risked costs exceed the project budget, or if the project budget is subsequently cut below the margin provided for risk, the plan should be modified, maybe by stretching out or delaying some activities or by reducing scope. The risk analysis can show the magnitude of the discrepancy between monthly or cumulative costs and the budget by taking account of the effect of risk on the outflow over time.

The results of the risk analysis combined with the organization's desire for cost and finish-date certainty will be used to choose the amount of contingency reserve of time and of cost from the time and cost histograms. These results are appropriate for the project plan and the identification and quantification of the risks to that plan. They do not anticipate changes that the project manager may make to the plan. The contingency reserves can be added to the end of the schedule and below-the-line of the cost estimate.

Contingency reserves should be included in the organization's promises for delivery to the final customer or bids if it is a contractor. Nobody believes that the projects are risk-free and it would be unwise to act as if there were no risks to time or cost by believing the results of the static project plan.

Traditional 3-point Estimates of Impact

To understand the benefits of the Risk Driver method of assigning risks to activities, we first introduced the traditional method using 3-point estimates for the activity durations. Traditionally the uncertainty of project schedule durations and cost elements has been represented by 3-point estimates applied to durations or cost estimates to represent the uncertainty of those values. For schedule these three duration estimates were the optimistic remaining duration, the most likely remaining duration and the pessimistic remaining duration since schedules include actual progress which is beyond risk. For costs the 3-points were the comparable optimistic, most likely and pessimistic values for the cost element.

There are several problems with the 3-point estimate approach to representing risk:

- Once the 3-point estimates are installed there is no one-for-one equivalence to an identified risk or risks that may determine these values, particularly if more than one risk affects the duration or cost. The risk interviewee or workshop participant needs to do some pretty complex calculation before deciding on the three uncertainty values to determine how those risks will determine the impact ranges.
- This traditional approach has been criticized for focusing on the impact of the risks rather than the risks themselves. Focusing on the impact of risks on activity durations and project element costs clouds the underlying forces that are causing the uncertainty in time and cost, namely the identified risks. Usually the risks can be found prioritized in the Risk Register.
- The 3-point estimate has no way to represent the probability of the risk's not occurring. The three points just record uncertain impact on the duration or cost. Suppose a risk is not 100 percent likely to occur. Then there would be some fraction of the iterations when it would have no influence on the activity or cost and the base estimate stands. With the 3-point estimate that addresses uncertainty in the duration or cost directly any adjustment of the impact that should be made for a risk that has a low probability of occurring has to be done off-line and in one's head, pre-processing the risk data during the risk data gathering process. Experience shows that the probability of a risk's occurring is generally not considered as risk data are gathered.
- An activity or cost element may be influenced by several different risks so it is important to identify the risks and uncertainties and sort out their influences since we mitigate risk but we cannot mitigate an activity or a cost element.
- A risk or uncertainty may affect several activities or cost elements but collecting data for the 3-point estimate of duration or cost is accomplished one activity or cost element at a time. In the traditional 3-point estimate approach the full impact of the risk will be lost because the impacts on duration or cost that a risk may cause on several project elements are not linked or associated with each other. There is no way to sort out the full impact of a risk or uncertainty that affects multiple activities

or cost elements. If a risk affects more than one activity or cost its full effect will be underestimated when the 3-point estimates are assigned one activity or cost at a time.

- It is known that correlation between activity durations and costs exists in most projects. Using the method of applying 3-point estimates directly to those durations and costs requires the specification of correlation coefficients between the activities to represent this phenomenon. The correlation coefficients are particularly difficult risk data to collect since interviewees or workshop participants have relatively little experience actually putting numbers to their correlation assessments. We frequently collect correlation data in workshops or interviews only to find that the implied correlation matrix is inconsistent and the simulation is not run.

Given these drawbacks, some analysts have insisted on returning to the fundamental drivers of uncertainty in cost and schedule, the risks themselves. That is what the Risk Driver approach does.

The Risk Driver Approach

The Risk Driver method starts with the Risk Register's prioritized risks. These risks will be strategic risks that have been identified and assessed as having serious impact on the project's schedule and cost. We have heard that these are the risks that management worries about. Generally some 20 to 40 risks will be sufficient to consider even for multi-billion dollar projects.

Starting with risks – instead of the risks' effect using the 3-point estimates – drives the analyst back to the fundamentals of the profession, identifying the specific risks that are the root causes of duration and cost uncertainty. It is the hallmark of the Risk Driver method. The benefits of this approach flow from this crucial starting point.

The Risk Drivers are usually identified and prioritized using qualitative risk analysis methods and shown in the risk register. These risks' probability and impact parameters are then characterized in risk interviews or risk workshops, although there is a concern about collecting data in risk workshops where certain organizational and personal factors may bias the risk data.

The risks are characterized by the knowledgeable interviewees in three ways:

- The probability that the risk will occur. Notice that this concept already provides more information than the traditional 3-point estimate on duration and cost, which only deals directly with impact. While the probability has been assessed during the qualitative risk analysis leading to the Risk Register, experience shows that it is a good idea to re-open for inspection the probability value and ask for specific probability values rather than the ranges of probability that are offered during the Risk Register data collection.
- The Risk Driver method collects values representing the impact range of the risk itself, expressed as 3-point estimates of impact on duration or cost in multiplicative terms. The multiplicative impact factors for each risk represent the impact of that risk on the activities and costs in the cost-loaded schedule that it affects if it occurs.

- The interviewees are asked to identify the activities that will be affected if the risk occurs in any iteration so they can calibrate the impact factors. They may say "construction" or "engineering design" or "procurement." There may be many activities in those categories. During modelling the analyst will assign the risks to the appropriate activities since the risks must be assigned to the lowest level of detail activities and costs.

- The Risk Drivers are used to influence the activity durations and costs of activities and cost elements that are already in the schedule.[3] The activities that are not already in the schedule but may appear with some probability, say recovery after possibly failing a qualifying test, can be handled as existence or Risk Register risks that can be used in the same analysis as the Risk Drivers method. Also, uncertainties with 100 percent probability such as cost or duration estimating error can be used alongside Risk Drivers and existence risks.

- Notice that the Risk Driver method collects the risk data that one would expect to characterize a risk event – both probability and impact. It still uses 3-point estimates but they represent the uncertainty associated with the risk impacts rather than the effect of those risks on the activities directly. Experience shows that people find it easier to talk about the risks and uncertainties than the effect of those risks and uncertainties on durations and costs, probably because they do not have to perform mental arithmetic to pre-process the traditional 3-point data.

- If the risk is not 100 percent certain to occur (that would be an uncertainty, not a risk event) it will appear in some fraction of the iterations and the activities that it influences will find their durations, burn rates or equipment costs multiplied by a value selected at random from the risk's impact range. If the risk does not occur, in all the other iterations, the risk factor is set to 1.0 and is neutral in the multiplicative sense so the durations and costs values are as estimated in the static schedule and cost estimate.

- The risks are also specified at such a fundamental level that they are generally independent, not correlated with each other.

- This does not mean that durations and costs of individual activities and project elements are not correlated – they are. They become correlated during the simulation. If a risk affects more than one activity those activities become correlated. If the risk occurs for one it occurs for the other, and the risk factor that is chosen is applied to the duration or cost of both activities. Since the simulation causes correlation between durations and costs in the natural way, as it occurs in nature, there is no more need to try to collect correlation data or deal with inconsistent correlation matrices.

- A major benefit of using the specific risks as drivers of project cost and schedule risk is that the most important risks can be identified individually and accurately. With the traditional 3-point estimate an activity's impact range can be influenced by several risks and their individual influence cannot be sorted out. Also, if a risk affects multiple activities, the analysis of the risk project risk looks at activities and costs one-at-a-time rather than taking the whole impact of the risk, which may affect several activities or costs. The traditional method of using 3-point estimates usually identifies high-priority activities or paths but cannot identify high-priority risks.

---

3   The Risk Driver method available today exists in the Risk Factors module of Primavera Risk Analysis, formerly Pertmaster, from Oracle.

With the individual risks driving the overall project cost and schedule risk, the analyst can identify the marginal impact of any risks just by taking it out of the equation and running the simulation again. The risk can be taken out by setting its probability to zero so it does not occur in any iteration. Interestingly, the marginal impact can be calculated at any level of certainty that is desired, say at the 80th percentile on the cumulative distribution.

Risk Drivers is a fairly new method, and it is still being refined.[4] The more it is used the greater the understanding will be and its use will spread. The module has been improved substantially since its introduction. The benefits are serious. Users have said that the Risk Drivers method is "logical," "transparent," and "the way risk analysis ought to be done." The ability to combine Risk Drivers with (1) the existence or Risk Register risks and (2) the traditional 3-point estimate that is often used to represent estimating error is convenient and powerful.

Organizational Culture is a Key Success Factor

The most important success factor in executing a cost and schedule risk analysis is the organizational culture's openness to risk analysis. The resources and time that a risk analysis takes is a concern for some project managers and they must see the benefits for the project's success to embark on the effort.

The biggest success factor from the organization's side is whether the organization wants to know the truth about the project so risk mitigation can occur.

- A project manager who deserves respect said, at the kick-off meeting for the risk analysis of his project: "There will be good, bad and ugly in this project and I want to know all three or I can't do anything about risk." Most of the teams got the word and tried their best to provide unbiased risk data.
- A supportive corporate general manager said, the first time he received the briefing about cost and schedule risk: "We must do this. We have never been able to quantify the risks. We cannot move forward unless the risks are quantified. Of course I do not want to lose my date, so what risk mitigations have you prepared for me?"

Corporate acceptance of project risk analysis starts at the top of the organization, or at least with a single "champion" of the method who is willing to try it. Often it is important to provide organizational independence of the risk analyst from the manager of the project that is under analysis so the project manager does not interfere with or bias the results. Of course the project manager must be part of the interviews and certainly the PM leads the risk mitigation efforts, but the risk analyst can produce objective results that do not have to please that project manager.

Another success factor is the collection of the best possible data about risk. A key element in achieving that is the ability to provide confidentiality for the interviewees, so

---

4   Pertmaster created the Risk Factors module in 2007 for a client. The author and an associate, Waylon Whitehead, specified the objectives of the module and de-bugged the initial versions. Since that time the module has shipped with Pertmaster / Primavera Risk Analysis.

that what they say is not identified to the person saying it. Some analysts are successful with risk workshops, but if there is pressure from management to achieve a particular result – usually to show little project risk to the customer – interviewing behind closed doors without the project manager in the room helps to result in unbiased risk data.

A common reaction of traditional cost estimators and cost risk analysts is to question the logic of starting the cost risk analysis with the project schedule. They are often unfamiliar with project scheduling and feel uncomfortable or inadequate when faced with the necessity to deal with project schedules. In fact, however, to be a cost risk analyst one needs to understand and incorporate the risk to the project cost that is caused by schedule risk; hence, the cost risk analyst needs to be comfortable with project scheduling or to cooperate with someone who is. Starting with the schedule is not just the best approach, it is essential. The organization should recognize the integration of the cost estimating and scheduling of a project and force the cost and schedule staffs to work together.

Of course in starting with the schedule the analyst will derive as an intermediate and simultaneous-available product – the schedule risk analysis results. We have shown that, in getting to the cost risk result the schedule risk result becomes available. And the schedule needs to be credible, since it forms the basis of a large portion of the cost risk analysis. Health-checking the schedule against best practices and debugging the schedule is important, both for static critical path method (CPM) scheduling and for risk analysis using Monte Carlo simulation techniques.

Cost risk analysts who ignore the schedule or try to incorporate indirectly the implications of a separate schedule risk analysis for cost risk are missing or mis-estimating a major impact on cost. The best way to be clear about the schedule risk to project cost is to model the cost risk within the resource-loaded schedule. Those who believe that resource loading a schedule is difficult and have never done it should take heart because summary resources may be used. It is just a way to get the risk-free project budget into the project schedule on the right activities for a time-phased cost estimate.

Cost Risk Analysis Maturity

There is a hierarchy of cost risk analysis maturity and it has steps:

1. Cost risk analysis using the method of moments or PERT-Cost instead of Monte Carlo simulation. This is all right if the cost estimates are just added down a column of numbers, since the central limit theorem drives the total cost distribution to the normal or Gaussian shape distribution.
2. Cost risk analysis, using Monte Carlo simulation of a cost estimate built in a spreadsheet using 3-point estimates that represent risks to cost elements.
3. Cost risk analysis using Monte Carlo simulation of a cost estimate built in a spreadsheet but conducting a schedule risk analysis and introducing schedule risk into the spreadsheet analysis (Hulett 2006). This is an indirect way to incorporate schedule risk into the cost risk analysis that can be conducted in a spreadsheet format. However, a schedule risk analysis will have to be conducted to get the schedule risk inputs to the cost risk exercise.

4. Integrated cost and schedule risk analysis starting with a project schedule that has been loaded with resources and the project budget (without embedded contingency), then simulating it using 3-point estimates with some risks directly applied to the schedule and with other risks applied to the costs. The risks to the schedule will affect cost if the risky activities have time-dependent labor-type resources. However, there are some risks that affect only the cost, either the burn rate per day or the capital equipment and materials estimate. These risks are time-independent and should be risked as well.

5. Execute point 4 above using the Risk Driver method for varying the durations and costs of those activities that are in the schedule. This approach is often combined with the use of the Risk Register/existence/probabilistic branching for discontinuous events causing new activities to be needed, and with traditional 3-point estimates on duration or cost to represent uncertainties such as estimating error. These three approaches work well together and can be used as appropriate.

6. Use the simulation model of the project and the Risk Driver method in point 5 above to identify the high-priority risks, understanding that some of the most important risks to cost are indirect because their initial assessment is that they affect the schedule. Use these high-priority risks to drive risk mitigation based on a mitigation workshop conducted with the project manager and team leads.

Integration of cost and schedule risk analysis has moved the professions of project management and risk management forward. The Risk Driver method allows the analyst to start with the fundamentals of the risk generation process, and to focus the project team on priority risks causing both schedule and cost risk to focus their risk mitigation. Some forward-looking organizations are already requiring their projects to be analyzed for both cost and schedule risk in an integrated fashion (NASA 2009).

References

Hulett, D. (2006). Integrated Cost/Schedule Risk Analysis. Crystal Ball User Conference, Denver, CO.

Hulett, D. (2009). *Practical Schedule Risk Analysis*. Farnham, England, Gower Publishing.

NASA (2009). Joint Confidence Level (JCL) FAQ, NASA Headquarters PA&E.

Index

Page numbers in *italics* refer to figures and tables. PEC refers to "project element cost"